T0251415

CISO LEADERSHIP
ESSENTIAL PRINCIPLES
FOR SUCCESS

THE (ISC)²® PRESS SERIES

CISO Leadership: Essential Principles for Success
Todd Fitzgerald and Micki Krause, Editors
ISBN: 0-8493-7943-X

Official (ISC)²® Guide to the CISSP® CBK®
Harold F. Tipton and Kevin Henry, Editors
ISBN: 0-8493-8231-9

Building and Implementing a Security Certification and Accreditation Program: Official (ISC)²® Guide to the CAPᶜᵐ CBK®
Patrick D. Howard
ISBN: 0-8493-2062-3

Official (ISC)²® Guide to the SSCP® CBK®
Diana-Lynn Contesti, Douglas Andre, Eric Waxvik,
Paul A. Henry, and Bonnie A. Goins
ISBN: 0-8493-2774-1

Official (ISC)²® Guide to the CISSP®-ISSEP® CBK®
Susan Hansche
ISBN: 0-8493-2341-X

CISO LEADERSHIP

ESSENTIAL PRINCIPLES
FOR SUCCESS

Edited by
Todd Fitzgerald, CISSP, CISA, CISM
Micki Krause, CISSP

SECURITY TRANSCENDS TECHNOLOGY®

Auerbach Publications
Taylor & Francis Group
New York   London

CRC Press is an imprint of the
Taylor & Francis Group, an **informa** business

Auerbach Publications
Taylor & Francis Group
6000 Broken Sound Parkway NW, Suite 300
Boca Raton, FL 33487-2742

© 2008 by Taylor & Francis Group, LLC
Auerbach is an imprint of Taylor & Francis Group, an Informa business

No claim to original U.S. Government works
Printed in the United States of America on acid-free paper
10 9 8 7 6 5 4 3 2

International Standard Book Number-13: 978-0-8493-7943-7 (Hardcover)

Library of Congress Cataloging-in-Publication Data

Effective leadership skills for the CISO / editors, Todd Fitzgerald and Micki Krause.
    p. cm.
    Includes bibliographical references and index.
    ISBN 978-0-8493-7943-7 (alk. paper)
    1. Computer security--Management. 2. Computer networks--Management. I. Fitzgerald, Todd. II. Krause, Micki.

QA76.9.A25E385 2007
658.4'78--dc22
                                          2007033737

Visit the Taylor & Francis Web site at
http://www.taylorandfrancis.com

and the Auerbach Web site at
http://www.auerbach-publications.com

Dedication

For those who took the time to teach me:
my parents — for the value of caring for people and hard work;
Grant and Erica — for the purpose of life; Kim — the courage of risk-taking;
and for my late brother, Jay, who taught me that our success in life
is defined by the passionate journey we embrace and
not by our destination.

— Todd

This book is dedicated to my Mom, the embodiment
of unconditional love and unrelenting optimism.

— Micki

Dedication

Contents

II A LEADERSHIP MANDATE

2 Who Companies Really Want to Hire: How to Advance Your Career and Have Great Success 31

JOYCE BROCAGLIA

3 The Evolving Information Security Landscape 43

WILLIAM HUGH MURRAY

Preface

The information security profession is in its infancy and hasn't had the good fortune of a structured and professional curriculum or reliable and useful mentoring, the lack of which leads to:

- Insufficient mastery for the skills and competencies required to succeed
- A tendency to revert to the comfort of techno-speak
- An inability to craft business strategies and demonstrate a value proposition
- A shortage of effective communication and relationship skills

What we have captured in this anthology is many, many years of hard knocks and success stories and, yes, failures, all in the hope that you, the reader, will learn from some morsel and apply the message to improve your lot.

Much of what we know, we have learned through experience; we have been there, done that, have the t-shirt and, yes, the scars. We have prospered in careers that we did not expect in a field that we helped create merely because that was the only way possible.

We recognize that it is our responsibility and obligation to support and develop the next generation of security leaders. For those of you who aspire to leadership, we want to help you qualify. For those of you who are not destined for leadership, we want to help you succeed and enjoy your success.

Surveys show that many of you may be frustrated by problems that we have solved and are troubled by questions that we have answered.

In short, we strive to mentor. We want to capture for you our collective and cumulative experience. We want to record for you the lessons that we have learned and pass them on to you in a useful form.

This is not intended to be a "how-to" book. It is not a collection of technical data. It is not about products or technology. It is not a recapitulation of the Common Body of Knowledge. It is about information security leadership. It is about having a successful career in the field. The book and its authors aspire to record and convey wisdom. What we offer are life lessons, from which you may pluck one or more plums.

Within each of the individual chapters, you will find heartfelt introspection that each author has been gracious enough to share. Collectively, we wish you the very best of luck in your professional endeavors.

About the Editors

Todd Fitzgerald, CISSP, CISA, CISM, serves as a Medicare systems security officer for National Government Services, in Milwaukee, Wisconsin, which is the nation's largest processor of Medicare claims and a subsidiary of WellPoint, Inc., the nation's leading health insurer. Todd was named as a finalist for the 2005 Midwest Information Security Executive (ISE) of the Year Award, nominee for the national award, judge for the 2006 central region awards, and has served as the global moderator for several Executive Alliance Information Security Executive roundtables. Todd has authored chapters on information security for *The 2007 Official (ISC)² Guide to the CISSP Exam, The Information Security Handbook Series, The HIPAA Program Reference Book, Managing an Information Security and Privacy Awareness and Training Program,* and several other security-related publications. Todd is also a member of the editorial board for *(ISC)² Journal* and *Darkreading.com* security publications, and is frequently called upon to present at international, national, and local conferences. Todd serves on the board of directors for the nationally recognized HIPAA Collaborative of Wisconsin, and is an active leader, participant, and presenter in multiple industry associations such as the Information Systems Security Association (ISSA), the Information Systems Audit and Control Association (ISACA), Blue Cross Blue Shield Information Security Advisory Group, CMS/Gartner Security Best Practices Group, Workgroup for Electronic Data Interchange (WEDI), and others. Todd has 28 years of information technology experience, including 20 years of management. Prior to joining NGS, Todd held various broad-based senior information technology management positions for Fortune 500 organizations such as American Airlines, IMS Health, Zeneca (subsidiary of AstraZeneca Pharmaceuticals), Syngenta, as well as prior positions with Blue Cross Blue Shield of Wisconsin. Todd holds a B.S. in business administration from the University of Wisconsin–Lacrosse, serves as an advisor to the College of Business Administration, and holds an MBA with highest honors from Oklahoma State University.

Micki Krause, MBA, CISSP, has held positions in the information security profession for the past 20 years. She is currently the chief information security officer at Pacific Life Insurance Company in Newport Beach, California, where she is accountable for directing the information protection and security program for the enterprise. Pacific Life is the 15th largest life insurance company in the nation, and provides life and health insurance products, individual annuities, mutual funds, group employee benefits, and a variety of investment products and services. She was named one of the 25 most influential women in the field of information security by industry peers and *Information Security* magazine as part of their recognition of Women of Vision in the IT security field, and was awarded the Harold F. Tipton Award in recognition of sustained career excellence and outstanding contributions to the profession. Micki has held several leadership roles in industry-influential groups including the Information Systems Security Association (ISSA) and the International Information System Security Certification Consortium (ISC)² and is a passionate advocate for professional security leadership. She is a reputed speaker, published author, and co-editor of the *Information Security Management Handbook* series.

Contributors

Joyce Brocaglia is the president and CEO of Alta Associates, Inc. (www.altaassociates.com). Founded in 1986 Alta Associates is widely acknowledged as the leading search firm in IT risk management, information security and privacy. Having successfully partnered with global enterprises for 20 years, Alta has built world-class IT risk and information security organizations. Joyce is sought after for her deep knowledge of market conditions and business intelligence and her ability to create industry alliances. With over 20 years of experience acting as a strategic advisor to her clients, she has gained the trust and respect of the industry's most influential executives. In September 2003, *Information Security Magazine* honored her with a "Women of Vision" award, naming her one of the 25 most influential women in the information security industry. In 2003, Joyce also founded the Executive Women's Forum on Information Security, Privacy, and Risk Management, a ground-breaking event for women executives in the information security industry to exchange ideas and best practices (www.infosecuritywomen.com). In 2005, she authored "The Information Security Officer: A New Role for New Threats" in Larstans's *The Black Book on Corporate Security*. In 2006, Joyce and the Executive Women's Forum partnered with Carnegie Mellon's Cylab to create scholarships for outstanding women to enroll in CMU's Master of Science in Information Security Technology and Management program. The first EWF Fellow was announced in 2007. Joyce is the career advisor of *CSO Magazine*. She is author of the monthly "Career Corner" column for the *Information Systems Security Association (ISSA) Journal*. She is on the board of advisors for the ISSA and International Information Systems Security Certification Consortium (ISC)². Joyce has appeared in *The Wall Street Journal, Network World, Network Computing, Information Security Magazine, Redmondmag.com* and *CSO Magazine*. Joyce is a speaker at industry events regarding career matters and emerging roles within the information technology and security community. She holds a bachelor of science degree in accounting from Montclair State University and is a certified public accountant.

Peter Browne, principal manager, Peter Browne & Associates, is one of the pioneers in information security, having started that function in the U.S. Air Force in the early 1970s. He is an independent consultant, serving mostly financial service companies, large and small. He also has worked in Herndon, Virginia, as the vice president and general manager of the Global Integrity Information Security business unit of Predictive Systems. He successfully merged two different cultures and philosophies as that firm struggled to integrate two well-regarded information security consulting organizations. Prior to joining Predictive, Peter retired as the senior vice president and division head for information security at First Union Corporation in Charlotte, North Carolina. He built a highly regarded internal information security organization that reported directly to the chief operating officer of the company. He was responsible for security policy and standards, network security, access control, disaster recovery, and business continuity. He led an active internal applications development security consulting group, which developed industry-leading techniques to verify and validate security in computer applications. He built a world-class security metrics and monitoring program to track compliance to corporate standards at the individual business unit and machine levels. He was one of the original institutional leaders of BITS, and participated in many of the pioneering activities of this technology arm of the Financial Services Roundtable, to include its Standards Committee, early information security projects, the Financial Services Security Laboratory, outsourcing project, and various institutional/ customer education activities. He was the co-chairman of the BITS Security and Risk Assessment Committee from 1998 to 2001, and was instrumental in growing that group from a half dozen active participants to over 45 institutions. His distinguished career has spanned over 35 years of service as a corporate information security professional and consultant. He formed well-regarded information security functions for the Air Force, State Farm Insurance, General Electric Corporation, Motorola, and First Union National Bank. He also formed two consultant companies in the field in the late 1970s and 1980s, which developed many of the precepts that are now commonly held as key information security philosophies. During this time, he consulted to over 200 organizations, setting up information security policy, standards, initiatives, and systems. He pioneered the concept of risk assessment as a driving force for making decisions relating to technology risk and security management. Peter has published over 50 technical papers, articles, and briefs, and has given over 200 speeches and public presentations. He has held local and national office in many professional organizations, including ISSA, the ACM, DPMA, International Information Integrity Institute, and BITS. He was recipient of the 1998 Fitzgerald Award as the Information Security Professional of the Year. He is currently an appointed member of the Computer Security Systems Advisory Board to the U.S. government, established by the 1988 Computer Security Act. He graduated from Syracuse University and holds an MBA from the University of Nebraska at Omaha.

Vaune M. Carr, principal and risk management practice leader, Chicago Consulting Group, LLC, has been a leader in information protection for more than 20 years and has consulted to major organizations in both the commercial and private sectors.

Vaune has helped a multitude of organizations design and implement cost-effective programs to protect against information threats. In a wide range of assignments, Vaune has assisted clients in safeguarding their digital assets, especially their key intellectual property, against the uncertainties of the dynamically changing global Internet. Vaune has been a leader in corporate America as well as an entrepreneur, including managing director in the North American Center for Excellence at Unisys Corporation and consulting practice manager for Sprint Systems Integration. Innovative, she has pioneered several emerging technologies, among them single sign-on and commercial grade wireless recovery. She is a past president of the Information Systems Security Association (ISSA) and one of the founding leaders of the International Information Systems Security Certification Consortium (ISC)², the internationally recognized Gold Standard for educating and certifying information security professionals. She is the recipient of the Diamond Award for Public Service from the ISSA, the global voice of the information security profession. Vaune is one of the authors of the Generally Accepted System Security Principles (GASSP). She has an MBA from DePaul University and an undergraduate degree from Purdue University. She earned the designations of Certified Information Systems Security Professional (CISSP) and International Information Systems Security Certification Consortium (ISC)². Recently she received the Information Systems Security Management Professional (ISSMP) designation and Information Systems Security Architect Professional (ISSAP) designation.

James S. Christiansen, chief information security officer (CISO) Experian, has more than 25 years experience in information security and systems management. Prior to joining Experian, James served as CISO for General Motors where his responsibilities included implementation of a worldwide security plan for the largest financial and manufacturing corporation in the world. Prior to joining GM, he was senior vice president of information security for Visa International, responsible for their worldwide information security program. James has been featured in the *New York Times* as one of the new leaders in information security. He has an MBA in international management, a BS in business management, and is a published author. James has been a prominent speaker for prestigious events such as the Business Round Table, Research Board, and the American Bar Association.

Robert Coles is a director at Merrill Lynch in London responsible for information security and privacy. He previously held various positions at the Royal Bank of Scotland Group including heading up incident and threat management, governance, and security consultancy functions, and before this he was the partner at KPMG in charge of information security consultancy for Europe, the Middle East, and Africa. He holds an MBA in finance from Manchester Business School/University of Wales and a PhD in the psychology of information and IT risk from the University of Leeds.

Michael J. Corby, PMP, CCP, CISSP, consulting director, M. Corby & Associates, Inc., has over 38 years of experience in IT strategy, operations, development, and security. Mike has successfully managed large projects and developed flexible IT infrastructures and sound security organizations for hundreds of the world's most successful organizations, most recently as a consultant with Gartner, Inc. He is also the founder of (ISC)², Inc., the organization that established the CISSP credential. In 1992, Mike was named the first recipient of the Computer Security Institute's "Lifetime Achievement Award." A frequent global speaker and author, he formerly held executive positions with several global consulting organizations including Netigy Corporation and QinetiQ and was a senior member of the Gartner and META Group consulting practice. He was also formerly CIO for a division of Ashland Oil and for Bain & Company. A business owner for nearly 20 years and community supporter, Mike has established a reputation for creativity and excellence in technology and its application to business needs. He holds a BS EE degree from Worcester Polytechnic Institute, is a Project Management Professional (PMP®) from the Project Management Institute and is a Certified Computer Professional (CCP) and a Certified Information Systems Security Professional (CISSP).

Harry DeMaio is an independent consultant specializing in information systems applications and practices. At the time of his retirement from Deloitte & Touche, LLP in June 2002, he was a director in their Secure e-Business Technology practice. Harry was also president and CEO of a wholly owned subsidiary of Deloitte & Touche — Deloitte & Touche Security Services, LLC.

Harry joined Deloitte in 1987 after 31 years with the IBM Corporation in marketing, systems engineering, software development, and information security. His last position with IBM was as corporate director of data security programs with worldwide responsibility for IBM's offerings, customer support, and external relations concerning information security, privacy protection, and information trade. Harry has written many articles for major data processing and accounting journals and legal and industry publications. He has been a frequent guest speaker at computer, audit and accounting, telecommunications, information ethics, law enforcement, and government programs and often appears in radio and television interviews. He wrote *Information Protection and Other Unnatural Acts — Every Manager's Guide to Keeping Vital Computer Data Safe and Sound* (1991, American Management Association, and 1995 in Japan by Diamond Publishing). He has supplied chapters addressing information protection for several books including the 1994 and 1995 *Handbooks of IS Management* published by Auerbach Publications. His professional book, *B2B and Beyond — New Business Models Built on Trust* was published in September 2001 by John Wiley and Sons.

Rebecca Herold, CIPP, CISSP, CISM, CISA, FLMI, has provided information security, privacy, and regulatory services to organizations from a wide range of industries. She has over 17 years of privacy and information security experience and was instrumental in building the information security and privacy program while at Principal Financial Group, which was awarded the CSI Information Security Program of the Year Award in 1998. Rebecca has been CPO for two consulting organizations. Rebecca is currently an independent information privacy, security, and compliance consultant, author, and instructor. Rebecca assists organizations throughout the world, of all sizes and within all industries, with their information privacy, security, and regulatory compliance programs, content development, and strategy development and implementation. Rebecca has written chapters for several books, hundreds of articles, and has been writing a monthly privacy column for the *CSI Alert* newsletter since the beginning of 2001. Rebecca has written multiple books; some of the more recent include *The Privacy Management Toolkit, Say What You Do, The Privacy Papers, Managing an Information Security and Privacy Awareness and Training Program,* and has co-authored *The Practical Guide to HIPAA Privacy and Security Compliance.* Rebecca also has been an adjunct professor for the Norwich University Master of Science in Information Assurance (MSIA) program for the past two years.

Stephen R. Katz, CISSP, has been directly involved in establishing, building, and directing information security and privacy functions for over 25 years. He is the founder and president of Security Risk Solutions, an information security company providing consulting and advisory services to major, mid-size, start-up, and venture capital companies. Steve is an executive advisor to Deloitte, is on the board of directors of nCircle, Inc., the technology advisory board of Phoenix Technologies, and the advisory board of *CSO Magazine.* Steve is also a member of the (ISC)² Americas Advisory Board for Information Systems Security. Steve organized and managed the Information Security Program at JP Morgan for ten years. In 1995, he joined Citicorp/Citigroup after the Russian hacking incident. At Citi, Steve was the industry's first chief information security officer. He spent the next six years directing Citigroup's global Corporate Information Security Office. Steve then joined Merrill Lynch as their chief information security and privacy officer, where he organized and instituted the companywide privacy and security program. Steve has testified before Congress on numerous information security issues, and in 1998 was appointed financial services sector coordinator for critical infrastructure protection by the secretary of the Treasury. He was also the first chairman of the Financial Services Information Sharing and Analysis Center (FS/ISAC) and is an advisor to the FS/ISAC board of directors.

Billi Lee is a speaker, columnist, author, and creator of Success Savvy seminars, whose worldwide following credits her insights and savvy strategies for many of their career successes. Clients as diverse as the CIA, Bank of Australia, IBM, the FBI, Time Warner/AOL, and the Republic of Buryat in Siberia count on her to help their people succeed in rapidly changing systems. Refreshingly candid and provocatively witty, Billi captivates audiences with her humor while daring and equipping them to lose their naïveté and get savvy. Billi speaks at conferences, conventions, and special events when the audience demands a dynamic, entertaining style and a thought-provoking message. Her newspaper column is eagerly read by fans throughout the world; her "boot camps for business" are filled with people who want to succeed in the game of work; and her seminars are required courses for many organizations. Featured on CNN.com as an underground career secret, Billi's pragmatism is just right for these challenging times. Billi holds degrees in French, speech pathology, and psychology. She has authored the book *Savvy: Thirty Days to a Different Perspective* and numerous magazine and journal articles. Two new books are in production. Billi also produces radio essays and audio/video programs. She lives in Denver and Ajijic, Mexico.

Lynn McNulty, CISSP, serves as the director of government affairs for (ISC)². He retired from the National Institute of Standards and Technology (NIST) in 1995, where he served as the associate director for computer security. While at NIST he founded and chaired the Federal Computer Security Program Manager's Forum and served as the executive director of the Computer Systems Security Advisory Board, presently known as the Information Security and Privacy Advisory Board. He was appointed to this board in March of 2005. During his government career Lynn worked in the field of information security at the Department of State, the Federal Aviation Administration, and the Central Intelligence Agency. He served on the board of directors of the International Information Systems Security Certification Consortium (ISC)², the governing body for the CISSP certification program from 1998 though 2005. He is a native of Oakland, California, and graduated from the Berkeley campus of the University of California with a bachelor's degree in political science. He also received a master of arts in international relations from San Jose State University and a master of science in administration from George Washington University.

Rolf Moulton, CISA, CISSP-ISSMP, CCP, is an international business executive with considerable management experience in both private industry and government positions. His key skills relate to the management of complex business, strategy, security, and governance opportunities in global, national, and local operating environments, as well as handling and resolving sensitive organizational situations. He is also an active participant in furthering the information and information security profession. His management accomplishments have included the creation and implementation of services programs in very large international organizations. This has included the creation and implementation of three enterprisewide information security programs. He has served as a board member and/or officer of (ISC)², ISSA, the Federal Information Processing Council, and the Data Processing Management Association, and has authored many professional articles and one security management textbook. Currently, Rolf is the director of Risk Reduction Solutions. Previously, he held the positions of president and CEO (interim) of (ISC)², head of IT risk management and information security at Unilever, manager of IT security at BP America, and director of the Computer Security Services Unit at the Department of Investigation, City of New York. He holds MBA and BA degrees from the City University of New York and served as an adjunct associate professor at Pace University.

William Hugh Murray, CISSP, is an executive consultant for Cybertrust Corporation and associate professor at the Naval Postgraduate School. He is a Certified Information Systems Security Professional (CISSP) and chairman of the governance and professional practices committees of (ISC)², the certifying body. Bill is an advisor on the board of directors of the New York Metropolitan chapter of ISSA. He has more than 50 years experience in information technology and over 40 years in security. During 25 years with IBM, his management responsibilities included development of access control programs, advising IBM customers on security, and the articulation of the IBM security product plan. He is the author of the IBM publication *Information System Security Controls and Procedures.* He has made significant contributions to the literature and practice of information security. He is a popular speaker on such topics as network security architecture, encryption, PKI, and secure electronic commerce. He is a founding member of the International Committee to Establish the "Generally Accepted System Security Principles" (GSSP, now referred to as the GISSP), as called for in the National Research Council's Report *Computers at Risk.* Bill remains as an active member of this committee. Bill is a founder and board member of the Colloquium on Information System Security Education (CISSE). He has been recognized as a founder of the systems audit field and by *Information Security Magazine* as a pioneer in computer security. In 1987 he received the Fitzgerald Memorial Award for leadership in data security. In 1989 he received the Joseph J. Wasserman Award for contributions to security, audit, and control. In 1995 he received a Lifetime Achievement Award from the Computer Security Institute. In 1999 he was enrolled in the ISSA Hall of Fame in recognition of his outstanding contribution to the information security community. In 2007 he received the Harold F. Tipton Award in recognition of his lifetime achievement and contribution. He holds a BS in business administration from Louisiana State University.

Mark D. Rasch, Esq., is a managing director in FTI's technology practice and is based in Washington, D.C. He brings over 24 years of experience in the information security field, having served for nine years as the head of the U.S. Department of Justice Computer Crime Unit, and having prosecuted key cases involving computer crime, hacking, computer fraud, and computer viruses. As managing director at FTI, Mark is focused on helping clients in the areas of computer security, privacy, and incident response. He has spent the last 15 years consulting with commercial and governmental clients on matters related to computer security, regulatory compliance, and electronic evidence handling and computer incident response. For the past three years he was the senior vice president and chief security counsel at Solutionary. Prior to Solutionary, Mark helped establish the SAIC Center for Information Protection (CIP), a business unit within SAIC dedicated to commercial information security consulting. Starting with nine people, the CIP developed first into Global Integrity Corporation, a wholly owned SAIC subsidiary, and then was acquired by Predictive Systems, Inc. Prior to that, he was in private practice with the Washington, D.C., office of Arent, Fox, Kintner, Plotkin & Kahn. While at the Department of Justice, he was responsible for investigations of computer hacking cases including those of the so-called "Hannover Hacker" ring (Kevin Mitnick), and was the lead prosecutor in *United States v. Robert T. Morris*, against the author of the Cornell Internet worm in 1988. He helped the FBI and the Treasury Department develop their original procedures on handling electronic evidence. He created and taught classes at the FBI Academy and the Federal Law Enforcement Training Center on electronic crime and evidence. He also investigated, prosecuted, and handled appeals on complex white-collar criminal cases involving consumer protection fraud, banking and securities fraud, insider trading, public corruption, Department of Defense procurement and contract fraud, counter-intelligence matters, export control, pharmaceutical fraud, and violations of federal mail fraud, wire fraud, tax fraud, and Foreign Corrupt Practices Act laws. He was co-counsel in *United States v. Lyndon LaRouche*, as well as complex cases against organized crime figures. He has taught evidence law at the Catholic University School of Law, and white collar and computer crime at the American University School of Law. He has taught other computer and privacy law courses and incident response classes at the University of Fairfax, George Washington University, George Mason University, and James Madison University. He has also lectured at Stanford University, Harvard University, and Harvard Law School. Mark is frequently featured in the news media on issues related to technology, security, and privacy. He has appeared on or been quoted by CNN, Forbes, Fox News, MSNBC, NBC News, *The New York Times*, NPR, PBS, *The Washington Post*, and other national and international media. He writes a monthly column in Symantec's *Security Focus* online magazine on issues related to law and technology and is a regular contributor to *Wired* magazine.

Randolph (Randy) N. Sanovic, CISSP-ISSMP, ISSAP, has been an information security professional since 1972. In 1978 he became manager, computer security planning, for Mobil Corporation responsible for its overall information security posture, strategy, programs, plans, and policies. In 1995, Randy became director, information systems security, for United Healthcare Corporation where he directed a staff of 32 information security directors, managers, and staff professionals. His responsibilities included reorganizing the corporation's disparate information security functions into a well-managed worldwide function, and developing an effective strategic IT security plan covering the corporation's distributed three-tier client server and Internet/intranet computing environments. In 1997 Randy became general director, information security, for General Motors Corporation responsible for GM's information security strategy, programs, plans, and global information security posture. Some of Randy's other professional affiliations include being a member of the board of directors of the International Information Systems Security Certification Consortium (ISC)^2 since 1989; treasurer and chairman of the board audit committee of (ISC)^2; co-chair of (ISC)^2's America's Advisory Board; and chairman of (ISC)^2's board of directors; a four-year member of the National Computer Systems Security & Privacy advisory board; and past chairman of the membership advisory committee of the International Information Integrity Institute (I-4). Randy presents at major national and international IT security conferences, publishes articles on IT security, and continues to serve on editorial boards of IT security publications. His educational background includes a BBA and an MBA.

Don Saracco, Ed.D., principal, joined MLC & Associates, Inc., with over 25 years experience in human resource and organizational development in manufacturing, health care, and government organizations as a manager and consultant. His background includes the design and delivery of corporate education and training as well as executive coaching, and facilitation of organizational change and process improvement. In addition, he has served as an adjunct faculty member for a state university and a private business school. Don served for several years as a faculty member of the Business Recovery Managers Symposium presented by the MIS Institute. His speaking credits include Business Continuity Planning and Y2K Preparedness workshops for the International Quality & Productivity Center (IQPC), Atlanta, Georgia; Orlando, Florida; and Las Vegas, Nevada; and the 4th International Conference on Corporate Earthquake Programs (ICCEP) Conference, Shizuoka, Japan, as well as the annual Contingency Planning and Management Magazine Conference and Exposition. In addition, Don has presented papers at national and international conferences sponsored by the International Society for Performance Improvement, the Association for Quality and Participation, RIMS, and Continuity Insights. He has also worked as an adjunct faculty member in graduate business programs at two accredited universities. Specific speaking credits include MIS Institute Business Managers' Recovery Symposium, San Diego, California, 2000, "Murder One: An Exercise in Team Development"; ACP International Symposium, Seattle, Washington, 2000, "Managing Psychological Contracts for Business Continuity"; ACPLA Chapter Meeting, Los Angeles, California, 2000, "Event Management"; ISPI Culture & Change Management Conference, Washington, D.C., 2000, "The Evolution of Macro-Cultures: Implications for Performance Management"; CASFAA keynotes for three regional conferences, 2000, "Peak Performance"; CPM Conference, Baltimore, Maryland, 2000, "Team Development"; CPM West, Las Vegas, Nevada, 2006, "Business Continuity Leadership"; and RSA Security Conference, San Jose, California, 2006, "How to Win Friends for Your Security Program."

Howard A. Schmidt, president and CEO, R&H Security Consulting, LLC, has had a long distinguished career in defense, law enforcement, and corporate security spanning almost 40 years. He has served as vice president and chief information security officer and chief security strategist for online auction giant eBay. He most recently served in the position of chief security strategist for the U.S. CERT Partners Program for the National Cyber Security Division, Department of Homeland Security. He retired from the White House after 31 years of public service in local and federal government. He was appointed by President Bush as the vice chair of the President's Critical Infrastructure Protection Board and as the special advisor for cyberspace security for the White House in December 2001. He assumed the role as the chair in January 2003 until his retirement in May 2003. Prior to the White House, Howard was chief security officer for Microsoft Corp., where his duties included CISO, CSO, and forming and directing the Trustworthy Computing Security Strategies Group. Before Microsoft, Howard was a supervisory special agent and director of the Air Force Office of Special Investigations (AFOSI) Computer Forensic Lab and Computer Crime and Information Warfare Division. While there, he established the first dedicated computer forensic lab in the government. Before AFOSI, he was with the FBI at the National Drug Intelligence Center, where he headed the Computer Exploitation Team. He is recognized as one of the pioneers in the field of computer forensics and computer evidence collection. Before working at the FBI, Howard was a city police officer from 1983 to 1994 for the Chandler Police Department in Arizona. He served with the U.S. Air Force in various roles from 1967 to 1983, both in active duty and in the civil service. He had served in the Arizona Air National Guard from 1989 until 1998 when he transferred to the U.S. Army Reserves as a special agent, Criminal Investigation Division, where he continues to serve. He has testified as an expert witness in federal and military courts in the areas of computer crime, computer forensics and Internet crime. Howard also serves as the international president of the Information Systems Security Association (ISSA) and was the first president of the Information Technology Information Sharing and Analysis Center (IT-ISAC). He is a former executive board member of the International Organization of Computer Evidence, and served as the co-chairman of the Federal Computer Investigations Committee. He is a member of the American Academy of Forensic Scientists. He had served as a board member for the CyberCrime Advisory Board of the National White Collar Crime Center, and was a distinguished special lecturer at the University of New Haven, Connecticut, teaching a graduate certificate course in forensic computing. He served as an augmented member to the President's Committee of Advisors on Science and Technology in the formation of an Institute for Information Infrastructure Protection. He has testified before congressional committees on computer security and cyber crime, and has been instrumental in the creation of public and private partnerships and information-sharing initiatives. He is regularly featured on CNBC, CNN, Fox TV as well as a number of local media outlets talking about cyber-security. He is a co-author of the *Black Book on Corporate Security* and author of *Patrolling CyberSpace, Lessons Learned from a Lifetime in Data Security.* Howard has been appointed to the Information Security Privacy Advisory Board (ISPAB) to advise the National Institute of Standards and Technology (NIST), the secretary of commerce and the director of the Office of Management and Budget on information security and privacy issues pertaining to federal government information systems. Howard holds positions on a number of corporate boards in both advisory and director positions and recently has assumed the role as chairman of the board for Electronics Lifestyle Integration (ELI). He holds a bachelor's degree in business administration and a master's degree in organizational management from the University of Phoenix. He also holds an honorary doctorate degree in humane letters. Howard is a professor of practice at Georgia Tech, GTISC, professor of research at Idaho State University, and adjunct senior fellow with Carnegie Mellon's CyLab.

Steven Skolochenko, CISSP, CISA, CISM, is an associate with Booz, Allen & Hamilton. Prior to joining BAH he served as an information systems security program manager for the Department of the Treasury. He also served as deputy director, information systems security staff, at the Department of Justice. He joined the Department of Justice from the U.S. Postal Service. Prior to joining the USPS Steve served in the Army as a logistician and data processing officer. His involvement with information security started in 1976 when he served as chief, Plans, Standards, and QA branch of the U.S. Army Management Systems Support Agency. While with the USPS he managed software design and development projects in the area of process control and information systems. He next served as manager, information systems security, for the USPS. In this position he established, implemented, and managed the corporate information/computer security program. He also has experience as a programmer, systems analyst, and program/project manager. He holds masters degrees from both George Washington University and American University. Steve is a frequent speaker at information systems security conferences and served as a member of the steering committee of the Federal Computer Security Program Managers Forum and is a member of the ISACA and the Computer Security Institute. Steve is currently working on IA and IA threats in the space environment.

Acknowledgments

The editors wish to acknowledge the following professionals who also contributed precious time and brainpower toward the formulation of this anthology:

William (Bill) Boni, corporate vice president, Information Protection & Security, Motorola, Inc.

Adel Melek, MSc, CISSP, CISM, CPA, partner, global leader – Security & Privacy Services, Deloitte & Touche, LLP

Eddie Zeitler, CISSP, executive director, (ISC)^2

A LEADERSHIP
DISCONNECT

Chapter 1

What You Told Us:
A CISO Survey*

Todd Fitzgerald

Overview

The emergence of the Chief Information Security Officer (CISO) as a valued position within government and private sectors is a relatively new phenomenon. Within the last five years in particular, there has been a significant emphasis on information security through emerging laws such as the Health Insurance Portability and Accountability Act (HIPAA), the Graham–Leach–Bliley Act (GLBA), Sarbanes–Oxley (SOX), the Federal Information Security Management Act (FISMA), and the refinement of supporting control frameworks such as ISO17799 (ISO27001: 2005), Control OBjectives for Information and related Technology (COBIT), Information Technology Infrastructure Library (ITIL), and others. Why is this significant? In the past, where information security was relegated to log-on IDs and

---

* Editor's note: The survey provided the basis for understanding the key issues facing today's security leader. Most of the contributors of the subsequent chapters met for several days to discuss the issues and clarify the content that would be most beneficial to the reader. Some charts may vary slightly from the data presented due to rounding. Rich insights were obtained from the extensive use of open-ended questions and excellent responses.

passwords performed somewhere deep in the information technology organization as an "IT" task typically performed by a lower-level associate, today there is an increasing recognition that information security is essential to the business. Along with this recognition is also the recognition that the CISO is an individual who needs to have a wide range of skills to be effective within the organization.

So what are these skills? How does an individual charged with the responsibility to lead the organization's information security practice meet the demands of the business and at the same time ensure that the business is not taking an unnecessary risk in doing so? To answer this question, a survey was constructed to get the views of leading security practitioners across a variety of organizational positions, industries, organization sizes, department sizes, and geographic locations. The survey was not intended to be a statistical sampling survey, but rather a survey to determine the types of issues that security officers were concerned with in their daily jobs and the skill sets they felt were needed most. The survey was focused on the security management function and primarily concerned with the "soft skills" that were necessary to get the job done. There are many great technical individuals who are not as successful as they could be and may not advance in their careers to the security officer position due to their lack of soft skills versus technical abilities. This survey is a different type of survey than most, and although numbers of incidents, viruses handled, technologies employed, dollars per employee spent on security, and numbers of attacks are interesting and necessary to track for the business, the focus of this survey was on the leadership abilities of the security leader.

Survey Population

Industries represented were primarily insurance (29.2 percent), healthcare and medical services (14.6 percent), financial (9.4 percent), and security consulting (7.3 percent). The survey included approximately 250 security leaders from well-known companies, with 99 respondents. The companies were predominantly mid-sized

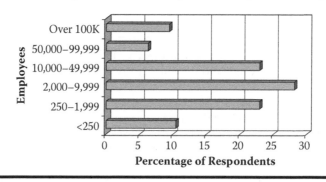

Figure 1.1   Organization size.

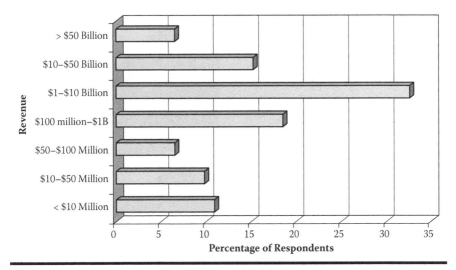

Figure 1.2   Organization revenue.

(2000 to 9999 employees) and large organizations (greater than 10,000 employees). Most of the revenue within the survey population was at least $1 billion. Figure 1.1 and Figure 1.2 show this stratification.

The CISO/CSO Title

It is clear from the survey results that although the role of Chief Information Security Officer (CISO) and Chief Security Officer (CSO) are the desired titles, organizations are still somewhat hesitant to create this role. Only 27 percent of those surveyed held the specific title of CISO, and significantly fewer individuals held the title of CSO (5 percent). The majority of the rest of the individuals held some variation of a VP/AVP/Director/Manager/Analyst role with respect to security, with some of the titles inferring that security was not their only responsibility. Roles such as compliance, risk management, enterprise architecture, and privacy appeared to be coupled with the security job responsibilities. Although much of the common security-industry press would lead individuals to believe that many organizations have defined the "chief" role, this appears to be only emerging. On the positive side of these numbers, it could be argued that approximately 32 percent holding the "Chief" designation would be substantially higher than five years ago, when the designation would have been virtually nonexistent in most organizations. This is analogous to the emergence of the Chief Information Officer (CIO), a position that is now taken for granted in most medium-sized to large organizations. As little as 15 to 20 years ago, this role was also seen as a role without much definition or presence even in large organizations.

Regulations have been largely responsible for establishing individuals in these roles. HIPAA, for example, requires that there be "someone accountable" for the security of

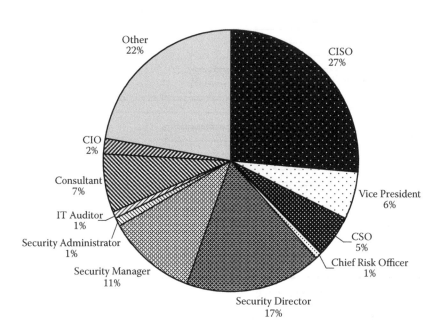

Figure 1.3 Security leader title.

the organization, and this could not be a committee. Someone needed to be appointed with this responsibility, which had the effect of organizations paying attention to the role and the types of individuals that would best be suited for the role. The term *Officer* in many organizations has special meaning and is reserved for individuals who have an executive presence at the CEO's table. The fact that many organizations still do not recognize the CISO/CSO role, as borne out by this survey (Figure 1.3), indicates that the security leader is still operating at a lower level in the organization than typically promoted within the industry (reporting at an executive level to another executive).

Security Leadership Themes

The survey provided many open-ended questions to get to the issues that security leaders must deal with during the course of their daily interactions with end users, middle management, and the executive suite. The observations from these individuals were grouped into 20 different "themes," or "issues," if you will, for which security officers attempt to find answers. The answers to the questions must be met with the typical consultant answer — "it depends" — because company size, culture, individual ability, maturity of the security program, influencing regulations, etc., will be factored into the specific response. However, the purpose of the survey was to uncover these themes so that others could perform more exploratory research into methods that have been successful and unsuccessful. The themes are shown in Figure 1.4.

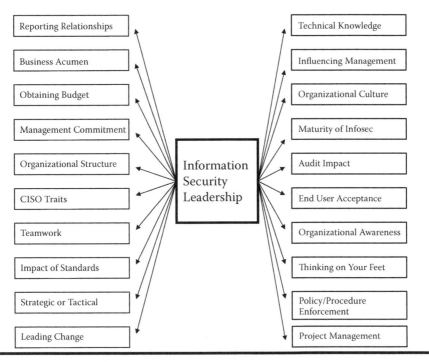

Figure 1.4   Survey themes.

The importance of the various soft skills were noted in Figure 1.5, where questions were asked about tenacity, perseverance, oral and written communication skills, strategic business planning, and so forth. These results will be referred to as the themes are explained in more detail.

Reporting Relationships

With as many articles that have been published that promote the ideas that security "is not solely an IT issue," "must be aligned by the business," or "is about risk management," one is led to believe that the function is reporting to the CEO, COO, or risk management executive. However, information security is still reporting predominantly to someone with information technology responsibilities (Figure 1.6). These include titles such as the chief information officer, VP of Information Technology, VP Architecture, and Director/Manager of IT. In fact, a full 65.2 percent of the security officers reported to an IT person, with 13.4 percent reporting to the CEO, COO, CFO, Risk Manager, Compliance Officer, or General Counsel — combined! Security is still seen, for the most part, primarily as an IT issue that is best understood and managed by the individual charged with managing the company's information systems. Obtaining a seat at the executive table was found to be

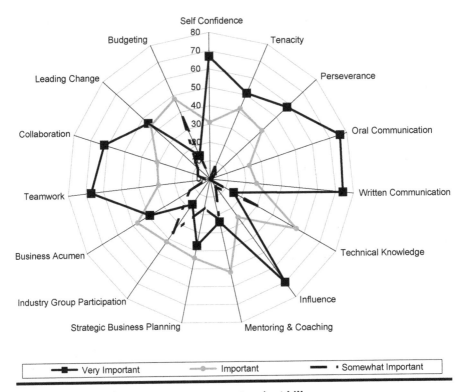

Figure 1.5   Security management competencies/skills.

a challenge; as long as security was grouped with IT, it was felt that IT would not be viewed as a "thought partner" but rather an "execution partner."

Several respondents noted that while the security organization reports to the information technology department, there is a perceived conflict of interest with this reporting relationship, and would prefer that it resided elsewhere within the organization. CIOs are driven by delivering high availability and new functionality to meet business requirements. Recommended alternatives were to have the security leader report to the CEO, CFO, or compliance officer to preserve the independence necessary. It was also suggested that the model works if the CIO understands the security issues; however, this also makes the security efforts contingent on the person versus the establishment of the information security program. Reporting to the CIO also reinforces the notion that information security is all about the technology. Good security practices may be sacrificed for what makes the CIO and the IT department appear successful in completing the projects on time and maintaining the original budget. Some CIOs viewed the CISO position as one that competes

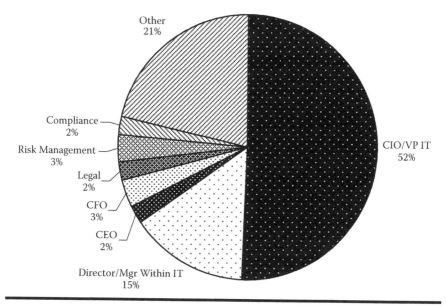

Figure 1.6   Reporting relationship.

with their own time for the board of directors, especially when competing for face time. Some also felt that reporting outside of the IT department provided greater visibility and ability to generate greater awareness of the security issues.

Others noted that the conflict of issues surrounding the CIO reporting relationship was overblown and poor results are really the result of poor executive management versus the reporting relationship. Some favored the reporting relationship, as they were much more in touch with the changes and new developments within the Information Technology projects (Figure 1.6). The personnel working on those projects were more likely to support the security initiatives if security was within the same organization. If the security leader is working closely with the IT personnel, it was felt that the security function takes on more of a focus toward security implementations versus risk, compliance, and managing auditing issues. Security operations work well within this model; however, one respondent felt that attention is applied to the operational issues at the expense of security governance, education, awareness, and architecture.

Some organizations had the reporting within the IT organization while there were immediate IT issues that needed to be addressed, but planned to move it to an independent entity outside of IT once the issues were sufficiently addressed. Several organizations that had the security leader report to the CIO or other IT management person also had a dotted-line reporting relationship to the CEO, COO, CFO,

Compliance Officer or the Board of Directors. This model provided the closeness of the IT relationships that provided an avenue for external reporting.

The comments seemed to infer that where some security leaders were not happy with the reporting relationship, and others were (with respect to the IT leader), the determining factor of success had to do with the CIO's support of the information security initiatives.

Business Acumen

The respondents indicated that business acumen was seen as a skill used often (54 percent) and always (32 percent), slightly higher than the importance of technology. In terms of importance, it is interesting to note that there is a significant difference between the "very important" views of technical knowledge (15 percent) versus that of needing business acumen (39 percent). While all respondents felt that both categories were at least somewhat important, business acumen appeared to be more crucial. This is an interesting observation, given the fact that most of respondents still maintain the security function within the IT organization.

It was noted that security professionals are constantly challenged to understand business processes, underlying processes, and the applications that support them. Business acumen is also not included in the training of most security programs on information security and is highly dependent upon the vertical industry to which the security professional is engaged. Another noted that security is viewed as a technology skill, and there is a definite need to understand the business, culture, direction, and goals before recommending security solutions.

Obtaining Budget

"Show me the money" might be the mantra of the security leader. With 99 percent feeling that budgeting was important, and with 62 percent feeling it was very important or important, 63 percent felt they were good at performing it. Respondents indicated that it was hard to convince the business unit management that spending money on security will add value to their business objectives. Budgeting is also difficult because initiatives are developed and funded within the business areas without the input of security. It was also noted that it is hard for the CFO/Finance Department to understand technical security terms, just as it is difficult for security professionals to understand accounting. Return on investment (ROI) calculations were viewed as less effective in advancing the security agenda. Some difficulties were also recognized due to the organization's capital planning and procurement rules. Even good ideas had pressures due to competition for resources and funding from other areas.

Funding for security projects was also viewed as difficult due to many uncertainties when the project begins, which created approaches where some contingency funding (padding) was put into the calculations to increase the likelihood of success of the effort. Budgeting also was seen as being difficult in those security functions that were not being given a separate, distinct budget for information security. Finally, one security leader indicated it was not an area he had particular interest in.

Management Commitment

One respondent noted, "Difficult to remain committed to a profession where the organization is not yet committed to backing the information security program, despite 'great presentations' and 'great programs,' executive backing is required." Another noted, "I do not understand the politics of getting things done, tend to get intolerant of those who disagree after I have made a good business case." Others referred to the importance of the tone at the top as essential for sustained security success, and the culture not providing security much visibility.

However, while some viewed obtaining management commitment as a major challenge; others provided insight into how executive management has provided the appropriate support to the security program. The following techniques were noted as examples of how executive management provided this support:

- Support for broad security awareness and education programs requiring all employees participate
- Announcements to management for major security program changes
- Evaluation of executives by tracking their compliance with security goals
- Support for the security oversight committees
- Providing capital and expense commitments
- Feature stories in the company magazine on information security
- Letters from the CEO, CIO, and CISO on a regular basis
- Security policies delivered by the CFO
- C-level incorporation of security into employee performance reviews
- Chairman created committee with his direct reports to oversee process with updates from the CISO
- Dedicated officers meet quarterly to discuss various issues
- Town hall meetings mentioning security from senior management
- Executive committee must approve all security policies and review security program annually; approval includes preamble from the company president
- Utilize outside consultants for risk analysis
- Communication by executives of need to comply with regulations

The responses made it clear that support from the senior executives was essential, but different security leaders face varying views of what support was necessary. For some, the acknowledgment of the security program and support of the training initiative were enough; for others, they desired a more active role such as the involvement of the executives in an oversight or steering committee. There appear

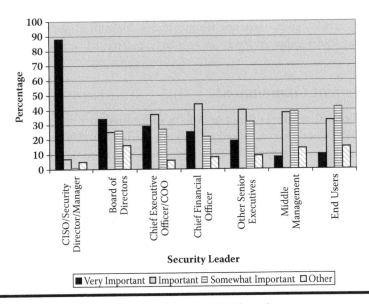

Figure 1.7 Perceived importance of the security function.

to be "pockets" of support across the organizations interviewed, with some cases showing strong support by the CEO, and mixed support across the other business leaders. The time executives devote to security issues was also noted as a limitation, with the held expectation that those assigned to managing security functions would take care of issues as they arose.

When the security leaders were asked what importance each of the management classes put on security, the "very important" scale ranged from ten percent (end users) to 88 percent (the security leader). Although they felt the board of directors viewed it as at least somewhat important, the results were somewhat evenly split between very important (34 percent), important (25 percent) and somewhat important (26 percent). The largest challenge appeared to be with middle management and end users, rating 39 and 42 percent somewhat important, respectively. These numbers suggest that while the awareness of security exists, it is not holding the highest level of attention of management. It is unclear what the high watermark should be within an organization, which might vary depending upon organization type. The results are shown in Figure 1.7.

Organizational Structure

Collaboration across business units was seen as a challenge, when it was noted that the business units themselves do not always collaborate with each other or see how security applies to them. Business group goals may also be different. Decentralized structures were noted as a hurdle as communication is more difficult and requires more attention. In addition, they were cited as being more difficult structures to implement common processes. Dotted-line relationships (i.e., to the CIO and to the CEO or the Audit & Compliance Committee) were viewed as challenging to implement.

Teamwork

In any organization teamwork is essential to get the appropriate perspective on a particular problem, and to ensure that individuals feel they are able to contribute according to their talents. Teamwork across business units can be especially challenging, particularly when the information security goals are perceived to be at odds with the immediate business goals and viewed as an impediment to delivering solutions that are inexpensive and are introduced quickly to the market place. Gaining consensus on the issues under these conditions is a slow process, as everyone has different agendas and the security leader must balance these various objectives to attain a solution that benefits everyone involved. Security leaders also noted in the survey that the security leader is trying to sell something that the business doesn't want and is perceived that it will make their jobs harder. Security immediately conjures up the word "no" and presents a barrier to the ability to communicate, which must be overcome. A majority of respondents noted that teamwork was a very important skill (67 percent) to be effective, and a full 61 percent indicated that they always exercise the skill. One survey respondent noted that it was important to have the involvement of people on the Information Security team who had prior functional IT experience beyond security, as it increased the working relationships to determine how best to meet the regulations.

Impact of Standards and Regulations

About one-third of the respondents had implemented some standard/control framework such as the Control OBjectives for Information and related Technology (COBIT) (34 percent), Information Technology Infrastructure Library (ITIL) (29 percent), National Institute of Standards and Technology (NIST) (32 percent), and International Organization for Standardization (ISO) (33 percent). Another 23 to 37 percent were either evaluating or would be implementing within the year, as shown in Figure 1.8. The predominant usage of these standards suggests the desire for a control framework to guide and base the security decisions of the information security program on something that has been blessed by a respected entity. Survey respondents also noted some difficulty in promoting some of these "best practices," particularly when they went beyond what is really required. Several security leaders were pushing ITIL, ISO, and Capability Maturity Model Integration (CMMI) certification within their organizations and saw these as tough challenges.

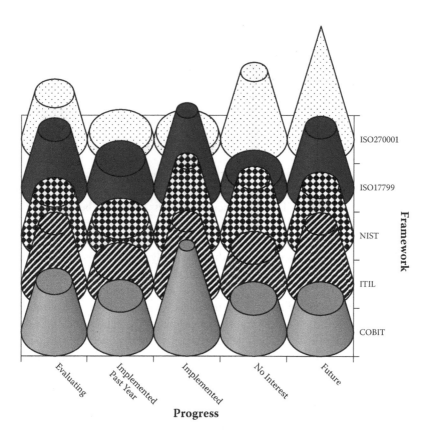

	Evaluating	Implemented Past Year	Implemented	No Interest	Future
□COBIT	21	15	36	14	14
◪ITIL	25	9	26	15	25
◨NIST	18	7	31	24	21
■ISO17799	24	12	32	7	25
◻ISO270001	19	3	3	28	47

Figure 1.8 Impact of standards.

Why are security leaders embarking on these challenges? The answers typically centered on the need to have an industry-accepted framework to demonstrate compliance with the emerging regulations. So what regulations have been pressing? As it turns out, organizations are being faced with multiple regulations (Figure 1.9), such as HIPAA (71.3 percent), GLBA (51.1 percent), Sarbanes–Oxley (62.8 percent), FISMA (22.3 percent), and a plethora of other regulations such as the Patriot Act, Securities Exchange Commission (SEC) regulations for trading partners, Food and Drug Administration security rules, Supervisory Control and Data Acquisition (SCADA), California Senate Bill 1386 on security incident reporting, state privacy laws, Payment Card Industry (PCI) standards, Office of Management and Budget (OMB) A-130 Circular Appendix III, SAS070 audits,

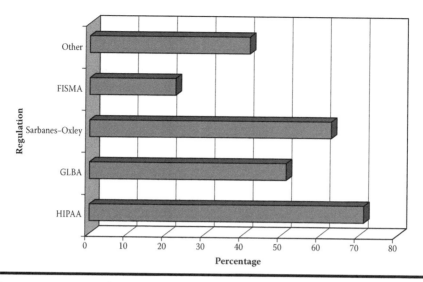

Figure 1.9   Impact of regulations.

and others. Each of these regulations introduces a slightly different focus or level of detailed analysis on the security program. One respondent noted that the pressure placed by one of the government regulators on the security programs forced the organization to embark on what seemed to be an impossible task of log management, only to have the effort result in receiving an innovation award by a respected industry publication. Several respondents noted involvement of cross-functional departments from Internal Audit, Information Technology, Human Resources, Legal, and the business units as a critical factor in developing the controls to achieve SOX compliance. One respondent noted that the operational risk environment was addressed through the use of a control framework, in their case COBIT, with security as a key function. The environment is now migrating to a risk management environment, which includes IT as one of the components of operational risk. Another respondent noted that the size of the project to define the control frameworks was daunting and the use of an outside consultant to build the framework was very helpful. Once the framework was defined, the current internal staff is handling the details without significant effort.

Information Security Perception: Strategic or Tactical?

Strategic business planning was noted as "very important" and "important" by 37 percent and 44 percent of the security leaders, respectively. With 81 percent viewing Strategic Business Planning as important, it is interesting to note that only 49 percent use this skill often and 25 percent use this skill always. This may be related to the placement of the information security responsibility within the IT organization. This may also suggest that there is room to enhance the strategic capabilities of the security organization to provide more emphasis to long-term issues in place of day-to-day operational concerns. Some security leaders expressed the sentiment that their organizations did not share enough information on the strategic plans, making it difficult to align security with these future initiatives. Others noted that alignment with business goals and objectives was most critical.

Leading Change

Leading change was also noted as an important skill of the security leader (46 percent "very important," 44 percent "important"). It was noted that this is difficult, as security practitioners are seen as conservative risk-takers and have the image of "more red tape" for people to get their projects completed. Some security leaders also view change as introducing risk, and if security education has not been properly communicated, those necessary to support the implementation may not understand the rationale for the changes. Change also tended to create an initial period of higher costs or effort. One respondent noted that bringing forward change was difficult from a security point of view, as the perception is that the security leaders are much more restrictive than their peers (in the industry); however, benchmarks have demonstrated that they are not. This makes advancing the security agenda more difficult.

In industries where constant change is the norm these days, such as the healthcare industry, it was noted that while business is faced with constant change in business strategies and reimbursement strategies, the security changes are competing with the same cultural changes. Leading change and "making it stick" in these environments was viewed as a constant battle.

Technical Knowledge

While 55 percent of the respondents rated technical knowledge as "important," only 15 percent of those respondents rated the technical knowledge as "very important." This is in stark contrast to the "very important" rating on the "softer skills" such as self confidence (67 percent), tenacity (55 percent), perseverance (58 percent), oral communication skills (76 percent), written communication skills (74 percent), influencing (70 percent), business acumen (39 percent), teamwork (67 percent), collaboration (62 percent), and leading change (46 percent). In fact, the only category that scores lower is budgeting (14 percent). This is very interesting, given that much of the literature and training within the security profession is still predominantly focused on developing the technical skill set, and that security is still viewed by many business leaders as a technical discipline. It is clear from these results that while technical knowledge is still seen as "important" (55 percent) and "somewhat important" (30 percent) by the respondents, it does not rise to the same level for this role as the other abilities. Some respondents noted the importance of keeping up with a certain technical level; however, the rate of constant technical change made this challenging. One respondent noted that it was difficult to keep up technically, while at the same time keeping their focus on the big picture. They viewed their role as a generalist and an evangelist for information security.

Influencing

Influencing was viewed by 70 percent of the respondents to be "very important," with 26 percent reporting "important." This skill area was seen as used most often (61 percent) by the respondents; however, with 30 percent indicating that they always used this skill, this suggests that there is room for improvement in the competency. This was seen as a challenging area, where different individuals have different ideas about what should be done and how it should be accomplished. It was also noted that improvement in this area would lead to getting security activities completed more efficiently and effectively. One respondent noted that individuals are motivated by many factors, some of which may appear to be irrational. Another noted that influencing is difficult because the audience (business areas) are seldom receptive to the message, because "nothing bad has happened here," at least that they are aware of, and don't see the information security issues which could negatively affect the company. Influencing individuals to view information security as a business investment instead of a business punishment was seen as a challenge. Influencing without direct authority over individual departments and end users that were necessary to implement secure practices was viewed as another challenge. The ability to influence those where no direct control is present is seen as essential to executive career progress in many companies.

"I am not a political animal by nature," indicated one respondent, which highlights the technical upbringing of many individuals within the security field. The individual indicated that he or she needed to work more at networking and helping others to believe that the security leader's ideas were actually their own ideas.

A balanced approach to security was suggested by another, whereby security leaders need to demonstrate that they understand the business needs and are concerned about them, as an alternative to "forcing information security down their throats." This was perceived to be the most critical factor in advancing the security agenda to meet the business imperatives.

Others noted that even though the common mantra was to show how security "enables" the business, in actual practice, this was difficult to demonstrate. Pragmatic, practical solutions between Information Technology and the business were suggested to provide the necessary controls. Some IT individuals were noted as tough to influence why security was needed at that level and would prefer a "live and let live"-type model. Finally, advocating a risk-based mentality in the influencing activities was viewed as beneficial, as business leaders understand the concept of risk.

Organizational Culture

Organizational culture sets the tone, framework, and operational context in which the security leader must operate. Culture, in many ways, is a nebulous word, which has different meanings to different people. Culture has been defined as "a way of life for an entire society" and, as such, it includes the manners, dress, language, religion, rituals, and norms of behavior such as law and mortality, and systems of belief. Not surprisingly, when asked the question, "What impact does your organization's culture have on the ability for information security to succeed?" a wide variety of answers were received, depending upon the individual interpretation of "culture." The wide range of answers suggests that the security officer needs to pay attention to these factors because no matter how subtle some of them may be, each has the potential to influence the success of the information security program. A synopsis of some of the observations by security leaders on culture included the following:

- Individuals who have been with the organization a long time are used to doing things a certain way and are resistant to change. Helping them to change and see the rationale for the change is a challenge.
- Culture is open and creative, which creates challenges for introducing more restrictive controls into the environment. These individuals do not accept control, policies, and procedures openly.
- Tone at the top is critical, as the lower-level management and employees look for clues to see if the senior leadership is in support of the security, audit, and compliance initiatives.
- Culture promotes responsible behavior and ethics by the organization and the individual, with information security being a key part of these goals to protect the client information.
- Moving from a culture where "everyone knew everyone else" to becoming more security conscious as an organization took about 3 years.
- Company operates in a highly regulated industry with much litigation, which forces us to pay close attention to the compliance issues.
- Information security is a relatively immature profession; therefore, it is underfunded and less understood.
- Security is not centrally managed, which creates challenges to implement common policies, procedures, and standards.
- Areas with a customer service focus as the driving factor were the most difficult to corral and comply with the rules.

- Banking and financial business is used to compliance with regulators, laws, regulations, and a large number of internal and external audits, making the information security sale easier. Due to this fact, in this organization, there is the support necessary.
- Information security is not provided much visibility.
- New companies do not have the legacy systems to slow down change.
- Business culture is risk averse and security/control minded.
- Too much trust within the organization, which makes implementing controls difficult. Security measures are viewed as "big brother" who undermines the high-trust norm within the environment. Therefore, a fine line has to be managed to demonstrate to the external world that it can be trusted.
- Risk-taking organization tends to take the approach of being "self-insured" and applies this to information security decisions, and may take more risks than necessary.
- Have found that including management in the assessments produces more buy-in for the future actions, which need to be implemented to enhance security.
- Culture is the core principles of the organization that govern politics, communications, willingness to share and evolve, competition, and entrepreneurialism. Culture in this sense is not defined as being a "security-minded organization," but must be considered in the broader sense.
- An open environment where individuals are free to communicate openly contributes to the success of the security program.
- Information Technology must be in sync with the business goals; otherwise, it is very difficult to inject information security practices.
- Intellectual property is a large asset in our organization; hence, the support for information security is there.
- Cultural changes are slow and require dedication and perseverance.
- Business plans and best processes are great, but if the culture doesn't support you, you can't be successful.
- "It is an Oil Supertanker, difficult to turn!"
- Company culture views security as a cornerstone to success, plus with the culture of a factory-worker mentality, where you do what you are told, makes for a straightforward communications and expectations-setting process.
- Fear of change is the mode of the culture, so, because security can affect many areas of the organization, the changes are usually debated and fought until they are defeated.
- Banking culture protects customer accounts; healthcare industry individuals are burnt out from other initiatives that have been more critical to them (i.e., creating more passion) than information security.

After reviewing the above snippets of insight into different organizations, it should be clear that cultures are vastly different and have different views of the importance of information security. The take-away is that the security leader needs to understand the culture of the organization that he is working within to be able to develop the program, which takes these factors into account. The survey results also suggest that success can be created in a wide range of cultures, provided that the security leader is willing to be adaptable in understanding the needs of the business areas that he is working to protect.

Maturity of Information Security Field

One of the challenges noted by several individuals was the relative immaturity of the information security profession. Although information security has been in practice within information technology organizations for several decades, the general population until recent years has not recognized the scope and importance of information security. As such, the profession is still at the state of convincing organizations of the need, defining roles, and securing the appropriate funding. Due to the regulations in some industries, some companies have become more accepting of the need for the role and have been staffing these functions. Government agencies have also increased the focus on information security through the appointment of CISOs and increased audits.

Impact of Audits

Although some respondents noted the amount of time involved with the auditors was significant, others noted that the audits were helpful in advancing the security program. Resources were allocated and management attention was generated as a result of the audits. Security controls become key factors in being able to achieve clean audit opinions to support the financial statements of the organization. Organizations were utilizing the regulators, internal/external audits, and escalation to the Audit & Compliance committees to raise visibility of security issues.

End User Security Acceptance

One respondent noted that employees were seeing the benefit of asking security questions and felt comfortable in doing so. Management was highlighted as "participants in information security and employees were taking their lead." Another noted that people (in banking) understand sensitivity and not making errors, but we need to teach them about unencrypted files, tracking shipments, and not protecting hard copy.

Organizational Awareness

Techniques utilized included newsletters; mandatory annual training; posters; Web sites; emails, etc. to management and end users. Others sent monthly reports to the board and senior management each month. Letters from the CEO, CIO, and CISO to the organization on a regular basis were utilized. Others noted no formal communication of security priorities.

Functions Supported by Security Leader

Several security leaders indicated that implementation of security policies was a big win for them which took perseverance and the involvement of the business units prior to approval by senior leadership. Of the functions reporting to the security leader, responsibility for security policies was noted as a responsibility by 82 percent of the respondents, the function most common to security leaders as shown in Figure 1.10.

Other functions that report to most of the security leaders polled include security awareness (81 percent), security strategy (77 percent), incident response (65 percent), security architecture (59 percent), audit issue management (56 percent), and research and development (53 percent). Fewer security leaders reported having the operational security responsibilities, such as security administration (48 percent), intrusion detection (39 percent), and firewall monitoring (34 percent). Although a fair number of security leaders have these responsibilities reporting to them, one could infer that the technical and operational activities are left to the groups that are handling day-to-day operational activities, which permits more focus to be placed on ensuring that the security strategy for the organization is being developed to meet the business needs. The combination of emphasis on security strategy, policy development, security awareness, and incident response is congruent with the fact that only 15 percent rated technical skills as "very important" for this role. Additionally, the fact that the security leader is having to focus on

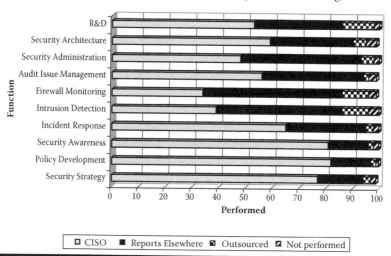

Figure 1.10 Functions supported.

strategy and policy development issues, which involve understanding the business and influencing the other business leaders, one can easily see where the "soft skills" in Figure 1.5 tend to take on greater importance.

Participation on Committees

Most security leaders were involved in a committee to advance the security agenda, as shown in Figure 1.11. The standing bodies were identified, as an opportunity for the information security function to identify value to the organization by working to support the business needs. Through these committees, it was generally felt that the security agenda was kept in front of the committees. Committees such as the Information Technology Steering Committee helped to secure funding for security initiatives, as all major projects had to pass through this committee. Representation on these committees is also typically composed of executives involved in the decision-making process. Committees such as Security Councils were utilized to make security strategy and policy recommendations to senior management for subsequent approval and dissemination across the organization.

One respondent noted that although these committees are effective in communicating with senior management, security awareness of the issues was not as well known at middle management levels. Generally, the involvement of senior management in these committees was viewed as a necessary step to influence management and obtain its support for the initiatives. Presentations to the board pitching security initiatives usually result in debates, which in turn end up providing the impetus for funding future security initiatives.

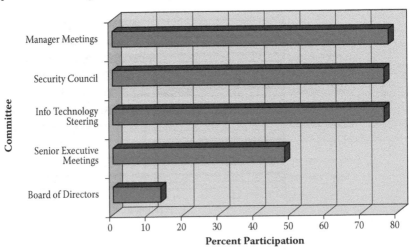

Figure 1.11   Security representation on committees.

Dealing with Different and Difficult People

Leading a security program requires the ability to work with many different people, often in different countries and companies. They often have different cultures, value systems, backgrounds, and personal and professional priorities. Security is apt to be met with resistance because many times it is perceived that it is inhibiting people's ability to perform their jobs, contrary to the desire by security practitioners to promote security as an enabler. The survey respondents were asked how they dealt with difficult people, and the following were some of the suggestions:

- Focus on win/win solutions, providing the other parties with something they need.
- Explain how the security controls are for the betterment of the company and will help in daily jobs.
- Keep communication on an open, honest, professional level and not be drawn into the toxic conversation.
- Try to understand their viewpoint and cooperate with them, but sometimes you must stand firm and indicate that these are the rules and they need to abide by them.
- Listening and trying to solve their problems.
- Active listening and showing support by echoing back their issue to demonstrate understanding prior to resolving the issue.
- Face-to-face communications are more effective when resolving conflicts.
- Make the issue about the facts and remove emotions as much as possible.
- Difficult people should be treated as any other challenge. As in the game of chess, when it appears difficult, you must continue and get more creative to make things go the way that will be most beneficial to the organization.
- It may be necessary to find other people who share your viewpoint to collaborate with, recognizing that this particular individual may never support your initiatives.
- Adjust communication based upon their personality style, as the security leader is part psychologist. Try to understand their style, determine if they are analytical, visual, or broad perspective-oriented and then try to match the style which makes them most comfortable.
- Engage them and make them part of the process.
- Try to understand the motivations that contributed to their point of view and understand the challenges that they may be facing.

Many of the responses seemed to suggest that many security leaders understood the importance of being open and listening to the concerns of the so-called "difficult" individual and subsequently trying to create a workable solution. It was also recognized that in so doing, there was not a one-size-fits-all solution that would be effective.

Successes and Failures

Individuals potentially learn as much from their failures as their successes. To that end, those surveyed were asked to identify some of their failures and what they learned from them. These lessons are expanded on in the security pitfalls chapter.

Demographics

The security leader sample was not a statistical sample and was answered on a voluntary basis for the purposes of understanding the issues that the security leaders were experiencing. It may be useful to understand the backgrounds of the security leaders to set the appropriate context, as well as to understand the education, credentials, salary, and reporting relationship of the survey respondent. The following are the demographics of the respondents:

- Security leader title (Figure 1.3)
- Reporting relationship (Figure 1.6)
- Work and security experience (Figure 1.12)
- Highest education level achieved (Figure 1.13)
- Total compensation range (Figure 1.14)
- Major certifications held (Figure 1.15)

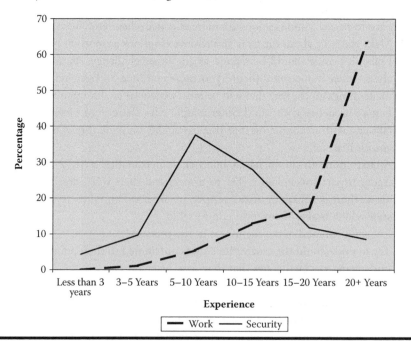

Figure 1.12 Work and security experience.

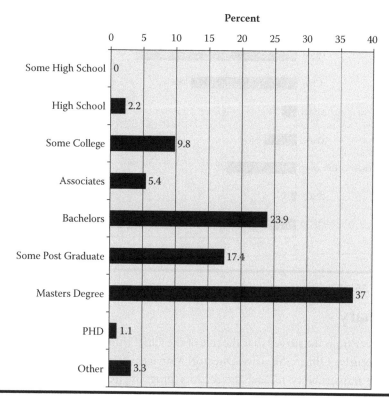

Figure 1.13   Highest education level.

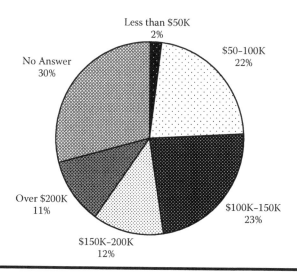

Figure 1.14   Total compensation range.

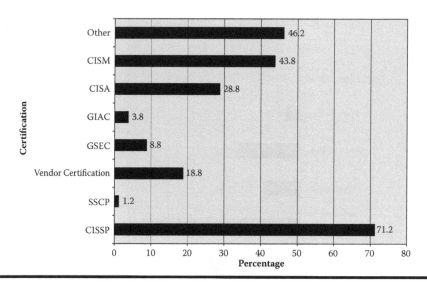

Figure 1.15   Certifications held.

Summary

It was clear from the survey that the role of the Chief Information Security Officer, Chief Security Officer, Security Director, Manager, or other individuals charged with the responsibility to lead the security programs readily identified with the need to work in some capacity with senior management to continuously promote the security initiatives. Although technical skills were still viewed as needed, there was much more emphasis on the "soft skills" necessary to adequately perform the function. Management commitment was viewed as essential to the security program and obtaining this commitment was highly dependent upon the norms and culture of the organization. It was also recognized that not everyone within the organization was "dipped in the security juice" and the effective security leaders recognized this and tailored the message individually to those individuals. Finally, in the end, everyone will still experience his or her failures as well as successes, which have the ability to prepare the individual for the next situation.

Recap

- Formal CISO/CSO title is still emerging, with 24.3 percent of individuals surveyed holding the title, with other titles such as Security Manager and Director performing the function.
- Most organizations have security officers reporting into the IT Department, while it is at the same time perceived as a conflict of interest by some.

- Management can provide very visible support for security through its actions in a variety of ways.
- Technical knowledge is still important, but does not rise to the same level of importance for this role as the soft skills.
- Success can be achieved in a variety of organizational cultures if the security officer can adapt to the changes.
- Management commitment is essential, and successful security leaders develop methods to communicate their security message.

References

1. IT Infrastructure Library (ITIL), http://www.itil.co.uk.
2. COBIT 4.1, IT Governance Institute, http://www.itgi.org.
3. ISO/IEC 17799: 2005 Information Security Techniques — code of practice for information security management, International Organization for Standardization (ISO), http://www.iso.org.

A LEADERSHIP
MANDATE

Chapter 2

Who Companies Really Want to Hire: How to Advance Your Career and Have Great Success

Joyce Brocaglia

This chapter will discuss the evolving role of the information security/IT risk professional, give you an insider's view of what corporations are looking for when hiring, and, finally, provide some practical advice for advancing your career. So how is it that I'm qualified to have an opinion on this topic?

In 1986, I founded Alta Associates, the leading executive search firm that specializes in IT risk management and information security. For over twenty years we have built corporate information security organizations, consulting practices, and security product vendors. This has earned us the reputation as a trusted advisor to our clients.

The network of relationships that we've developed over the years has provided us with tremendous exposure to the inner circle of the industry and a very unique perspective of the evolution of the role of the IT risk and information security officer.

In the two decades that I've been recruiting in the security and controls industry I've witnessed many dramatic changes. With the number of threats and vulnerabilities constantly increasing, and regulatory requirements setting new standards for security strategies, the role of the security officer continues to evolve, and so do the skills necessary to be successful.

When we first began filling CISO roles we looked for the most technical person. We are now replacing technology-focused managers with executives who take a more holistic approach to technology risk management. Clients are asking us to find executives who understand operational effectiveness, governance, and partnerships, and who possess leadership skills.

We've witnessed the corporate culture of global organizations shift from placing focus on the technical aspects of information security, to focusing on managing the overall operational risk of the organization. IT security is being viewed as a slice of the much larger operational risk pie.

Operational Risk

So what is operational risk, why do companies think it's so important and what does this have to do with being a successful security executive?

Operational risk is "the risk of loss resulting from inadequate or failed internal processes, people, and systems or from external events, including loss related to legal risk." Besides technology risk, operational risk can include areas such as:

- Consumer compliance
- Legal and business continuity
- Fraud and theft
- Business processes
- Financial reporting
- Vendor management
- Human resources

In the past, organizations primarily focused on credit and financial risk management with a lesser focus on operational risk. Part of the reason is that operational risk is so expansive that it's hard to define and effectively address. However, as organizations face increased risks that fall outside of market and credit disciplines — such as risks related to technology and security, environmental risks (think pandemic flu, hurricanes, global warming), regulatory/compliance-related risks, and even new areas of risk (such as losing in litigation due to the inability to access information, i.e., e-discovery-related risk) — they are focusing on the development of enterprisewide operational risk-management capabilities that are more holistic and comprehensive.

Importance for Information Security Executives

The big picture is that your company's most senior-level executives and board of directors rely on timely and actionable risk information to enhance their ability to make decisions that will drive corporate efficiencies and operational effectiveness. These leaders realize that effective risk programs will ultimately improve customer service and increase shareholder value.

Many companies feel so strongly about this that their executives' incentive compensation models have a component driven by the results of their internal risk versus return performance measures. Forward-thinking companies recognize that business and IT executives need to establish standardized, repeatable ways to identify, prioritize, measure, and reduce business and technology risks, both collaboratively and effectively. This means that security executives who were accustomed to working in their own silo must now consider all business-related risk areas to align investments properly with exposures.

Because information risk management is becoming integrated into overall risk management, companies have redefined the successful traits of an information security officer. Executives are being sought who can understand and manage technology risk in a way that allows their company to meet organizational goals. They are no longer seeking security technologists to solve specific problems.

Insider's View: What Companies Want

So what really goes on behind the scenes when we are called upon by a client who wants us to partner with them on making a strategic hire?

When we begin a search for an information security executive our first step is to have an in-depth conversation with the executive management team. It is usually with the CIO or CTO, and sometimes the General Counsel or even the CEO of smaller companies. The initial discussion usually centers on defining what they are trying to accomplish with their security and risk organizations. I think it's important to note that this conversation seldom centers on the technical aspects of the role.

The Requirements

At the highest level, they talk about the importance of their ability to:

- Maintain confidentiality, integrity, and availability of services.
- Act competitively, while being secure and meeting privacy and regulatory requirements.
- Enhance the brand and overall reputation of the company.
- Speak in terms that have a bottom-line effect on the overall operational success of the business.

At a more tactical level they want someone who:

- Can manage the creation and implementation of enterprisewide solutions. Creation is the most important word here; they are looking for someone who has actually created enterprisewide solutions, not someone who just implemented other people's solutions.
- Has a thorough understanding of the business. It is essential to find someone who understands the operational risks associated with their particular business.
- Is aware of regulatory/legal/privacy implications. Successful candidates need to understand the impact that these requirements have on the risk programs they are implementing.
- Develops relationships and communicates and sells ideas effectively to senior management. We often do searches where there is a technically competent information security officer already on board, but he or she lacks the ability to formulate risk strategies and sell them effectively within the organization.
- Can apply a technology risk management approach. They understand that information security is not a technology issue; it's a business issue.
- Build the department's credibility. The key to success lies in building credibility. Start by tailoring your security posture to the specific needs and risk appetites of the business. Speaking in terms of operational risk will give you a common language of understanding. Developing common ground is going to make it easier for you as a security practitioner to gain credibility and support. If you want to be effective you have to start thinking in terms of operational risk now.

The Unwritten Requirements: There's More to the Job Than the Job Description

I'm sure you have seen many job descriptions posted internally in your organization or externally on job boards. Security postings usually focus on the technical requirements. What many people fail to recognize is that this is just the price of admission and far from a guarantee that the job is yours. It's true that in the past, if your background matched the requirements profile in an information security job description you were well on your way to landing the job. This was partly due to the lack of qualified, experienced candidates and partly because the profession was not as mature as it is today. Although many people focus on these written requirements when interviewing, it is your ability to fulfill the unwritten requirements that will ultimately land you the job.

Soft Skills

The unwritten requirements are traits that you have to make evident to your current employer or have the ability to convey to a potential employer. I speak often about differentiators, your ability to articulate the value you add to the overall success of your team and your company as a whole. Among the greatest differentiators are the soft skills that you bring to the table. It is essential that you recognize the importance of conveying these skills to a potential employer.

Communication Skills

Communicating your differentiators is one of the keys to success. You could be the most qualified person for the job, but if you are ineffective in conveying that to the prospective employer you're not going to be selected. Even the most accomplished individuals sometimes get tongue-tied when it comes to selling themselves.

I like to use the acronym STAR when advising candidates on how to describe their experiences. Think of a relevant Situation or Task that will describe an accomplishment that either generated income, saved time or expenses, built or leveraged relationships, or was an innovative solution. Articulate the Action you took and explain the Result it had on the organization. Keep it simple and to the point, and select the accomplishments that are most relevant to the position at hand.

Desirable Personal Attributes

The five most important personal attributes that companies look for when making strategic hires are:

1. *Leadership:* The most sought-after trait. Former U.S. Secretary of State Colin Powell is credited with the following quotation that I think especially applies to security officers: "Great leaders are almost always great simplifiers who can cut through argument, debate, and doubt to offer a solution everybody can understand."
2. *Confidence with humility:* You must display a mature sense of purpose and confidence in yourself, your abilities, and the importance of your mission.

You're only an expert for a few minutes … there's always someone who knows more. Displaying arrogance is not the way to build consensus. You'd be surprised how many professionals don't get job offers simply because of their cavalier attitudes.

3. *Passion:* The willingness to display the strength of your convictions. Tenacity is key in the face of never-ending and ever-increasing challenges. If you don't believe in your mission, why should anyone else?

4. *Personal integrity:* Integrity is the foundation on which our industry is built. Always tell the truth. Your peers, subordinates, and managers all must trust your personal and professional ethics.

5. *Sense of humor:* In this job you need to roll with the punches. Having a sense of humor is a necessity for your own survival and the well-being of your team.

Many intelligent, knowledgeable candidates fall short on interviews because they underestimate the value of their soft skills in obtaining a position. Whether you are interviewing or not, do a little soul searching and ask yourself how you measure up on the unwritten requirements scale. The time to think about where you need improvement is now. Corporations are shifting their culture and adding much more value to technology professionals who display strong soft skills and business acumen. It is just as important for you to let these qualities shine through with your current boss and clients as it is with a potential employer.

Now, let's assume you've either gotten a new job or decided to climb the corporate ladder at the company where you are currently employed. How do you ensure that you're not one of those security officers I'm asked to replace?

Collaboration Is the Key

As companies are forced to deal with the complexities of risk from doing business in a global economy they have recognized the important role that risk management plays in achieving their business goals. In doing so, they have to constantly align their information security, compliance, governance, business continuity, and operational risk and audit activities. When you consider that information security executives now play an integral part of a larger risk organization, you begin to understand the importance of collaboration. I think everyone would agree that our success as individuals and the success of our companies rely on interdependent technologies and relationships. Managing risk successfully requires collaboration between information security, privacy, risk management, and governance functions. Companies are interested in hiring professionals who are capable of connecting the dots.

Managing by Influence

When we talk about people, process, and technology, there's a reason why people come first. If you can't positively influence the people, all the processes and technology in the world aren't going to do it for you. Our more progressive clients are beginning to ask the question, "How do you socialize your security program?" What they want to know is, how you achieve results without having direct authority or staff. You must be able to give examples where you were able to leverage your influence and get positive results. You must be able to highlight your organizational agility. Organizational agility is knowing who to influence and when and how to get things done through formal and informal channels. Whether or not you are interviewing, assess the strength of your organizational agility and work on making it better. Security is about solving complex problems and the only way that's going to happen is by bringing people together.

Articulating Business Value

The only way you can communicate effectively is to articulate the business value. Know your audience and talk in a language that they understand. One of the most difficult tasks for a technical information security professional to master is messaging. You have to learn to deliver the appropriate message to the audience. To do this you first have to understand security from a broader risk perspective. Then it is extremely important to tailor your security posture to the specific needs and risk appetites of the business. Speaking in terms of operational risk will give you a common language of understanding. It's one that business managers have lived with for years. Be prepared to give examples of where you have utilized this common ground to build credibility and gain consensus.

Execution: The Ability to Get Things Done

My clients are all results oriented. At the end of the day you have to prove your ability to execute and complete tasks successfully. Companies look for a track record of successful execution in their leaders. Find ways to say "yes" to your internal or external clients and customers. Make security an enabler, not a roadblock, and you will be considered an invaluable part of the team

Breaking the Glass Ceiling

Everyone talks to me about reporting structure and wanting a seat at the table. Good leadership skills can really make a difference in being invited to that table. But you have to recognize that to be invited back to the table, you have to have good table manners. That means you have to step out of your comfort zone and do what it takes to gain the business understanding and executive-level presentation skills.

So many security professionals experience a conflict between their desire to move up in the organization and their instinct to remain in their comfort zone. In effect they have created their own glass ceiling. Until these attitudes change, technology risk professionals will never succeed in becoming a part of the executive team. Many technology risk professionals don't recognize this limitation and it's holding them back. By no means should they turn their back on technology, but they must start thinking of technology in terms of how it supports the business.

This same advice applies to gaining adequate funding for your security initiatives. Technology risk professionals must learn not to sell all the bells and whistles of the newest technology, but rather to make a clear and compelling business case to senior executives on how technology will enable them to achieve their objectives. You're more likely to get approval if you can provide them with real examples of how the investments they make

- Contribute to revenue
- Reduce costs
- Provide a competitive advantage, or
- Increase customer confidence

The bottom line is, technology is a means to an end, not the end in itself. As a security executive, you must recognize the different levels of risk that each business line is willing to accept and assist them in making strategic decisions based on this information. By directing your approach along these lines, you'll earn more credibility and find it easier to gain support and funding.

Finally and most importantly, if you're already doing this, then your goal is to figure out how to make each member of your team understand this. Remember, if the goal is to make InfoSec a part of the overall corporate culture, you need as many agents of influence as you can get, so start by cultivating your staff.

If you want to change perception of information security within your organization, you're going to have to begin in your own backyard. Take this as a call to action. You have to nurture and develop the thought leaders of the future. Remember, your success will be judged by the effectiveness of your team and its ability to add value, not on your individual contributions.

Building a Team

- When genuine teamwork is created, the whole is always greater than the sum of its parts.

- Good leaders build good teams. They recognize that to be successful they need the right mix of talent who can produce and message their results to stakeholders.
- When you are building your organization there are a few important steps to consider:
  - First, recognize that you and your team must make a commitment to devote the proper time and energy to the process, regardless of your busy schedules.
  - Partnering with an experienced recruiter will extend your leverage into the community, provide access to passive candidates, manage their expectations, and bring the search to a successful conclusion.
  - If you don't make the interview process a high priority, both the candidate and the recruiter will recognize your lack of commitment and will lose interest.
  - Begin by setting a formal process and time frame in place. Commit to scheduling a 15-minute call every week with your external recruiter and internal HR partner specifically to talk about feedback and scheduling. Timely and detailed feedback is essential to refining and completing a search.
  - Clearly define the role and responsibilities of the position and make sure that everyone interviewing the candidates understands the skills that should be evaluated. Be thoughtful when selecting the people who will do the interviewing. They are the face of your department and the message they communicate will make a significant impression on the candidate.
  - Make sure that someone is designated as the final decision maker with the authority and ability to work with Human Resources to ensure that things gets done.
  - Keep in mind that the candidate is evaluating the company throughout the entire interview process including the delivery of the offer. The smoother the process, the more likely the candidate will have more confidence about joining the team.

In summary, finding the right person takes time and effort from you, your staff, your management, and your recruiter. The longer the period of time from the first interview to the extension of an offer, the less likely you are to close the candidate. So make a true commitment and partner with a recruitment firm dedicated to do the same.

Personal Career Advancement

At the risk of sounding self-serving, there's a reason why movie stars and sports figures have agents: it's because there's a tremendous advantage to being represented by a professional. Think of the time that you've devoted to your craft as a security professional. Now imagine the benefit of partnering with a firm that has devoted that same level of commitment to helping individuals and organizations achieve their professional goals. Take control of your career, take control of your hiring process, and invest the time it takes to build a trust-based relationship with a recruiting firm.

Networking

Ask yourself, "How strong is my business network?" "Do I know whom I can count on for support within my company?" "How many people can I rely on from outside my company for sound advice?" No man or woman is an island. His or her ability to build a network of relationships provides the foundation for a true leader.

To build trust-based relationships, a leader needs to be a sophisticated networker capable of connecting with people at a deeper level. This takes time and effort, but a powerful network delivers high-value results.

Networking is a build-it-before-you-need-it process. You need to find a venue that best fits your personal goals. In 2003 I founded The Executive Women's Forum on Information Security, Privacy and Risk Management (www.infosecuritywomen.com), a gathering of over 200 of the most senior women executives in the security and risk industry who get together to discuss best practices and lessons learned. By participating, these executives build lifelines that they can rely on long after the conference is over.

Actively participating in a group like The Executive Women's Forum increases a circle of reference and influence. It's essential to your career development, success, and recognition as a leader to be involved in industry-recognized events and associations. Find one that fits your needs and it will provide an enormous return on your investment.

If your business networks are limited, so is your potential for success.

Soul Searching

- Do you have a vision of your next job? If not, why not? If so, how are you preparing yourself for it?
- Have you identified your weaknesses, and what are you doing to address them?
- How do you define success?

These are the types of questions that you should include in your personal career self-assessment. If you haven't defined your own career goals and objectives, you're not likely to achieve them. Make sure you do regular self-assessments and grade yourself on what you've accomplished to date, and then determine what next steps you need to take to prepare for the future.

In summary, the most successful ISOs are adaptive and enjoy the challenge of their constantly evolving role. Be open to new ideas, work diligently in creating and nurturing internal and external trust-based relationships, develop a generosity of spirit, and work toward enabling others to achieve success. If you can strengthen these characteristics, you'll hold the key to your personal success.

Recap

- Employers are now searching for security executives who can understand and manage technology risks in a way that allows their company to meet organizational goals.
- Speaking in terms of operational risk will give you a common language of understanding.
- The soft skills differentiate you. They include:
  - Communication: Think of a relevant situation that will describe an accomplishment that either generated income, saved time or expenses, built or leveraged relationships, or was an innovation.
  - Leadership: The ability to cut through an argument, debate, or doubt, and offer a solution everybody can understand and accept.
  - Confidence with humility: Display a mature sense of purpose, confidence in yourself, your abilities, and the importance of your mission.
  - Passion: Tenacity; the willingness to display the strength of your convictions.
  - Personal integrity: Honesty and ethics.
  - Sense of humor to roll with the punches.
- Managing risk successfully requires collaboration between multiple functions. The following attributes are critical:
  - Organizational agility: Knowing whom to influence and when and how to get things done through formal and informal channels.
  - Articulate business value: Tailor your security message to the specific needs and risk appetites of the business.
  - Execution: Find ways to say "yes" to your internal or external clients and customers.

Chapter 3

The Evolving Information Security Landscape

William Hugh Murray

This chapter recapitulates the emergence of the concept of information security and the requirement for it. It describes the enterprise response to that requirement. It discusses the careers of those who work in the field.

Next it presents a model of careers in general. The model can be used both to understand and plan careers. It suggests that all careers can be viewed as a series of phases, similar to those of schooling. After describing the model, the section applies it to security careers. Finally, it applies the model to the chief information security officer position and to those who aspire to that position.

Where Security Came From

The idea of information security originated in the late sixties and early seventies, in the era that the Association of Computing Machinery (ACM) has called the "golden age" of the mainframe. As with any new technology, the computer brought with it opportunity for crime that did not exist before. The advent of multi-user shared-resource computers brought with it a concentration of sensitive data. One concern was that the computer was necessary for access to this data. If it were damaged or otherwise unavailable, it might damage the health or continuity of the enterprise. This was complicated by the fact that computers were capital equipment, built to order, on delivery schedules measured in months.[1]

In the early days of the computer, efficiency increased with scale. Herbert R.J. Grosch observed that "the cost of computer systems increases at a rate equivalent to the square root of their power." Said another way, the cost of the computer rises linearly while the power grows exponentially. The faster the computer, the lower the cost of its use. Grosch said, "Things can get worse without limit."

The military found they were using larger and larger computers, for more and more sensitive applications, and shared across greater numbers of users. Much of this sharing was in what was called "time-sharing" mode, intended to exploit Grosch's "law." The Department of Defense (DoD) in general, and the Air Force in particular, were concerned that classified information might be observed by computer users who were not cleared for it, and that it might leak from one person or process to another. To a lesser extent, they were concerned that two or more people might cooperate to share information in violation of policy, as expressed in its security classification, and in ways (covert channels) not obvious to the managers of the computers, the information, or the users.

The DoD was also concerned about information leakage from electro-magnetic emanations from computers and input/output devices (TEMPEST). IBM's first product security manager was named in response to emanations from the early IBM 2260 CRT terminal.

Another driver was the concern about the impact of computers on personal privacy. It seemed obvious that as the cost of collecting and storing information fell, there would be more and more of it. It would be misused and inaccurate, would mislead, and it would leak. All of this has proven to be true, but only recently has it become a serious problem.

As the user population of mainframe systems began to exceed the low tens, the size of mutually trusting groups, it raised the specter of the rogue user who might use the computer to gain unintended access to another's data. The complexity and scale of the computer might cause errors and mask malice.

In this era rogue hackers began to emerge. They were few in number and their fame exceeded their cleverness. Like today, their primary attack was "social engineering," i.e., fraud and deceit. Unlike today, their motivation was less information than expensive computer and communications capacity.

The golden age of the mainframe ended with the introduction of the computer on a chip. Moore's law replaced Grosch's law. Moore observed that the number of circuits on a chip doubled every 18 months, that speed increased as the circuit size decreased, and that both power and cooling efficiency improved. The result has been exponential growth in use, uses, and users. As the use, uses, and users of computers grew, so did the risk. As the risk grew, the information security profession emerged to manage it.

The responsibility for protecting assets cannot be separated from the privilege of using them. The executive or manager who exercises the authority and discretion to say how and by whom an asset will be used has the responsibility to say how it will be protected. This executive or manager is often characterized as the "owner" of the data; that is to say, he exercises all of the organization's ownership rights in the asset. He must instruct the custodians and users of those assets on who is to protect them and to what level of risk.

However, the massive application of information technology within the enterprise often obscures the lines of authority and responsibility. It may also change the risks, i.e., the threats, vulnerabilities, and potential damage to the assets, in ways that may be novel or obscure. As a result most large enterprises have staff, managers, personnel, and resources to advise management on how best to assign responsibility for assets, how best to protect them, how to coordinate efforts, and how to measure the results. These staffs draft policy, develop standards and guidelines, monitor compliance, note variances, measure results, and recommend corrective action.

In the past, in very large enterprises, the enterprise staff responsibility for information security might have been in the corporate security function, sometimes in the records management function, in some banks in the risk management function, and in the defense industry in the DoD industrial security program. For reasons relating to the complexity, not to say the mystery, of information technology, a new, electronic media-focused staff emerged in the information technology (née data processing) function. This staff has evolved into the modern information security function. By the mid-seventies, information security (née data security) was emerging as a permanent business staff function.[2]

Current Status

Today the computer is ubiquitous. There are now adults who cannot remember a world without computers. Infants now learn to use a mouse before they learn to use a crayon. We now use computers for applications that would have been unthinkable a generation ago. These include image capture and storage, communication (e.g., voice and video teleconferencing), and entertainment (e.g., music and video). The computer has brought professional-level creativity into the hands of the amateur.

The Internet is revolutionizing business. Not only does it make trade more convenient, it makes markets dramatically more efficient. This is true not only in consumer markets facilitated by eBay® and PayPal®, but in almost every specialized industry and commodity market.

Computer performance continues to increase rapidly; Moore's law still holds. However, storage is improving even faster than performance; while the cost of computation halves every 18 months, the cost of storage halves every year. Cheaper storage results in more records, more databases, more machine-readable metadata, and more value.

Problems that were barely identified a generation ago are now routine. The anti-virus industry is now a multi-billion dollar business. In addition, we have security problems like spam, "phishing," and spyware that we did not even foresee. Network-based attacks are a daily occurrence and every enterprise must have perimeter defenses to resist them. Major leaks of personal data from lost media are reported weekly.

Information, more specifically intellectual property, is the asset of interest in the 21st century. We no longer have "cages" for cash, negotiable instruments, parts, tools, or office supplies. Thieves bypass most desktop computers to target those containing sensitive databases.

There is a shift from authorization controls to detective controls in business functional applications. For example, employees now make purchase decisions and place orders directly without pre-authorization. Businesses now pay for materials received before ensuring that they were ordered.

Security mechanisms lag the requirements and their application lags even further. A major function of the information security staff is to tell IT and general management where to spend the next dollar and hour. Security in the Internet is never better than it needs to be.

What's in a Name?

Before passing from history to careers, it would probably be a good idea to mention the way the subject field is styled. As has information technology, the field has enjoyed a number of names that reflect its emerging significance and breadth. In the early seventies the field was called data security and privacy. As the relationship between them was better understood, these two terms separated. The early staffs and managers were called simply data security. As the data processing function became information technology, the field became information security, and then information protection. The government, who often leads in nomenclature, now calls the field information assurance. This reflects a change in the government's emphasis from one that focuses on the confidentiality of classified information to one that includes integrity and availability. In this book, we may use any and all of these terms, but we are concerned more with what it is than with what it is called.

Career Model (Milestones)

This section will propose a career model or road map. People who are early in their career may find it a useful guide. Perhaps those late in their careers will find that the model describes their career.

In this section we will treat the professionals in generations. We will talk about the first generation, the pioneers, and the ones that were more chosen by the field than chose it. This generation lasted from the early seventies to the early nineties. This generation counted themselves in the hundreds to low thousands. The second generation, dating from the nineties to the present day, consciously chose to work in this field. They number themselves in the tens of thousands. The next generation will find that, like physicians, they will have to choose the field early just to qualify. There may not be as many of them as accountants and auditors, but they may still number in hundreds of thousands.

We do a pretty good job of giving young people a road map for their schooling. Every kindergartner knows about first grade, every college undergrad knows about graduate and professional schools. We do not do a very good job of giving them a road map for their careers. This may manifest itself in worker disorientation, unrealistic expectations, and sometimes in bad career decisions. This failure results in part from the absence of a map and in part from a failure to recognize the value, not to say the necessity, of having one.

The model proposes that all careers can be divided into phases. The first phase, let's call it Phase Zero, is the phase in which one gains the minimum entry requirements for the chosen career. These requirements may be limited to simply knowing how to read, write, and do simple arithmetic. For most careers it will require a high school diploma, technical school, or a college degree. A few will require professional school, a master's degree, or a doctorate.

For example, if one wishes to be a carpenter or other craftsman, reading, writing, and arithmetic may be sufficient entry-level credentials to get a job as an apprentice. If one wishes a career in the military, one must have a high school diploma to be a noncommissioned officer or, to be a commissioned officer, a college degree. To be a registered nurse, one needs a high school diploma and technical or nursing school. To be a physician, one must have a medical degree.

Note that Phase Zero does not qualify one to build houses or practice medicine. It merely qualifies one to enter the field. Phase Zero is also characterized by the fact that one is not paid for it. Indeed, one or one's family or community must pay. The duration of Phase Zero can be as little as six or eight years or as much as twenty, depending upon the field or career.

The first generation of security professionals usually had a degree in liberal arts, business, engineering, or accounting. Although the second generation may have these same degrees, many have degrees in the newly emerging computer science programs. Many of the third generation will have professional degrees from the dozens of schools now offering graduate degrees in information assurance.

Qualification

Phase One can be called "dues paying." Phase One is where one acquires and practices the knowledge, skills, and abilities to make a living in one's chosen field. For the carpenter, Phase One is called apprenticeship. For the physician, it is called internship. For the accountant, it may be junior auditor or bookkeeper. For the IT professional, it may be junior programmer, operator, or administrator. People in Phase One are paid. However, because they are not fully qualified and must be taught and supervised, they are normally paid less than their true economic value. Phase One may take as little as three years, but more likely as much as five.

In the first generation of information security, there were no entry-level jobs in the field. Most paid their dues in related fields like IT, intelligence, law enforcement, industrial security, audit, or records management. Today, there are entry-level jobs in the field and most will pay their dues in these jobs.

Phase Two may be called "masterwork." Masterwork is that phase of careers in which one matures. One does that piece of work which demonstrates that maturity and establishes one's identity among one's peers and colleagues. For the carpenter, this is journeyman. For the physician, it is residency. For the young auditor, it may be lead on an audit; for the programmer, lead on a system or application. Like Phase One, Phase Two normally takes five years. In Phase Two, one is paid at about one's (increasing) economic value.

As the first generation usually paid its dues in related fields, it sometimes did its masterwork there. Indeed, it was often that masterwork that cemented the association with the field. One might have developed controls for a system or an application. One might have led the investigation of a computer-related crime. One might have done security-related research in computer architecture. One might have done a security-related system or application audit. One might have developed controls and procedures for a system, application, or organization.

Today, young information security professionals do their masterwork in the field. They may have responsibility for an organizational unit, a system, an application, a product, or a management system. They may develop enterprise standards or guidelines.

Phase Three may be called "establishment." The established carpenter, plumber, or other craftsman is called "master." The military NCO is master sergeant or chief petty officer. The commissioned officer is commander or colonel. The public accountant or attorney may be senior or partner. In enterprise, establishment may be associated with titles like senior manager or director. In public accounting or law, think partner. Save for incompetence, death, or disgrace, "everybody makes establishment"; it is a matter of time, and the maturity and experience that goes with it. Established people are often paid more than their economic value and accumulate some capital, mostly because they train, and exploit, use, or leverage those in Phase One paying their dues. Most people will spend the majority of their careers in establishment and retire from it.

Although almost everyone makes establishment, only a small number even aspire to leadership, or Phase Four. In the military, leadership is associated with titles like senior chief, sergeant major, captain, colonel, admiral, or general. While learnable knowledge, skills, and abilities suffice for the basic career, leadership requires special attitudes and aptitudes. It requires vision, initiative, creativity, and what we may call for lack of a better word, charisma.

In the information security field, leadership positions include the chief information security officer (CISO) and the chief security officer (CSO). These are both roles and titles. The roles emerge in most organizations. The titles are conferred in recognition of the leadership provided by the incumbents and that they are members of the executive ranks of the enterprise. The CSO role is mature in most enterprises. The CISO role has only recently emerged and only in the second generation of the field. It is increasingly likely that those experienced will fill the CSO position in information security and from the ranks of CISOs.

Other leadership roles in the field are in the information security industry. These may include practice leaders in consulting practices. It includes those leaders in academia who have led research and established programs, laboratories, and centers.

Candidates for security leadership, like those for other leadership positions, may be expected to have advanced academic training. They may have MBA or MS degrees in information technology or computer security. They will have in-depth experience and will have excelled in most phases of their career. They will have held management, staff, and technical positions. Many will have held management positions in the mainline of the business or industry activity. They will have demonstrated initiative and self-motivation throughout their careers.

Candidates for leadership will have networks of colleagues and reputations in the field and in the enterprise. They will know who to call in any situation and will be recognized when they call. They will have participated in training, programs, conferences, and governance outside the enterprise. They will have trained and published.

Although most leadership positions are filled from within, organizations that are trying to initiate or revitalize a program will often look outside for fresh leadership. Most security leadership positions are filled with those experienced in the field. Rarely these positions will be filled with executives who do not have security experience, but who are chosen for their demonstrated leadership.

Summary and Observations

The first generation of security professionals usually did most of the phases of their careers in the same enterprise. This reflected the times, in which there was a premium on employee loyalty and tenure. In the second generation, it was more common for each phase to be completed in a different enterprise. In the 21st century, most of us will spend at least part of our careers in service organizations, rendering service to organizations that engage us, but do not employ us. Our value will be related to the breadth of our experience across enterprises as much or more than for our experience within a single enterprise.

Note that one can change careers, for example, from NCO to commissioned officer or paralegal to attorney. One might even change from physician to clergyman. This will often involve returning to Phase Zero for additional credentials and paying additional dues.

A word of caution is in order. It is the journey, not the destination, that is important. The purpose of paying dues is to contribute, learn, and enjoy. It is not to get to masterwork. One should focus on the career phase that one is in, rather than on getting to the next one. Most of us will not become CISOs any more than we will become CEOs, governors, senators, or presidents of the United States. The idea is to make a mark and to have a good time. The best way to advance one's career is to do one's job.

The entrepreneur is an exception to the career model. The entrepreneur makes his own rules and sets his own schedule.

The Future

Asimo™ (the humanoid robot) can already fetch and carry. Computers already talk and listen. Children play with robot pets and toys. Bill Gates is giving away what can only be called robot developer tool kits. Robots will build our houses, cars, appliances, roads, schools, and hospitals. They will fight our fires, grow our food, operate our mines, perform medical procedures, and entertain us. Already computers monitor their own performance; they self-diagnose and self-repair. They assist in their own design and accelerate their own fabrication. They assist in complex decision making that defies the human brain.

Ray Kurzweil predicts that in 2023, give or take a year, one will be able to buy the computing power of the human brain (hardware only) for $1000 and that by 2050, give or take a decade, there will be automated personalities that assert that they are self-aware. In the process, technology will revolutionize what it means to be human. It will create wealth and leisure on a scale that we can now hardly anticipate. It will solve problems that now seem intractable and create some that are now unimaginable. It is not an exaggeration to say that we face change on a revolutionary scale.

Perhaps not this generation of information security leadership, but certainly the next, will have to deal with this revolution. The job of this generation includes identifying and developing that leadership.

Notes

1. In 1956 IBM had entered into a consent decree with the Department of Justice. One of the provisions was that orders would be filled in strict order of their receipt. While IBM might replace destroyed equipment from its own installed machines, it would never commit to do this in advance.
2. Legend has it that GE Information Systems named Peter Browne as the "first data security manager" in 1973.

Chapter 4

Business Drivers for Information Security

Harry DeMaio

> Note to the reader: Throughout this chapter, we use the term "business" in the broadest possible sense. In fact, "enterprise" or "organization" or "institution" would be equally appropriate. If, for example, you are employed by a government agency, educational or medical institution, organized religion, or any of the countless entities that don't usually identify themselves as businesses, you will still find that the principles and recommendations in this chapter are applicable, often without any modification. As you read, feel free to use any term you please. The underlying theme of this chapter is your own adaptability.

Obviously, if you're reading this book on CISO leadership styles, you are taking your career development in information security management seriously. Implicit in this attitude is a desire to be recognized as a key member of the organization's mainstream management. And implicit in that desire is a need to make information security as realistically and continuously relevant to top management as possible.

In this chapter, we cover those

- Characteristics
- Business principles

- Objectives and priorities
- Operating modes
- Environment and constraints

of the enterprise that should influence how you design and develop your security organization and your career.

How do you become "realistically and continuously relevant" to business management? We all know that periodically "scaring the hell out of them" accomplishes neither. It may result in short-range programs and funding, but it usually does nothing to elevate your function on a permanent basis. In fact, quite the opposite may be true, even if you are right. Consistent bearers of bad news often get shot, shunned, or outsourced.

An organizational analogy: The Legal Department. Too many corporate lawyers see their mission strictly in terms of prohibition and risk avoidance. Stay out of court, keep a low profile, and settle whenever possible. All necessary, but very incomplete! The truly effective law departments are those who earn their keep by facilitating and enhancing the strategies, programs, product and service development, relationships, campaigns, and image of the organization. In the words of a chief executive known to the author, "Don't tell me what we can't do. Tell me how to do it legally, ethically, and effectively." Recognize anyone?

What to do? How do you turn what is often regarded as a burdensome, scary, and poorly understood overhead function into a positive force within the business? First, let's talk about you for a moment and why you bought this book.

We will assume that your knowledge, experience, and performance in the technical and operational arts of information security are above reproach. But it is highly likely that you suffer from the same "geek" image that afflicts the majority of IT as well as IS professionals, including many CIOs and IT directors. Even if you do not belong there, conventional management wisdom will put you in this category until proven otherwise. Nothing wrong with being a "geek!" Our technology would collapse without them. But a "geek" by definition falls outside the mainstream, and isn't that where you want to swim? So, the first thing you must project to your management, your people, and the external world is your increased breadth of knowledge and (this is most important) interest in the business. Then, display the fact that you are managing your operation with this knowledge and interest as a top priority.

You may understand encryption algorithms, but do you understand the fundamentals of cash flow within your organization? Can you read and understand the basics of the annual report? (Forget about the footnotes!) Assuming it's listed, what are the market forces that are affecting the value of the company's stock? What affects its reputation? Who are your competitors by strength and market segment? Who are your most powerful customers? Which of your products or services are on the upswing, holding their own, or dying? You can probably answer most of those questions, but can you then articulate your understanding and, in a meaningful way, connect it to the information security function?

Yes, we know that you are overworked and underpaid. No, we are not suggesting you go out and get an MBA, although it could help. (Full disclosure: The author of this chapter is an adjunct professor in a graduate school of business.) But let's get some of the business basics out on the table and map them against both information technology and information security functions. Important point: As you well know, the perceived value of the enterprise's information protection program is a direct function of the perceived value of its information and information processes. (C'mon, that's InfoSec 101!) Yes, but unless you can truly understand and evaluate the business that employs you, you can't accurately and forcefully strategize, deploy, and, most important to your career, communicate the value of your protection functions. And that, dear reader, is what you must do.

Enough prologues! Let's get on to the subject at hand.

As mentioned above, in the remainder of this chapter we will explore the organization's characteristics, business principles, objectives and priorities, operating modes, environment, and constraints that will bear on information security. There are more than you may think, especially in the networked world.

Characteristics

Figure 4.1 is a heavily modified version of a table that appeared in *Business Week* magazine in 2001. It maps a pair of potential target end points for each of 14 characteristics that can describe an organization's dynamics over time. Your job is to analyze each characteristic as it applies to your organization and put a mark (right, left, center) under the "Trends" column at the point where you believe the organization currently stands, and an arrow and comment indicating its course and speed.

Each characteristic can yield different results. For one, your organization may not be moving at all. For others, it may be advancing to the "future" state at a variety of speeds and circuitous courses. Or it may be retreating with burned fingers.

The purpose of the grid is description and understanding, not judgment or evaluation. There are no right or wrong answers. Some businesses and organizations, especially those that are heavily constrained by regulation, may stay firmly in the "Traditional" column, but still meet or beat their objectives repeatedly. Conversely, some of the "Futurist" organizations may be going off the rails. A few of the characteristics such as "inventory turns" may not seem to apply in your case, especially in a service industry. But if you take inventory to mean service cycles (calls answered, reservations placed, consulting contracts fulfilled, kids taught, souls saved) the category can still be very meaningful.

We'll take you through a few examples of how to use the grid, and then demonstrate how to apply your conclusions toward further insights about information security. After that, it's up to you to finish the exercise. OK, on to Figure 4.1.

Characteristics	**Traditional**	Trends	*Future*
Organization	**Pyramid**		*Web–Network–Exchange*
Focus	**Internal**		*External*
Style	**Structured**		*Flexible*
Strength	**Stability**		*Change*
Structure	**Self Sufficient**		*Interdependence*
Resources	**Physical Assets**		*Information*
Operations	**Vertical Integration**		*Virtual Integration*
Products	**Mass Production**		*Mass Customization*
Reach	**Domestic**		*Global*
Financials	**Quarterly**		*Real-Time*
Inventory Turns	**Months**		*Hours*
Strategy	**Top Down**		*Bottom Up*
Workers	**Employees**		*Employees/Free Agents*
Improvement	**Incremental**		*Revolutionary*

Figure 4.1 Enterprise characteristics analysis grid. (Adapted from *Business Week,* 2000. With permission.)

Clearly, any functioning organization is going to look both ways. But the differentiating points here are scope, emphasis, course, and speed. Is the business becoming more externally focused through partnerships, increased vendor dependencies, outsourcing, new market development, new venues for production, or new research agreements? Does business trust take on a whole new meaning in this environment? If so, what implications should you draw for the present and future of your security program? For starters, there will be far more players involved in information processes, players who will have a significant effect on everything from access management, network protection, backup and recovery, to data integrity. Players you should be dealing with as part of your mission.

Much as you might like a permanent, centralized security program that evolves in a calm and stately fashion, it may not be in the cards. Envision a conglomerate that will remain under the corporate umbrella only so long as the member companies or divisions meet profit, market share, and revenue objectives. Spin-offs and spin-ins, all striving to maintain high levels of autonomy. Visualize a company whose products suffer from instant obsolescence and must continue to switch R&D, vendors, production, and marketing outlets. Imagine a company that flirts with, commits, and de-commits to outsourcing. Or a company that itself is a prospective target for merger or acquisition. Now, what is the likelihood that any security program you institute here will have a long and unperturbed life? To cope with these conditions, can you develop programs that distribute functions and responsibilities to the lowest feasible level? Can you tolerate methods, software, and procedures that are different from unit to unit? Are you capable of being an effective coordinator between these units sufficient to maintain a balanced level of security throughout the enterprise without beating your fists bloody trying to impose a single model that may or may not fit?

Here's a characteristic that may not be self-evident. We're all familiar with vertical integration, an extreme case being a company that owns the mines from which the iron and aluminum ore is extracted to go into their sheet metal production and rolling mills that supply their vehicle assembly lines. Few, if any, of these extremes still exist, but core vertical integration is still a favorite of businesses that are seeking to protect themselves from supply risk and are also interested in dominating their market segment.

Virtual integration comes about as a result of more loosely binding agreements that still have a similar effect. For example, a grocery chain that works with independently owned farms, processors, canneries, packagers, transport, and distribution facilities dedicated to supplying some, and often a major, portion of their output for the store's own brand name. Have you ever held a chain store's proprietary brand in your hand and thought, "I wonder who actually produced this?" Or been told by a store manager that their tuna fish is processed on the same line as a famous name brand?

What has tuna fish got to do with information protection? This: the degree to which your enterprise depends on these outside sources and conversely the degree to which those sources depend on your enterprise are critical. They will foster a level of cooperation or contentiousness that will reach right down through enterprise resource planning, customer relationship management, and R&D. You may recall the push back that arose when several major retail chains tried to force their suppliers to use RFID devices instead of, or in addition to, UPC codes on their packages. Is accurate and reliable product identification ultimately a security concern? You bet! Is it easy to maintain? Not when there are battles over technology types and costs, corresponding identity procedures and control between *virtually related* participants.

Let's look at one last characteristic as an example before we turn you loose to map your own enterprise against the grid. Quarterly and year-end financial reporting by publicly traded companies is almost as old as trade itself. The signed and audited annual report is supposed to be a bastion of reliability and transparency. Well, maybe. But, in today's universe, where corporate stock values are reported to the world second-by-second and analysts and reporters seem to wander freely in and out of every company document including e-mails and phone logs, financial "reporting" (or more appropriately, "external discovery") has become a very real-time thing. Few corporations like it. Many resist it. A few facilitate it. They all live with it. Now it's not just the official financial data that counts. It's every document that has money, strategy, performance, or liability content. Uh, oh!

We hope you can see where we're going with this exercise. Covering the company's mainframes, servers, data farms, LANs, WANs, WiFi, hard drives, and flash memory is only part of the story. Beyond the technology, interpreting impact based on the nature of the business is essential. But it's more than just risk assessment. It should also be a forward-looking analysis of how best to support proactively the business as it develops, grows, and, hopefully, provides you with opportunities for growth.

Business Principles

Statements of business principles are easy to come by. Just pick up any mission statement, new employee handbook, or annual report, or go to the "who we are" section of the organization's Website and you'll find more than enough to satisfy your needs. The obvious question is whether these statements of principle are indeed guiding doctrine or just created for external consumption. A review of some of the "principles" literature from companies recently indicted for fraud or other misconduct may lead you to a somewhat cynical view. Nevertheless, it is extremely important for an organization to clearly and consistently articulate these principles and to "walk the walk." One of your major tasks is to make a significant contribution to both the "talking" and the "walking."

Sure, but what principles are we discussing? The first that bounds on the stage in any information security dialogue is that old favorite: risk aversion. Entire security programs are built around this principle, but unfortunately, often only this principle. Clearly, risk aversion and the degree to which the enterprise subscribes to it will be the fundamental motivator for your security operation. Whether we are talking about financial risk, market risk, stakeholder risk, legal risk, competitive risk, labor risk, regulatory risk, physical risk, criminal risk, or catastrophic risk, no doubt you have received explicit or implicit direction from management. (Or have you??) You have translated these requirements into programs to deal with unauthorized access, business interruption, data and process integrity, attacks, errors and omissions, and all the other issues that bedevil the information security practitioner. Defining, locating, assessing, preventing, and mitigating risk in the realm of information is what it's all about. All?? Not quite!

There are other proactive principles that should also be major drivers for you, and these often resonate better with business management than dealing with risk. They can also change your image in their eyes. Let's take a few:

- Quality: The quality, integrity, completeness, and timeliness of information is basic to all the products, services, and dealings of the enterprise. Ask any manufacturer who has sustained a major recall. You belong in that process.
- Respect for the individual (employee, customer, business partner, the public at large).

- Ethical behavior and fair dealing including mutual protection.
- Trustworthiness: Not just ethics but demonstrable competence.
- Marketplace image: It only takes one slip, e.g., lost customer data, to cause a major black eye or worse.
- Civic responsibility: At many levels and venues.
- Excellent performance: Measured in dollars and cents (euros), customer satisfaction, market share, profitability, employee pride.
- Leadership: It's interesting how many organizations that proclaim a desire for leadership are only interested in "middle-of-the-pack" information protection.

There are others, of course, but these are enough to make the point. The business principles that have an effect and are affected by information security are more than risk aversion. Use them all.

Objectives and Priorities

Here's where things can get personal. Not you, top management! After all the principles and policies and directives have been enunciated, what objectives and priorities really head up their hit parade? We hasten to say that we are not accusing management of having conflicting agendas. Rather, some things are so fundamental to the business management mentality that they appear more frequently in actions, rather than words. The best way to discover these is to examine the metrics that management uses to measure performance and, more often than not, compensation.

- If market share growth dominates the corporate landscape (often to the detriment of profitability), you'd better line up behind fortifying market research, R&D, customer relationship management, distribution, and other functions that directly impact both growing the marketplace and growing the business's share of that marketplace.
- If revenue is king (queen), market dominance may be subordinated to developing, serving, and reaping rewards from those customers (sometimes a very small number) that represent major income sources. In that case, special attention has to be paid to the needs, wants, and mutual security responsibilities these relationships demand. Keep the big kids happy.
- If profitability and shareholder return is in the number one spot (believe it or not, it isn't always, especially in growth companies!), then cost control, cash flow management, and detailed financial reporting will dominate. This environment may be tough for you, especially if you are regarded as necessary but unwanted overhead. Play the control card. Develop security approaches that enhance business controls that rein in costs. And don't unleash long-range

projects with millennial paybacks when cash flow is a major issue. By the way, this applies equally to not-for-profit organizations. "Not-for-profit" does not mean running at a loss (intentionally). It simply means that net income is cycled back into the program rather than paid out to shareholders. Most "not-for-profits" live off endowments, capital and operating contributions, and new income from whatever money-making activities they are engaged in.

And of course, there are institutions, government bodies, the military, and regulated industries where compliance rules. Here you have to determine how strictly compliant management wants to be. Incidentally, market-driven organizations that have been hit with a deluge of lawsuits (antitrust, product failure, employment practices, safety, predatory practices, international violations, etc.) may start to behave exactly like highly regulated organizations.

Most enterprises seek to balance all of these objectives but, on demand, will shift from one priority scenario to another. A couple of lousy quarters that cause the stock price to tank can trigger a drastic change in what's important. Or, the sudden opening of formerly restricted international markets can bring on land rush behavior. New competition in the market can bring about deadly price wars. And of course, emerging from bankruptcy has a rubric all its own.

No matter what, make sure you have a good sense of the organization's behavioral priorities. They will shift. And it is the wise security manager who seeks guidance, analyzes, and acts on these shifts. Information underpins all of these scenarios. Make sure you demonstrate an appreciation and responsiveness to where things are heading and how to add safety to the mix. (And watch out for curves and sudden stops!)

Operating Modes

We covered many of these in our discussion and your mapping (we hope) of your enterprise's characteristics. We won't repeat them. However, there is one additional modal question that should be surfaced and realistically answered. Is your organization driven by formal policies, standards, specs, and compliance measurement, or are operating tradition, low-level procedures, management experience, and departmental lore the primary way things get done? Let's not get into a discussion of how things should be. In this chapter at least, we're discussing how things are.

How many information protection managers have slaved (and spent major sums) to produce comprehensive, state-of-the-art, professionally approved sets of policies, standards, and procedures, only to have them gather dust or appear only at internal audits? How many awareness programs have played to inattentive audiences? How many desktop gizmos and bulletin board announcements have ended up covered over by the results of the office fantasy football league?

At this point the information security manager traditionally sings the universal and eternal lament: "If only top management would pay attention and support the 'program,' we'd be making progress." Also at this point, the security manager often buys a new piece of software for updating his or her resumé. Granted, support from the executive suite is essential, but examine carefully what you are asking them to support. If what you see as professional good practice appears to them as bureaucratic overload, you have a perception problem to deal with, and they have the advantage. They're the ones with the perception

Do not misunderstand. We are not suggesting abandoning the codification of good practice. Quite the contrary, we are suggesting that you adapt the look, fit, and feel of your code to local practice, even if it runs somewhat contrary to conventional security wisdom. Managerial informality does not necessarily mean sloppiness or inattention. After all, these are the managers who, for better or worse, are the engines of the enterprise. Don't be blinded by your specialized expertise into undervaluing their input or understanding. In short, don't look and sound like a "geek." Especially an arrogant "geek" preaching from the moral high ground!

So, to adapt your program, spend as much time as you can with the managers who are going to affect and feel the effects of the program most. Do not approach top management until you have those managers in your corner. You can start by indicating that you are there to listen, not to dictate, and by demonstrating that you are acting on their input.

The traditional primary players in the realm of internally oriented information security are:

- Executive management
- The governance groups (e.g., Legal, HR, Government Relations)
- Financial
- Compliance officers, of which you may be one
- Audit, internal and external, especially in these days of Sarbanes–Oxley
- IT in all forms
- And, often most important, the business operations, processes, and units

The business units, all too frequently neglected by IS or approached secondhand through IT, are actually where your active, face-to-face liaison may pay the greatest dividends. Getting unit management on your side and getting them to act on behalf of a security program they understand and appreciate are worth all the time and effort. You may have to approach them singly. Design one less handout or cancel a couple of awareness sessions and make the time. Then and only then will you have a chance to produce a program that is responding to the major internal drivers of your business.

Environment and Constraints

But your employer does not exist in a vacuum and neither does your security function. We'll conclude this chapter by examining some additional aspects of the outside world that will have a bearing on your success or failure — what the economists refer to as "exogenous influences."

And let's begin with the economy as it affects your company and, eventually, you. At any given moment, some major market sectors will be robust, some flat, or feeling severe pain. Some geopolitical environments will be more (or less) favorably disposed to your organization's presence and prosperity. A wayward competitor may have blown the reputation of the entire industry. Special interest groups may have you in their sights. An overzealous media may convince the population that identity theft, for example, is an even greater threat than global warming, and that it's your organization's fault. Wars, terrorism, and government brinksmanship may lay waste to the company's international development plans. Nationalized industries and government-sponsored union activities that discriminate against your business and similar organizations are rife. They usually don't respond to conventional management wisdom, either. There are many more examples, and we invite you to entertain yourself (and others) by coming up with a realistic list that most applies to your business world.

In these and similar cases, the security manager is often faced with a dilemma. Sometimes, a security program designed to deal with the situation may actually exacerbate it. Several examples follow:

■ Somehow the media has gained access to your company's e-mail repositories or a stray hard drive or two and is using that access and journalistic imagination to weave a public spider web of intrigue, conspiracy, and dirty doings that may or may not have any basis in fact. True to the media principle of guilty even after having been proven innocent, public opinion is stirred, investigations are launched, and a couple of congressional committees are organized. And the stock may drop in value.

  Query: Is now the time to tighten up security, clamp down on all access, shred repositories, issue strong warning advisories, and slam all the information hatches shut? Or will that just inflame the conspiracy theorists who, having imagined smoke, are now seeking fire? Sorry, we're not going to answer the question because there are so many free radicals (no pun intended) in the formula. But, get together with your PR, legal, and executive management and discuss such scenarios before they occur. It's another variant of risk management, but it's one that could get you favorable executive-suite exposure as well as cooperation from other concerned functions in the organization. And it has a reasonable probability of happening.

■ The company is downsizing because of economic problems or has been granted very favorable production, tax, and labor status overseas, and is outsourcing at top speed. Jobs are disappearing. There is labor unrest. State and local politicians are taking shots. Local leaders and the media are citing the death knell of their communities.

Query: Should you upgrade security to forestall sabotage or leaks, or will labor charge that this is just another example of management insensitivity? If you do strengthen security, can you do it in such a way that it does not seem discriminatory against a certain class of workers, a certain location, or a certain process? Once again, we're going to duck providing a school solution. (There isn't any.) However, here is another case where getting ducks in a row prior to making and publicizing any downsizing or outsourcing decision is key and may stand you in good stead with top management.

Anyone involved in information security is familiar with constraints. In fact, we are agents of constraint. Mention the word and the first items that usually come to mind are regulation, litigation, and legislation. As they should! If you are not familiar with or, worse yet, if your legal department doesn't have a good handle on law-driven conditions that will affect the company's information program (defined in the very broadest sense), get on it … now! This topic like many of the others mentioned in this chapter will come up again in the advisory chapters that form the rest of this book.

■ Your organization's business partners. In the networked world, information security does not begin or end at your firewall. Your business will be communicating, transacting, developing, and sharing information-laden traffic with a very large number of partners, customers, third parties, and even competitors.

Query: Are they an asset or liability to your protective strategies? Conversely, are you a liability to them? (Let's face it, some security programs are better than yours.) Can you and do you wield any influence in this area? Are you open to being influenced by them? Is your top management even aware of this aspect of the relationship? Who's on first?

■ Is your organization a subscriber to, or bound by, external business standards? These may range from military contract requirements to professional ethics considerations and a wide range in between.

Query: Do they vary? (Of course they do!) For example, in pharmaceuticals, what information security requirements are triggered by double-blind formula testing on volunteer subjects? Do transportation safety regulations reach down to travel agencies and tour companies? How must you protect EPA data? And then, there's the all-time favorite, patient records. Many of these concerns are so fundamental to your organization that to ignore them would approach malfeasance. But there may also be peripheral or second-order influences at work. This may be especially true if your information or practices make their way into research and teaching institutions or, oddly enough, into regulatory agencies. Because they monitor and use but do not directly own the information resources or participate in the information processes, critical information can lose its importance and protection in their hands. It shouldn't.

■ Finally, there is privacy protection. Libraries have been written (and are still being written) on the topic. It's combustible. It varies widely from venue to venue and is all too frequently in the eye of the beholder. But as you well know, ignoring it can be fatal. Some security managers have tried to organize privacy protection out of their purview, hoping it will lodge with legal, HR, and privacy policy specialists. That tactic is seldom successful and may expose the company and yourself. You are usually the only one who has any grasp of the tools, techniques, and practices required to support the protective functions of the program. You might as well take credit for your contributions. You'll certainly share the blame if anything goes awry.

So, business drivers constitute a wider world than many information security texts will have you believe. You are, of course, a specialist. But enclosing yourself inside that specialty to the exclusion of all other considerations that drive, influence, and constrain the organization you work for can have only one end result: your exclusion from the mainstream.

Recap

■ First, you must project to your management, your people, and the external world your increased breadth of knowledge and (this is most important) interest in the business. Then, display the fact that you are managing your operation with this knowledge and interest as a top priority.

■ Understand the compelling business drivers of your organization and align the security strategy closely to them.

■ Understand the culture of your organization and adapt the look, fit, and feel of your code to local practice, even if it runs somewhat contrary to conventional security wisdom.

■ Getting unit management on your side and getting them to act on behalf of the security program they understand and appreciate are worth the time and effort.

■ The exclusion of all other considerations that drive, influence, and constrain the organization you work for can have only one end result: your exclusion from the mainstream.

Chapter 5

Security as a Business Function

Peter Browne and Stephen R. Katz

To be relevant and successful, an information security organization must be managed and treated as a business function. It essentially becomes a business within the business. As with any business there is a planning component, a sales and marketing component, a production or build function, and an operational or delivery capability as well as a financial and program management and control component. The primary mission of the security function is to assure the integrity, confidentiality, and availability of information. However, this mission must be accomplished within the context of security as a facilitator for the development and delivery of the organization's products and services. Security must be viewed as the organization where one goes for answers about how to securely move forward with a new product or service and to ensure that the company's trust commitment to its customers and partners is being achieved. This must be accomplished through an effective business risk management approach to developing alternative solutions.

Organizational Structure

It is important first to distinguish information security management functions from the purely operational tasks necessary to functionally secure a given system, network, application, or data store. In many, if not most organizations, these operational tasks are the responsibility of the organizations responsible for application development, systems, and database administration or network management. The role of the security organization will be to set, monitor, and help enforce a policy and standards framework that will demand accountability from the various operational and business entities. If, as sometimes happens, the security organization is also responsible for security administration, then the policy function needs to be separated from the operational function. The assumption in this book and certainly in this chapter is that the two functions are in different organizations, and we are focusing on the policy and enforcement aspects of information security.

Culture

The first task in developing or reviewing a security function is to assess and understand the organization's culture. The personality of an organization is rarely defined, but is crucial whenever policies and standards need to be developed, approved, and implemented. Information security is very much a change agent, changing policy, activities, processes, and functions. Thus the culture of the organization needs to be considered and addressed. This is very difficult. Culture within an organization consists of assumptions, values, normative behavior, and expectations. Is it an academic culture, where people work together for common goals? Is it a sports team culture, with great competitive energy, or a club culture, where everybody must "fit in"? Is it a high risk, entrepreneurial organization where people feel free to assume risk on their own? Or is it a fortress culture, where everybody else is "the enemy"? Are business and technical functions decentralized and autonomous, or is a centralized organizational model better suited for success?

The attitude toward risk is certainly a cultural issue. A risk-averse organization will have a strong tendency to stick to the "letter of the law" when implementing security. A risk-taking organization may be more likely to "push the envelope" and take a looser interpretation of policy and standards. Learning to deal with the culture is an essential element of a successful security function. Another key cultural issue has to do with how a company interprets and approaches legal, regulatory, and audit guidance.

Once the legal, regulatory, risk, and business drivers are understood, and a security organization is being established or reorganized, some key questions need to be posed and answered:

- What will the enterprisewide security governance process look like?
- What will be included/omitted from the charter of the security organization?
- Will a risk-based methodology be used for making information security decisions?
- Will the security organization be centralized, decentralized, or a combination of the two?

- How and where does the security organization fit in the organizational structure of the company?
- How will information security relate to other business functions?
- What is the level of management commitment and budget oversight?
- How will information security relate to other control functions such as audit, compliance, risk management, and physical security?
- What functions "belong" with the CISO? What functions will not belong to the CISO, and how will overlap issues be decided?
- What is the balance and organizational relationship between the policy functions and the operational aspects of security?

No one structure fits all. There are significant differences in how organizations function and are managed. However, one common thread is that the business processes of budgeting, marketing/sales, planning, building, producing, and operating are all part of treating security as a business function.

Organizational Placement

Historically security organizations have reported to a low-level department within the information technology hierarchy. A more recent practice is to report to the chief technology officer (CTO) who manages the computer and network infrastructure. Another attribute of a historical approach is to have more than one information security function without having any organization with overall responsibility for the program. This is especially true where technology is itself fragmented. This approach is shown in Figure 5.1.

In large organizations today, the information security function will often report to the senior executive responsible for technology such as the chief information officer (CIO). Oftentimes, this would put the head of security/CISO at the same level as CIOs within the business.

Another possible approach would be to have the information security function report outside of the IT function to a specialized risk officer role, e.g., chief risk

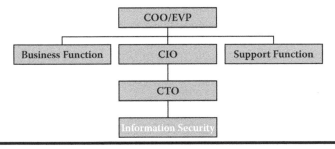

Figure 5.1   Traditional information security placement.

Figure 5.2 Information security reports to risk officer.

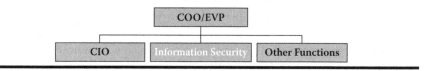

Figure 5.3 Information security reporting to chief operating officer.

officer (CRO), in which other control elements such as audit, physical security, and risk management may report as shown in Figure 5.2. This assures requisite independence and oversight. The negative aspects are that the function must have the credibility and support of the CIO to be able to affect change and to influence the direction of technology. If this mutual respect is missing, then all the issues relating to having an outside "control function" would come into play, including the concept that cooperation will be, at best, an arms-length relationship and, at worst, very strained.

A more optimal version of this is to have dual reporting roles. The security function would report dotted line or dually to both the CIO and the CRO.

Another model would have the function report directly to a chief operating officer, the same person to whom the CIO would report, as depicted in Figure 5.3. This has been used successfully in cases where independence is desired, but that there would be collegiality benefits resulting from being on the same staff together.

Correction Strategies for Organizational Placement

In a case where the organization does not appear to be functioning effectively, a number of initial activities can be undertaken to improve the situation:

■ *Consolidate disparate functions.* If the function is fragmented, it should be a goal to at least consolidate multiple instances, based, if on nothing else, the need for efficiency and cost savings.
■ *Separate policy from operational aspects.* As pointed out earlier, it takes different skills to manage a consultative versus an operational function. The separation may also help with some of the "political" issues that need to be addressed.

■ *Benchmark others.* A fundamental question that the head of security/CISO will be asked is, "How does our company compare with its peers?" Having an accurate answer will significantly improve the chances for organizational changes as well as developing and implementing policies and standards. Numerous security benchmarking studies have been initiated within and across industries in recent years.

■ *Hire a consultant.* Having an opinion from a credible and recognized outside organization will help develop and implement an effective action plan for the security function and program. This is especially true if the outside opinion comes as a result of an assessment of the viability of the overall information security program.

The organizational structure and responsibilities of the security function must fit the overall organization's culture. The reporting level needs to be high enough to influence change and not be "unduly constrained" by other organizational functions. Whether the information security organization is centralized, decentralized, or a combination of the two is a factor of organizational culture, and may change based on evolution of the function. Generally speaking, there tends to be greater levels of centralization in the earlier stages of the life cycle when the program is being developed.

In any organization, whether commercial, government, or nonprofit, a successful business function is led by a person who can effectively communicate and collaborate with other executives, managers and staff. The leader must develop a level of credibility where his or her perspectives, recommendations, and decisions are respected. One of the objectives of the security program is to develop an appreciation for the need for, and responsibility of, security at all levels of the company, from the board room on down. All levels within the company must understand that good security is "owned" by everyone, not just the security organization. Achieving this objective is at the core of the security marketing and sales function.

A successful program is scoped right, has the right people in place, and is organizationally effective.

Functions of a Security Program

We are focusing on a security program that is primarily consultative in nature, not operational. It should be thought of as a business unit, with its own marketing, sales, design, production, delivery, and budgeting processes. This is true even in nonprofit and government organizations.

The plan-build-run model is a useful way of looking at the totality of any organization. It was originally designed to help structure a total information technology organization. It is an equally useful approach to view the functions of an information security program.

Plan

An information security program needs to be based on a business plan, which states clearly the goals, vision, and mission of the function. The action plan states the objectives and timeline to implement desired future projects and ongoing tasks. The business plan, including objectives, projects, performance metrics, and budgetary requirements for the information security function is an essential element of success, and must map into the corporate or overall organization's strategic planning process.

Some or all of the information security function may be funded by business and operational organizations in the company. The CISO must negotiate with business and operations management to take a risk-based approach to funding the organization and must include specific operational, performance, and financial metrics. A component of the process will leverage the control structure imposed on the organization via legal, regulatory, and internal control requirements. In many industries and in government, security and control requirements are driven by regulation. In many cases an internal audit will reveal opportunities for improvement.

The budgeting process must start with an understanding of who pays for security and why that payment is a sound investment. In most organizations, those who implement security or who design/build application systems pay for it, and it is not directly funded by the information security organization. Therefore the CISO's job is complex, because he or she must convince others to put money in *their* budget. This requires that the CISO establish a reputation for credibility and achieving objectives. Pure information security tools, which include monitoring and control systems, are often in the CISO budget. However, the CISO still needs to be able to convince business and operational peers that the budget and expenses are justified. Sometimes the necessary or desired systems are costly, and so the CISO has to understand the organization's capital budgeting process.

In negotiating the budget, it will be necessary to articulate the benefits and consequences of funding options. Being able to articulate budgetary requirements in terms of cost, benefit, and risk is absolutely necessary. The time of the "scaremongering" is over. The CISO needs to be able to justify costs in terms of business benefit and risk mitigation.

Build

The *build* of information security focuses on the policy and standards framework, the processes to be put in place, the tools to make or buy, and the metrics to assess risk and security. Metrics are left to another chapter of this book.

Policy Framework

Security, like software development, has its own life cycle, as shown in Figure 5.4

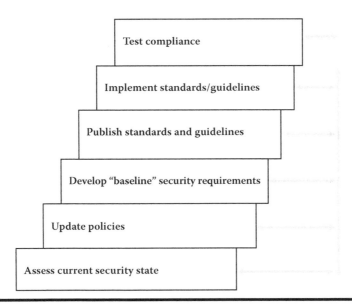

Figure 5.4   Security life cycle.

A first step is to assess the current state, and to keep reassessing it on an ongoing basis. This establishes a baseline for making changes and ensuring relevancy and currency. The assessment can be accomplished by the internal audit function, by the external auditor, by a government compliance organization or by a third party. Scope, depth, and cost effectiveness are all considerations. Often a qualified and credible third party is better positioned to be independent and not tied to internal management precepts, formulas, or politics.

Policies provide a broad statement of intent and set expectations for compliance and accountability. If the organization is a regulated entity or deals with the government, the policies tend to be more precise and strict. An entrepreneurial organization is likely to have less stringent policies. In any event, security policies must say *what* is to be protected, *why* it must be protected, *what* is appropriate (or not appropriate), and must include an enforceability requirement and penalty for policy violations. Policies are organizational in nature, though sometimes the word is used to define the instantiation of security policy on a particular machine or platform.

Standards provide statements of what to do. They are an extension of policy, and many times explain the application of policy in terms of particular technologies or functions and assign responsibility. They must cover all elements of the information security program. They provide the cornerstone for compliance. Again, an implementation of a policy for a particular technology is often based on industry or manufacturer standards for that unique technology.

Practices explain how to do something that meets standards. They generally provide examples and configuration recommendations. Because the underlying platform technologies change so rapidly, it is critical that they are kept current. Again, a particular implementation of policy for a particular machine or platform is based on practices. This is where the standards are put into specific actionable implementation.

Processes

The desired state of security allows the controls in place to be commensurate with the value and sensitivity of the underlying information assets. This means that security must be:

- Incorporated into the software (or product) development life cycle process
- Part of the overall technology and infrastructure architecture
- Part of the business management, project management, and information technology management process
- Part of the product planning, system administration, and network planning functions
- Kept current with changes in the business and technology

The range of security-related processes that need to be developed or implemented include:

- Those that support the policy framework as discussed above. There must be a process in place to periodically re-evaluate policy, standards, and practices, and to update them as needed.
- Those that provide for assessment of security, in specific technologies and types of platforms and systems. This can be performed by an internal group either within the security function or by an audit or may be performed by a third party that does security assessments. This assessment may include ethical hackers who will thoroughly look for security vulnerabilities in a network, system, or product.
- Those that monitor for and detect security breaches. Monitoring can be outsourced or accomplished in-house, but it is a critical function.
- Those that determine security requirements, identify potential solutions, validate solutions, and then implement them. Again the CISO organization may not do all of these functions, but must of necessity guide and support the processes.

The CISO must be able to understand the elements of sound business process management.

Tools

Since business offerings, technologies, and systems are always changing, security is seen as chasing a moving target, and, therefore, there is always a need to look at new controls, security, and tools. There is a wide variety of security tools, and more come on the market every day. The security organization may not directly use or implement these tools, but it will certainly have a hand in their specification and maybe their evaluation. The tools address large numbers of requirements, from access control to cryptography, and include products that help assess security. One of the authors of this chapter developed an in-house measurement tool that accomplished a monthly compliance audit of the security of every single system in the entire company, with results published to top management, comparing the security "status" of every business unit in the company. It was amazing how the overall state of security improved over time.

The evaluation of tools that are bought from outside needs to follow a rigorous process, with the same care devoted to any major purchase. In this case, beside the evaluation for total cost of operation and ownership, ease of use, and the ability to integrate into the business process served, the evaluation needs to consider the risk that is reduced by using the tool. In considering whether to build a tool internally rather than buying it, development time must be considered. In most cases it is better to buy and adapt it rather than build it in-house.

Run

The types of functional roles of a CISO organization include:

- Assessing security
- Acting as an internal consultant
- In some cases, operations
- A most critical marketing function to "sell" security to the rest of the organization

Assessment Function

As pointed out earlier in this chapter, the security life-cycle process starts with assessment. An overall security assessment can be performed by many outside consultants, and costs several tens of thousands of dollars. It might be a good way to get started if there is no existing security organization or if a serious shortcoming in the overall program is suspected. In addition security assessments by an impartial third party can be an excellent way of measuring the baseline and trending progress. There are several opportunities for smaller, more targeted assessments of single systems, a given business unit operations, or a type of technology, such as all Internet-facing applications.

Many security organizations have assessment-skilled people on staff that can test application systems. Certainly the CISO must know where and when to acquire assessment resources.

Consulting Functions

A primary role of the security organization is to serve as an internal consultant to other organizations — to help them design and build security into their own business processes, and to help them secure their systems and data. A working knowledge of business process engineering and an ability to write guidelines and procedures is required.

A consultative-oriented CISO will take every opportunity to work with management of all the business units and technology providers in the entire organization. He or she will routinely meet with and maintain an ongoing relationship with business, technology, and operations management. He or she is really running an advisory service, not an enforcement unit. Success depends on working to ensure that security is seen as an enabler, not a disabler. The attitude should be that security should not stand in the way, but a given function needs to have security "built in" as part of the initial requirements and design. The security organization's motto should be "Let's find a way to get the functionality you want and do it securely."

CISO staff should be a part of any project's design team, and should help build functional requirements for new systems. This requires some depth of technology skills in the security staff, but not necessarily in the CISO's resume.

Operations

Usually security operations are handled by organizations other than the CISO. However, one of the authors of this chapter was given the responsibility for security administration and had to mange this function, which did not fit easily in his consultative-oriented organization. This required having the function managed by a person who is operationally focused and experienced in dealing with a short turnaround process that is supported by good rules-based decision making. That person should not be the CISO, but could report into the security function. In this instance, it was essential that there was a separation of duties in place.

Experience in designing operational processes for others is useful when it has to apply to one's own organization.

Internal Business Functions

The CISO organization must provide for the usual business functions such as administration, finance, research, and management. The CISO will be contacted constantly by vendors who have the next greatest thing, and so must be able to delegate answering the phone and dealing with external forces. Because the key to success is effectively communicating the message, time must be spent with internal management at all levels. These ancillary business functions must be budgeted, staffed, and effectively supervised.

Security Awareness and the Marketing of Security

If a CISO were CEO and could dictate security, it still wouldn't happen. The CISO must earn and maintain the respect of senior and executive management within the company and must do it while being the "chief security evangelist" within the company. In all organizations, security will compete with functionality, time to market, speed, and cost. The security program must be based on an understanding of risks and their consequences to the overall organization. If that understanding is communicated effectively and persuasively, then success in implementing the necessary security controls and systems will be possible.

Commitment is more than just putting information security in the appropriate organizational box and feeding it with sufficient budget and the right people. It is getting security put into the mindset of all who develop and offer products to customers and who use and support technology. This is not an easy task, especially because security has often been viewed as an inhibitor, slowing down time to market.

So the critical success factors are an educated executive and senior management team, a complete understanding of risk, and the application of security early in life cycles of business product, software, and infrastructure planning.

Top Management Involvement

Part of the commitment comes from involvement. One of the effective ways to get that involvement is through a top level steering committee or council, in which senior executives from the business units and from technology meet on a regular basis to approve policy, adjudicate differences, set or approve budget, and deal with issues, including responses to new threats or risks. In some organizations a senior operating risk council or committee serves this function and covers more than just information security. The key is to have a standing group that will meet regularly to give focus to the control issues around technology.

Additionally, the council needs to receive regular reports on incidents and results of periodic security assessments. The key performance and compliance reporting discussed in the next section can also be targeted to the executive level.

Risk Management

There are three areas of risk that need to be addressed by the CISO: financial, reputational, and operational/technological. Communication of risk needs to be on simple terms at a high level. The standard risk paradigm shows in inverse correlation between probability of an event and the associated loss.

- Low probability, high impact
- High probability, low impact
- Low probability, low impact
- High probability, high impact
- Medium probably, medium impact

In any event, it would pay to know three important facts about any risk that is to be discussed in management terms:

1. The impact to the organization
2. The likelihood of a loss-producing event
3. The likely cost of loss over time

In all cases, the CISO needs to look at the risk in terms of probability of occurrence, impact of occurrence, and in terms of risk avoidance, risk mitigation, risk acceptance, and risk transference (insurance), and make appropriate recommendations to management. At the very least, a documented and approved process to address risk is required.

This book is not the venue to discuss risk measurement. Suffice to say it is not an easy or intuitive process, and so a much softer approach is to dimension risk in terms of scales or values such as high, medium, or low, as long as the definitions have precise and quantitatively bound limits.

If a security "event" impacting the organization were to occur, the organization is possibly facing an unplanned cost, both in terms of recovery and in terms of mitigating future similar events. As an example, what is the cost of replacing 100,000 credit cards after a security breach? It is a lot more than a dollar a card.

Leveraging the Industry

A final approach to management commitment is to use what others are doing as a benchmark. Generally an industry benchmark will resonate, especially if others are more advanced in their dealing with information security issues.

There are a number of associations such as the International Information Integrity Institute (I4), the International Security Forum (ISF), and the Financial Services Roundtables, which under strict nondisclosure agreements allow member organizations to share policies, techniques, information about vendors, and solutions with each other. In this context the members believe, even though they may be competitors in business, an information security breach at one of them will harm them all.

Industry and professional associations are also good clearinghouses for information, as are the conferences sponsored by them. The Information System Security Association (ISSA), the International Information Systems Security Certification Consortium (ISC²)®, Systems and Network Security (SANS), the Computer Security Institute (CSI), and the audit associations (IIA and ISACA) all contribute to the sharing of information across companies.

With the encouragement of the governments of several countries, including the United States, Information Sharing and Analysis Centers (ISACs) are being formed to share security event and vulnerability information under strict security controls. The purpose of such centers is to quickly provide "early warning" information for other industry members in case of cyber-attacks or easily exploitable new vulnerabilities affecting platforms, technologies, or systems. Within individual organizations, the notion of a corporate-level ISAC is also coming into use. This is especially useful in a technological and geographically diverse organization.

In summary, the messaging about risk management must be consistent, clear, and suited to the audience.

Final Business Function Thoughts

Business requirements drive the information security function. Taking full advantage of these drivers involves the following:

■ Being proactive about delivering on the company's trust commitment to customers, partners, and staff.
■ Reacting efficiently and effectively to the latest threat, attack, or vulnerability. Ensure that a process is in place to track all that comes in from the outside, and to react in case an attack to the organization succeeds, or there is a new threat (virus, Trojan horse, worm, etc.) that is otherwise not planed for.
■ Putting a security compliance program in place. Measure security compliance and work to make sure the compliance numbers trend upwards month to month. This will assure not only continuity, but also as a continuous improvement. Such is the raw material of a Baldridge Quality award.
■ Ensuring a proactive information security organization. Make sure that the right people lead it and it works effectively within the overall enterprise.
■ Building effective information security processes. These should stand the test of external review, and should focus on both efficiency and effectiveness.
■ Communicating on a continual basis with management and staff. Management commitment is essential, and that won't be a factor unless risk, value, vulnerability, and threat are all communicated upward and sideways, and in business terms.

There is no guarantee that all the risks will be covered, or that a disastrous security breach won't occur. However, with a proactive program (outlined in this chapter and elsewhere in this book) focused on the business drivers for security, any enterprise can rest assured that it has done all the due diligence that is required for an effective posture of information security.

Chapter 6

Security Leadership

Michael J. Corby and Vaune M. Carr

There are many excellent security managers. In fact, most of the people that I have known in the security profession are excellent managers. Bad managers don't seem to be attracted to security. It's too hard. It almost always involves trying to resolve a new crisis, break new ground, anticipate all possible conditions, and react perfectly with only a few shreds of real facts. Security is an area that breeds the need for good managers.

Security leadership is not about just being a good security manager. Leaders in any field or profession have a common set of traits that make them exceptional leaders. What those traits are may be hard to identify or quantify, but the effects of those traits are quite visible. Leaders attract the attention of others. Not in an obvious way, however. Not in the same way that a famous movie star, a Hall of Fame athlete, or a person of position attracts an entourage. Leaders have a knack for being used as a role model. Leaders discover that their casual phrases become part of the language without any effort on their part. One leader that I worked with used to say, "People can only do two things: point with pride or view with alarm." The phrase stuck, and throughout the organization some derivation of it was heard in technical settings, manager meetings, in human resources, finance, engineering, and sales. Some people didn't know who said it, but it stuck. Leadership often goes stealthily throughout an organization.

Occasionally leaders are youthful. When true leadership emerges while its host person is still in the thirties or even twenties, it often becomes newsworthy. The Boston Red Sox general manager is a notable leader more for his youth than his position or his decisions. A young Ted Turner achieved leadership status in his relative youth when he organized a new venture to offer 24-hour news. People who fundamentally change our society during the first half of their lives demonstrate some aspect of leadership. The computer field is crowded with executives, but few true leaders. Think about it.

Along with the young, rarely will leaders achieve recognition in their very advanced years (at least advanced by common standards of age). I'm not talking about people who are leaders already, and then grow older. Many of them continue leading and contributing well past the time that mere mortals choose to relax and retire. Leaders continue to be leaders until the day they die. Leadership doesn't retire. Only occasionally, however, will leadership emerge much later in life. Typically, leadership was already there; it's just that we became aware of it only late. Mother Theresa of Calcutta had been a leader in her community for many, many years, but backed into public leadership acclaim as an older woman.

Leaders have established a track record of being credible, believable, but not just being truthful. A leader weaves together several ways of presenting facts so that they are understood, are memorable, and even call people to act or at least reflect. Following are some traits to avoid or adopt in your quest for leadership.

Chicken Little

Leaders are optimists. Some have portrayed security as a technical field that delivers "bad news." This is a somewhat true generalization, but we view that as a shortcoming of individuals, not an attribute of the profession. I know people, and I'm sure you know them also, who are known for "lighting their hair on fire and putting it out with a hammer." Characterizing security by these dramatic security spokespersons as bad news purveyors is only looking at a small component of security — the part that has failed. Security as an attempt to restrict productivity against an inevitable security breach is misleading. Air travel could be similarly categorized as a fruitless attempt to defeat the forces of gravity. Leaders use a pervasive negative categorization as a ripe opportunity to offer solutions that can become a viable way forward to achieve new benefits. Not in an unrealistic way, but as something that is graspable, achievable within the near-term career of those near to the issue. Leaders don't panic or cause others to draw dire conclusions. They don't shy away from proposing solutions; yet present solutions in practical, realistic, achievable terms.

...By the Company You Keep

Leaders hang with leaders. But they are not seen as exclusionary, snobbish, or condescending to others. I've been lucky enough to be invited to several events that have attracted people of leadership caliber. The general atmosphere is warm, friendly, and very approachable. Some professional groups are designed to attract this type of crowd. One of the semiprofessional social groups in my past was the Young Executives Council. Unfortunately, I'm no longer invited, because I'm either not young or not an executive in the local area, but I found it a good place to see and practice leadership demeanor. I never got business or directly asked for referrals in such a group, but was more than once given an opportunity because I was with the people who were known to be in the Young Executives group.

Some Chambers of Commerce or other area business groups have the same effect. What I have observed is that joining does not result in immediate benefits. I have been a member of several organizations for decades and have only just recently started to feel the effect of "running with the big dogs."

Once inroads have been made in this circle, leaders do not rest, but seek to enlarge the circle. Hard to imagine a former world leader taking on a leadership role for simple home-building to benefit the poor, but in many ways, Jimmy Carter has become better known, and arguably more favored, as a participant in Habitat for Humanity than he was for being the President of the United States.

Storytelling

Leaders entertain. Everyone loves a good joke or a well-told story. There is a fine line between having an engaging style and trying to be a stand-up comic. Leaders are able to make the most mundane story sound like a world-class adventure. Having the descriptive phrases of a great novelist and the timing of George Burns, the legendary comic, can make even a budget presentation an enthralling, memorable event. Does this come easily? No, it doesn't, but it takes practice. Some need more practice than others, but it is important to observe those who do it well, even imitate them, and keep the skill fresh. Use it often, but be careful not to wear it out. Jesus was a master of story-telling, using the many parables that related to the people who were listening. But he didn't always speak in parables. Leaders know when to be regular people, too.

Are You Having Fun?

Are you passionate? Finally, one last common trait of true leaders. They live the order: "Find something you love and figure out how to get paid for it." The hardest days I've ever spent in my life were the ones where I was forced to do something I didn't like. Leaders are passionate about what they do. If they don't feel passionate, they don't do it. People can tell when a person is fully charged and engaged or "on." Leaders are always seen "on." Oh sure, they take time to drop down a few notches and relax the smile, nod off, or just sigh out of exhaustion, but they will never be seen in this "off" mode. As a leader, you will need to love your job — always! Not just from 9 to 5, or 8 to 4, but be willing to let your eyes twinkle when the topic of security comes up in conversation. As always, there is a word of caution: twinkling is almost always better than bubbling. Being passionate can be seen in a nonverbal response. If left unchecked, that passion can become verbal, and soon result in the overenthused leader being stranded alone as an evangelist. Silent passion is an often unused and undervalued commodity. Make it work for you in your quest for leadership.

Setting Yourself up for Success

Leaders create the setting to succeed. Always begin with the end in mind. Everything else that needs to be done will fall into line. Like an athlete visualizing an athletic achievement, a security leader visualizes what the achievement will look like when the project or security program is complete. Carefully laying out the steps to that achievement draws the leader and the team closer to the ultimate goal. It increases your chances of reaching the goal. This step towards success may be a small undertaking in a small organization and increasingly more difficult when organizations are larger and projects have a broader scope. Starting small and grasping the concepts and achieving success will build confidence and speed with repetition. This process does require visualization to keep the project or program on track.

If you don't have the luxury of starting small, for whatever reason, a proof of concept is one way of achieving success, trust, and building a foundation for the remainder of the effort. Time and costs will have their own role in the success of any project, so a successful proof-of-concept model demonstrates the effectiveness of the solution by allowing the security leader to contain costs and hold to a schedule, while at the same time proving the model will meet the expectations. You avoid the pitfalls of fragmentation and confusion when projects become drawn out and people lose sight of the vision or it becomes vague.

Another method of implementing a security system is to "pilot" the system. The implementation of an IT security system is when the system is launched first to a single group or area before being rolled out to the rest of the organization. Those who receive the technology are termed the "pilot" group. When the pilot is performed for part of an organization or part of a single project, the "users" are allowed to evaluate the pilot before implementation across an entire organization. The careful collection of feedback on the pilot and the correction of the design to "remove or change" those parts of the pilot which were unsuccessful or that brought negative feedback from the organization are a critical part of the security leader's final steps in the pilot.

An example is the steps one leader took in the deployment of token technology. Several different products are available on the market to be deployed. For each of the products, the security leader took great care to provide accurate documentation and training. At the end of the pilot, the "client' or "users" provided feedback on the token of choice. When users shopped and compared, they chose the product that was the easiest to use. All other factors being the same, the security leader took the input from the user and moved forward in the rollout with a single token. The leader had offered choices, and then carefully collected the feedback and achieved success with the technology rollout because he adjusted his plan to accommodate the preferences of the client. After the pilot, the rest of the rollout became easier and much faster. The leader received recognition and had gained the trust of his community of users for the successful implementation of the control. Proof that if you lay out the steps and practice, you can learn to be a leader.

Once you achieve success and visibility within the organization, the "rain" comes early and often. The plate is typically full for the security leader, and "food" on the plate seems to change quickly. Keeping ahead of the game is a challenge as in any information technology profession, but more so in the security arena, where anything you do right goes unnoticed, but when it's wrong, "look out!" Everyone notices. System access is a privilege, but the fact remains that when there is a problem with access the security leader can become the focus of the users' complaints, sometimes legitimately and other times not. When this occurs, the level of trust is broken and it is sometimes difficult to recover from a business disruption caused by a failure of security controls.

All things being equal, the number of projects does not exempt the leader from proper prioritization and assessment of the risk to appropriately address the projects. When a leader takes on too many projects at once, it can be a disaster. Be careful not to overcommit as missing targets and deadlines has the same effect on a security leader as any other leader: it dissolves trust in one's ability to deliver as expected. Communication is key to helping gain the understanding of all levels of the organization in what is being done, when, why, and how.

Overcommitting stretches resources and tends to add to confusion as to why various projects are being done, what they are supposed to achieve, when they will be completed, and other particulars. Remember, most people in the organization are giving very little thought to the security of the enterprise and may have limited understanding of what the various parts of the overall security program are. Security awareness classes, advisories, and other communications help the user community appreciate what security is doing to reduce risk within the organization. Help the organization understand what is your responsibility and what is their responsibility for each of your projects.

Another quality that exemplifies great leadership is being able to "pick the right battles." Too much conflict casts a negative light on any individual. Knowing when to take a step back and be cooperative instead of getting into a battle is a fine quality. These minor concessions can be accumulated to be used positively in a real battle as they indicate the leader's ability to work with others. Knowing how to manage your battles will improve your image and earn you respect.

While you are taking that step back, it is important for you to be inspirational. Great leaders inspire people to help move their efforts closer to organizational goals.

Keeping the end in mind will help your team get there. Being inspirational requires that you understand the individuals enough to be able to present that inspirational message so it has the proper impact on each one on your team.

How Is Your Performance Rated?

Positions of leadership, especially in the security field, are not won by a popularity contest. Not everyone is going to like you. This fact should tell you that you need to develop a certain persona or way that people perceive you. There are several outstanding qualities for a security leader. It is important to be viewed as honest. There is a large technical aspect to the security field and therefore being competent is also important. The speed at which the environment is changing should tell you that you need to be always forward looking. You want to be perceived as one who consistently achieves superior results.

People who consistently achieve their goals are usually effective in setting them. To do this, you will want to define in detail what you want to accomplish. The nature of security projects usually requires some sign-off or commitment by various levels of the organization. Preparing and communicating through high-level presentations is an excellent way to get "buy-in" from the appropriate groups in the organization.

Outline for yourself all of the things you would do if all the right conditions existed. Thinking through and defining your goals will give you the ability to recognize when there is an opportunity. When the timing is right, you will be able to take advantage of the opening to introduce one of your own projects. Don't be afraid to start the project and turn it over to someone else for completion. Getting the project plans and direction set is a great way to get work done through others.

If you have followers within the security group, that's one thing; however, the ability to listen carefully and communicate well will help build your image as a leader. The trust that is given to leaders also seems to provide an energy or empowerment to individuals to see the vision the leader has and to help the followers be able to commit to it. The leader's own commitment builds trust and relationships. Open dialogue and respect for others fosters movement toward the goal even more.

A great leader celebrates achievements as well as measures performance. If there is one thing I enjoy doing, it is celebrating the accomplishment. It helps show gratitude for those who are involved and creates a bonding effect for the team. Good memories can be shared as well as an exchange of what could have gone better. It marks a milestone in the project and is a positive take-away for the team.

The leader can help individuals overcome failures and even develop rewarding career paths. A great security leader challenges assumptions and needs to be innovative to provide what is required in a given situation. One example is when single-factor authentication was replaced by two-factor authentication. The security leaders had to educate as to why the new form of authentication was stronger and why it was necessary. Knowledge, persistence, competency, and a strong desire to make security better while reducing the vulnerabilities all played a role in the implementation of two-factor authentication. The same will be true for the technology you will implement.

Great leaders are almost always on the same level plane when it comes to their behavior. People come to expect it and can "rely" on it. Too many incidents of not being on that balanced level of steadiness can take away from credibility. If you are not positive about the outcome of your project, how can anyone else be? It's impossible. You need to be assertive, direct, and decisive when leading others on security. There is a huge difference between managing the projects and leading them. Keeping a consistent attitude and working towards the vision will help keep projects on track and contribute to your success.

Have a passion for what you are doing. It will influence those around you to be excited about your undertakings. People get caught up in the excitement and they begin to want you to succeed. They will encourage you and often want to become a part of the project or in some way connected to your success. This is a winning combination and worth keeping aware of the possibilities for making it happen. Know your allies and help them become knowledgeable of your work and its progress.

Accepting challenges will help you overcome fear. Fear of failure is a common emotion for people. Once you accept a challenge, you will be on your way to success. Just take it one step at a time. Every success will be a building block to your next success. Do it because you want it. Want creates a desire, an intent, and action. These are the steps that will help you reach your goals.

As you gear up to begin a project, it is important to recognize the amount of power you will have because of the amount of information that you will be privileged to access. As you succeed, that power will become more influential to your achieving the next success. Never stop believing in yourself as that will help you achieve the next success. Moving ahead with confidence will help you make it through challenging times. Whether in your leadership role or in a managerial role, you must have confidence that you will achieve your goals.

Nothing is as critical as clean, concise communication of your goals. Break the large goals into smaller tasks. For example, instead of saying you intend to work hard to achieve your goals, say that you will work from 9:00 am until 7:00 pm five days a week to achieve your goals. That way, when you try to decide if you met your goals, you will be able to determine what was done to complete them.

All else the same, your attitude is very significant to the outcome. Stepping into the project, you must possess the positive attitude that will help you overcome all obstacles. It will be your strength during trying times.

Leaders are leaders because they set out to express themselves rather than to prove themselves. Leaders don't set out to be leaders, they just want to freely express themselves. Adults learn best when they direct their own learning. Leaders agree that leaders are not born, but they are made. For the leader, life becomes the career.

It is a simple process to becoming a leader and it allows you to rely on yourself and your judgment. Of course you must accept responsibility for your actions. Blame no one. You have to be willing sometimes to make a fool of yourself. Being able to laugh at oneself allows you to keep progressing on the leadership path. Some people believe that the real role of the security leader is to make diverse elements and people work together. Security projects that have an enterprise scope and goal make it easy to observe all the elements and people a security leader must make work or "play" together.

Encourage yourself to be innovative and experimental and to take risks. These three elements will enable you to grow and experience success. Little setbacks are a part of the process of learning and growing. Learn to accept them as normal rather than abnormal. Think globally rather than locally. Security is highly visible and attracts the attention of the organization when anything goes wrong.

The next generation of security leaders will have some traits in common that help them become very successful, as shown in Figure 6.1. Security leaders must take in information, process it, and apply a lot of common sense. They understand the big picture in organizations (especially after a bit of experience) and can visualize what will work and what won't work. This can save time and money, unlike some individuals who must jump at the latest technology only to end up dumping it in a few months (if the vendor doesn't drop support first). Technology is only a piece of the puzzle. There are many solutions out there looking for a problem. You must know what will actually work, and then focus on leading the effort rather than applying a quick fix or putting out a fire.

Keeping control of resources is an excellent way to gain success on a security project. You can demonstrate sound business judgment and protection for valuable resources at the same time. Security leaders are good business leaders. They are weighing the risks, prioritizing the projects, examining the overall architecture, and developing real solutions. When you examine how efficient and effective security leaders are, you will note that even projects of enterprise proportions use only a fragment of the budget normally used for projects of the scope and size. All of these resource-conserving factors contribute to the success of the security leader.

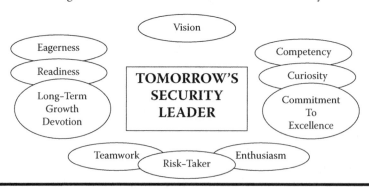

Figure 6.1 Skills of tomorrow's security leader.

Be strategic. It is important to sharpen your skills so that you can continue to look out at the security horizon. Picturing what is coming next will help you to be better prepared for your next success. Be careful not to overstep your bounds though, as the final call on security belongs to the ones who are responsible to the shareholders. Ensure that the executives are properly educated in what the risks are so they can choose to accept them or address the vulnerabilities with risk mitigation.

Security or protection specialists have the unique opportunity to blend the technical with the people side of the issues. If you want to be successful in security, pay attention to the people side of the problem. This is one field that will be very unforgiving if you forget this important point. People are what make leaders, not technology. Followers, managers, and other leaders are key to your success. Always remember the role that they play in your success. Putting people first will help you become a successful security leader.

There is an interesting soft-sell side to security that used to be very hard-sell. It has often been compared to selling insurance. The risk is there, but you may never need it. Recent events have found the risk to have increased vulnerabilities causing money losses, so the selling of security is not as difficult as it used to be. If you don't have it, an organization may not survive an unexpected threat, or may spend more money to "fix" something after the fact. You may feel like an evangelist at times, but you are selling what you believe the organization needs to reduce its risk. No one has to buy it, so you need to be persuasive. It can be as direct as explaining the return on investment, specific metrics, or risk reduction, but making your case will be critical to your having success as a security leader.

Being a successful security leader is a little like being any other type of leader. Survey what's out there. Get your focus or vision. Lay out your plans. Follow them religiously. Be determined, creative, and persistent. Always remember to be yourself. For in life:

> "There is only one success — to be able to spend your life in your own way."—Unknown

Professionalism

A leader is known as a consummate professional. What does that mean? Does it apply solely to practices that require special skills and inherent training and maybe even licensing, like physicians or attorneys? A professional may fall into one of these notable categories, but a person can also be viewed as a professional, even if their training is merely the basics of school and their permit to practice is that they have the job. Professionalism isn't just a piece of parchment or letters after a name. It's an attitude and an aura that surrounds the person. It's probably easier to describe what a professional attitude is not, than what a professional attitude is.

A professional doesn't look at the clock in the middle of a meeting or discussion and announce that it's 5 o'clock and time to go home, and then proceed to close up the folder and walk out. Professionals absorb the importance of the day and see it through to a logical rest point, even if not finished. Stop at 5:00? Not really. Stop when it is time to stop, reflect, and rest? Absolutely! Professionalism is the appropriate channel for enthusiasm. Workaholics are obsessed, not professionals. A leader strives to never confuse the two.

How does one recognize a true professional? The most commonly used phrase that I've heard to describe a professional is that they are always thinking of ways that they can use their knowledge and abilities to make an improvement in their employer's or client's position or value. Some also add something about taking a personal interest and having a stake in the success of their employer or client.

Finally, it is important that leaders can help cement their own credibility with peers by going the extra mile to speak in a vernacular that they can understand. Great leaders do not use acronyms; they cite examples that are meaningful to the audience and are willing to learn from others at any level. When speaking to farmers, tell farmer stories, use their terminology. When speaking to shepherds, use shepherd terminology and stories (forget the shepherd jokes!).

Be careful not to insult those people who are not present. A real leader treats all people as valuable. Even a very nationalistic society that may be highly prejudiced against others is not seen by real leaders as an opportunity to join in abusing others who have been without leadership. Stories that are directly in line with the listeners' key concerns should stop short of mimicking their own personality or societal failures. Leaders rise above taking sides.

Pretty much all that happens in the security field is related to one or more factors of people, process, or technology.[1] Historically, much of what has been said or written is heavily slanted to the technology. Come to the process. The success of a security program is weighted heavily on engaging people, such as recognized by the Human Firewall Council initiative. In 2000, a consortium of industry, government, and academic representatives formed the Human Firewall Council, established on the premise that information security is a people problem, a managerial problem that does have some technical solutions.

A successful leader puts in play all the people relationships they have nurtured through the years. I have a personal "rolodex" of over 7000 names that I have used from time to time throughout my career. The trick is not to become an expert in everything, but instead to pick the right expert for the need.

Vendors can be leveraged from a product or service vendor (trade value for cash) to a business partner (trade risk for a "piece of the action"). This can negate the gravitation attraction toward an adversarial relationship, which can be damaging.

Over all the specifics, we can do a significant amount to helping to establish common measurements of competency. There can be a world of difference between education, training, certification, and accreditation:

- Education primarily provides the theory and perhaps the understanding through a variety of formal teaching techniques.
- Training is typically a "hands-on" experience that transfers working knowledge of a function using a knowledgeable individual who has the skills needed to provide a full range of experiences in the knowledge transfer.
- Certification is a formalized validation that the skills and functions meet predefined criteria.
- Accreditation is also a formal process that establishes a predefined level of performance, typically for a computer system or process.

Each of these techniques can be applied in varying measures to assure that the people are performing at an appropriate level and that the processes achieve what they are intended to achieve. Leaders invoke the most appropriate technique and don't hesitate to use multiple ways to assure that the technology is balanced with competent people and reliable processes.

Leaders can also use the knowledge of business partners to help drive the security message into areas where it will be understood more clearly. For example, an aspiring security leader will work with external auditors to help communicate good security practices to the CFO.

Very, very few organizations have security alone as their business goal. It is almost always in concert with delivering customer value, creating solutions, maximizing investor appreciation, and providing services. The effective leader knows this and always is able to relate security activities to one of these corporate mantras.

A wise application systems guy once said to me; "The most important part of a system project is to know when it's done." Over the years, I've reflected on variations of this gem several times. In sales opportunities: "How do you know when we've satisfied your requirements?" In risk assessment and management projects: "How do you know when we've reached the point of acceptable risk?" And in personal career management: "How do you know it's time to move along?"

Making a transition from an outstanding security expert to an effective business executive is a daunting challenge. Not only do you have to demonstrate all the aspects of brilliant leadership, but all the cultural factors of the organization need to be aligned in your favor.

Early in my career I had the opportunity to move from an operational position in the data center to an advisory position in the IT research group. My new responsibilities would be to teach programmers and analysts how to design and create effective systems, provide highly productive support systems for them to do this, and to participate in resolving "nearly impossible" technical challenges. With the natural tension that existed between development groups and operations, the transition was not difficult technically, but it was a challenge culturally. For me to be effective, I needed to have the ability to create a gap between my old and new job functions that was large enough to virtually erase my past involvement. Fortunately for me, I was a young participant, and I had a supervisor who used many very creative ways to bridge this gap and establish me as a highly sought advisor to the company's most prestigious development teams.

Still, despite this excellent planning, my upward mobility was limited. When the former head of the data center became a senior vice president of administration, I had the opportunity to be on a business trip with him. He was pleasant during the trip, but when he returned, he questioned why I was able to attend this planning meeting in view of the fact that I was only a night-shift employee of the data center. No matter what I did, I would always be cast in the light of a good worker, not a fellow executive and potential leader. Time to move on.

When Is It Time to Move on?

What are some of the signs that your path to leadership may not be as attainable as you might like? Well, there are several signs that are indications that "you might not be tapped as a leader" (borrowing from a comedy routine). You might not be recognized as a leader if:

- You attend an executive meeting, and your peers keep asking where your boss is.
- The same executive is asking you the same technical question over and over.
- You plan to discuss some important strategic ideas at a dinner meeting, and someone has your seat moved to the auditor's table

Three Envelopes

You get the picture. Time to get out the resumé and make a career move. Which reminds me of a related humorous story: A key executive was having a "going away" party, and his successor was alone with him in his office. The successor asked him quite seriously: "To what do you attribute your success and long career with the company?" The executive answered: "Three envelopes. My predecessor gave me three envelopes and told me to open one whenever I was facing a crisis that I couldn't handle." And with that he handed the new incumbent three sealed envelopes and walked out the door. Years passed, and the new executive was doing quite well. One day, the company was facing a crisis that threatened to reduce the market share and stock price to mere peanuts. He went to his top drawer and pulled out the first envelope, opened it, and read on a small slip of paper: "Call a press conference, acknowledge that mistakes had been made and they overestimated the customer loyalty, and promise that a new vision will turn the company around." A press conference was called, the statement was made as prescribed, and immediately the company turned the situation around.

More years passed, and again the company was facing a crisis that threatened to cost them millions and jeopardize their very existence. He went to his top drawer and pulled out the second envelope, opened it, and read on a small slip of paper: "Call a press conference, and admit that the company had underestimated the cost to provide the level of customer service that was required, but a new vision will turn the company around." A press conference was called, the statement was made as prescribed, and immediately the company again turned the situation around.

Still more years passed, and again the company was facing a crisis that threatened to bring them to the brink of failure. He went to his top drawer and pulled out the third envelope, opened it, and read on a small slip of paper: "Prepare three envelopes."

Good leaders know when to prepare three envelopes.

Jump the Shark

Sometimes, the roadblocks to true leadership are placed there by yourself. Leaders are not perfect. Sometimes there is a single event that becomes a watershed or "fold in time" that divides all events. If this event doesn't go well, it may become almost impossible to make a correction. The situation continues to deteriorate and the best leader in the world is helpless. A culture has been formed that attributes this situation to the entertainment industry, when a television series makes a blunder from which it cannot recover. In the popular television series "Happy Days," there was an episode when the character Fonzie was water skiing. In that episode, Fonzie actually jumped his water skis over a shark. From that point on, the character and the series became a parody of itself, a fate from which it would never recover.

Sometimes leaders can "jump the shark," and there is no realistic recovery without a complete change. A wise leader is ready to sense when events or actions have taken on a higher degree of importance and will, for the long term, overshadow everything that is done. The leader becomes a parody of his or her own leadership.

You may have jumped the shark if your advice is sought on all decisions including when to serve meat loaf in the company cafeteria. You may have jumped the shark when, as a presidential candidate, you stick your head out of the turret of a tank, and flashbulbs start popping.

The actual situation is impossible to predict, but as a leader, you will recognize it, and as a leader you will act.

Recap

- Leaders attract the attention of others and are used as role models.
- Security leaders are good business leaders.
- A leader weaves together several ways of presenting facts so that they are understood, are memorable, and call people to act or at least reflect.
- Leaders present security as more than an attempt to restrict productivity against an inevitable security breach.

- Leaders don't panic or cause others to draw dire conclusions.
- Leaders don't shy away from proposing solutions; yet present solutions in practical, realistic, achievable terms.
- Leaders are good story-tellers.
- Leaders find something they love and figure out how to get paid for it.
- Leaders create the setting to succeed; they visualize the end and work backwards to achieve it.
- Leaders look for small successes that build on one another.
- Leaders under-commit and over-achieve.
- Leaders pick the right battles; accept responsibility for their actions; blame no one.
- Great leaders inspire people to help move their efforts closer to organizational goals.
- Leaders listen carefully and communicate well.
- Great leaders celebrate achievements as well as measure performance.
- Leaders know when their ideas may have "jumped the shark."

Note

1. See IT Infrastructure Library (ITIL), process documentation at www.itil.co.uk.

Chapter 7

The Public Sector CISO: Life in the Fishbowl

Lynn McNulty

Introduction

This chapter will examine the role of the public sector chief information security officer (CISO) and discuss the environment in which he or she operates. It will also seek to identify several of the significant differences between the operating environments of the public sector CISO and those employed by business enterprises.

The term "public sector CISO" is used to refer to those individuals who serve as the chief information security officer for a branch of government. In the United States, this usually means that the individual is employed by a component of the federal, state, local, or tribal government. The term could also be widened to include individuals who work for nonprofit organizations such as the Red Cross or the American Association of Retired People, to name two of the larger nonprofit organizations. Finally, the term "public sector" also includes employees of international organizations such as the United Nations or the World Bank.

Information security has long been a concern within the public sector. Beginning with the long-established national security focus on preventing the unauthorized disclosure of classified information, it was natural that this concern for security would be extended to computer systems, as these devices became used for processing and storing sensitive information.[1] In fact the early years of information security are marked by a heavy focus on protecting classified information held by the defense and intelligence establishments. This was the era of the dedicated computer system located in a secure area, protected by fences, armed guards, snarling dogs, and heavy doors equipped with large locks. These systems were operated and maintained by individuals with security clearances. In addition the use of telecommunication links to the computer were closely controlled, with a heavy emphasis placed on the use of National Security Agency (NSA)-approved encryption performed in large hardware boxes.

As computer technology evolved, these systems became widely used by the civil agencies at all levels of government to support a wide variety of functions ranging from tax administration, benefits processing, air traffic control, internal management, and regulatory functions. The security of civil agency systems, and the information processed by them, was not a primary concern when these systems were designed and implemented. In the early days of information processing by civilian agencies, security was viewed as an expensive luxury. In most instances only minimal security controls were instituted for these applications.[2] The author wishes that he had a dollar for each time he discussed security with responsible individuals at various civil agencies and was told, "the information is not classified." The implication of this response is that there is no need to protect it. Public sector CISOs are still paying the price for this negative attitude towards computer security.

The one issue that did drive information systems security in the "unclassified" world in the 1970s was the concern for the protection of personal information. The passage of the Privacy Act of 1974 forced government managers to address the security issues inherent in the use of computers for the processing of personal information. Although the Privacy Act mandated no specific safeguards, it did establish a new level of due care that forced federal managers to examine the security environment for systems that processed information covered by the Privacy Act of 1974.

The Regulatory Environment for Today's Federal CISO

A complex mosaic of statute and internal government regulation that has evolved over the past 20 years drives much of the contemporary information security environment within the federal government. This is one of the significant differences between the public and private sectors' attitudes towards information security. Although the private sector CISO does have to address regulatory requirements, the primary impetus for his or her program, as viewed by the senior executives of the enterprise, is to support and protect the profitability of the corporation. In contrast, much of the authority and basis for public sector information security programs is derived from various statutes passed by concerned legislators who are attempting to correct identified problems that have resulted in the compromise of citizen information or the loss of taxpayer dollars.

At the federal level, today's CISO must deal with a complex regulatory environment. One piece of legislation stands out as the key source of authority for the federal agency CISO. The E-Government Act of 2002 contained Title III, the Federal Information Security Management Act (FISMA).[3] It required each federal agency to develop, document, and implement an agencywide information security program to protect the information and information systems that support agency operations and control agency assets. The law also extended coverage to systems managed by another agency or operated on behalf of an agency by a contractor organization. FISMA also assigned the responsibility for the implementation of information security programs to the agency or department chief information officer (CIO) and stipulated that each major agency would designate a chief information security officer, who would report to the CIO. The function of the CISO is to execute the CIO's responsibilities for information security.

The FISMA legislation set forth several specific requirements for federal agency information security programs. It is not the purpose of this chapter to enumerate and discuss the specific provisions of the FISMA legislation. However, it is interesting to discuss the public reporting process that has been established by the FISMA law, for this underscores one of the major differences between the public sector CISO and his or her private sector counterpart.

One provision of FISMA requires federal agency CIOs and inspectors general (IG) to accomplish annual reviews of the agency information security program. These reviews are accomplished in accordance with guidance issued by the Office of Management and Budget (OMB) in May or June of each year. The FISMA reporting system is basically a parallel process where the office of the agency CIO prepares a report on the status of the agency's compliance with established government-wide information security goals. These can range from maintaining a complete and accurate inventory of all information systems operated by or on behalf of the agency, to reporting the status of completing certification and accreditation actions of agency applications.

While the CIO office is preparing its report, the IG organization is also preparing a similar report that contains their independent finding on the status of the agency's compliance with the FISMA requirements, NIST publications, and OMB guidelines. Both reports are submitted to OMB with a transmittal letter signed by the agency head. In some instances the independent program evaluation prepared by the IG is posted on the IG part of the agency website. Once these reports are received at OMB, they are reviewed and consolidated into a governmentwide report that is submitted to the Congress.[4] This document is also a publicly available report and is posted on the OMB website. It contains agency-specific information that discusses the issues and problems identified with respect to each major agency of the federal government. OMB uses the information provided in the FISMA reporting process to address specific issues with senior agency management personnel. In some instances specific program mandates are included in the agency's fiscal guidance, i.e., certify and accredit all information systems by the end of this fiscal year.

The appropriate committees of the Congress are given copies of the agency CIO and IG reports. To rate these federal agencies, the House Government Reform Committee has used these reports to derive an annual report card grade for information security. These grades are publicly released at an annual committee hearing on the status of information security in the federal executive branch.[5] At this public hearing several CIOs, primarily drawn from the agencies that have received failing or poor grades, are placed in the public spotlight and asked very sharp-edged questions about why their agency did not do better on that particular year's FISMA report.

Impact of FISMA on the Federal CISO

FISMA has been criticized as being a very inefficient and ineffective way of achieving a very desirable objective, the improvement of information security across the federal government.[6] One particular problem that has been cited is that as a compliance process, FISMA does not equate to good security. Other criticisms of FISMA focus on the emphasis of bureaucratic paper-bound processes, such as certification and accreditation, which some believe to be a nonproductive misallocation of agency resources that detract from more productive activities. However, there is general agreement among all parties that FISMA has significantly elevated both the status of information security as a mainstream program and the role and stature of the CISO within the executive branch of the federal government.

The issue of the position and stature of the federal agency CISO since the implementation of FISMA warrants additional discussion. Before the passage of the FISMA legislation in 2002, the term "CISO" was not part of the array of bureaucratic titles within the federal career service. By the year 2000, most federal agencies had established information systems security programs, but these programs were generally understaffed, underresourced and in some instances they were organizationally placed as to be ineffective. In fairness it must be acknowledged that this characterization applies more to the civil agencies of the government as opposed to the defense and intelligence components.

However, with the implementation of FISMA, there have been noteworthy changes in the federal information technology workforce. Most CISOs now hold senior executive service positions — the equivalent to flag officer status in the civil service. Information security is now a recognized career field within the government's personnel system.[7] There is now an established career ladder for individuals who enter government service in the field of information security. From a base salary perspective, government information security professionals are well compensated. Finally, information security has become a priority program in federal agencies, to the dismay of some long-term information technology veterans who fondly remember the days when security issues could be ignored with impunity. For example, in FY2005 federal agencies spent approximately five billion dollars on information security, approximately one eighth of the government's information technology budget.[8]

Other Legislation and Policies That Impact the Federal CISO

FISMA is not the only piece of government policy that federal government CISOs must factor into their operating environment. If the agency is a defense or intelligence component, there are separate policies aside from FISMA that apply to these components. The director of central intelligence has long-standing polices that prescribe security policy requirements for the processing of intelligence information. The National Security Agency, through the Committee on National Security Systems, also establishes security polices that cover government systems that process classified information. In some agencies, like the State Department or the Energy Department, the CISO may have to address systems that fall under three different security policies.

If the agency is in the healthcare business, such as the Department of Veterans Affairs, it must also comply with the security requirements of the Heath Insurance Portability and Accountability Act of 1996 (HIPAA). Many agencies are also bound by program-specific legislation that mandates the specific protection requirements for various types of information. Examples of these agencies with unique statutory-based information security requirements include the Bureau of the Census, the Environmental Protection Agency, and federal law enforcement agencies.

Finally, the concern for the protection of personal information has produced a patchwork quilt of privacy laws that impact federal agency CISOs. The Omnibus Privacy Act of 1974 provides the basic framework governing the protection of personal information held by federal agencies; however, there are some agency-specific privacy requirements that add other layers of policy complexity to the CISO's operating environment. The privacy issue is becoming increasingly complicated in the post-911 world. The strong emphasis upon the use of data mining tools, expanded access to federal databases, and information sharing among all levels of government is producing a corresponding concern about the privacy issues inherent in these programs. Privacy concerns also extend to the state and local government CISOs, as federally mandated counter-terrorism programs also produce similar information access and data sharing issues for state and local government CISOs.

Resource Constraints

Public sector CISOs must operate in different budgetary and staffing environments than their private sector counterparts. At the federal level, information security has traditionally operated on a very limited resource base — both staff and financial. Given the complex nature of the budgetary processes for public sector organizations, it is difficult for information security components to secure a defined, or line item, position in the agency budget. Many programs have had to live on resources that have been redirected from other operational programs, which have existing budgetary authority.

In a previous paragraph, five billion dollars was cited as the amount of funds expended by federal agencies for information security in fiscal year 2005. However, it would be incorrect to assume that the office of the CISO at the various agencies which comprise the government spent all of this money. The great majority of the funds cited in the OMB report are resources spent by lines of business components for security-related functions that are inherent in developing and operating enterprise information systems.[9] Consequently, many believe that the amount of fiscal resources allocated to public sector CISO organizations is in many instances insufficient to fully address the requirements that fall upon the CISO. This situation is compounded as one looks at the situation of state and local government CISOs. One recently completed study found that 40 percent of the 50 state governments responding to a survey indicated that they did not have a defined budget for the state CISO.[10] At the federal level, the level of budgetary resources have improved over the past few years, particularly after the passage of FISMA; however, these are still inadequate to fully address the challenges faced by these organizations.

Another factor that complicated the work of the public sector CISO is the politicization of the budget process. As of March 2007, five months into FY2007, all agencies of the federal government, with the exception of the departments of defense and homeland security, do not have a congressionally approved appropriation to fund their operations for this fiscal year. As a result they are operating on "continuing resolutions" which effectively force these agencies to operate at the spending levels of the previous fiscal year. New programs or technology initiatives included in the FY 2007 budget must be deferred until Congress passes the necessary appropriation bills, which may not occur until the FY2008 bills are passed. In addition the budgetary pressures created by the need to fund the war in Iraq by reducing domestic spending are also impacting federal agency information security programs.

The staffing problem also underscores another difference between the public and private sector CISOs. Many public sector CISOs manage what was recently termed a "blended workforce" consisting of government employees and on-site contractor employees.[11] Budgetary realities and Bush administration policies have effectively capped government employment and required federal agencies to augment their staff with individuals obtained from private sector contractor organizations. Information security has become one of the major growth areas in the federal outsourcing arena. Private sector employees perform a wide variety of functions for federal information security programs to include policy writing, performing security audits, preparing contingency plans, and staffing intrusion detection centers. It is quite common to find private sector contractor employees equipped with business cards bearing the logo of their client agency.

Government information security programs are staffed with a nucleus of career employees. Many of the individuals have years of experience with the agency or with other federal government organizations. They have experienced good times and difficult times as information security professionals, but they have made major contributions to the security of federal information systems. Several recent programs have had significant impacts upon the government information security workforce.

The first of these was the inclusion of information security in the government-wide information technology job series. Although this may not seem to be important to the reader who has no experience with the civil service system, it marked a major milestone for the government information security careerist. Before this change, individuals who worked in the field were placed in many different job series ranging from computer operations to computer scientist to traditional security officer. Being part of a dedicated information technology career field results in the establishment of a recognized career ladder for information security professionals. However, as a sub-series in a larger field, information security personnel still have not achieved full recognition as a separate, distinct career within the larger federal personnel system.

Another recent event, which probably has no corollary in the private sector, is a recent decision by the Department of Defense (DOD) to professionalize their information security workforce through the use of professional certifications. In 2004, the DOD adopted a policy that requires all information security personnel (military, reservists, civilian employees, foreign national employees, and contractor employees) to obtain an approved professional certification within three years.[12] Budgetary realities have extended the mandatory date for compliance with the policy to October 2009. It is estimated that approximately 100,000 individuals will be impacted by this policy requirement. It is quite likely that the adoption of professional certification as a workforce metric by the DOD will be adopted by other government agencies.

The question about where the next generation of federal CISOs will come from is being asked with increasing frequency. The future implication of the aging government workforce extends into the field of information security. The Scholarship for Service (SFS) program is providing a nucleus of highly qualified and motivated entry-level information security personnel for federal agencies. A presidential executive order established the SFS program in 2000, with implementation responsibilities divided between the Department of Homeland Security, the Office of Personnel Management, and the National Science Foundation (NSF). NSF transfers federal funds to various universities for the purpose of providing scholarships to selected students who have chosen information security as their career field.[13] These universities are chosen as program participants through a rigorous competitive selection process. In return for receiving the two-year scholarship, the student is obligated to work for two years for a federal agency following his or her graduation. Many of the SFS graduates are entering the federal workforce with masters and, in some instances, doctorates in the field of information security. It is quite likely that some of the future federal agency CISOs will be alumni of the SFS program.

Public Oversight

Another area where public sector CISOs operate in a different environment from their private sector counterparts is the degree of public oversight that program deficiencies and problems receive from a variety of audit agencies, legislative branch components, advisory boards, and the press. Although the private sector CISO does not operate completely behind closed doors, there is a considerable difference between the degree of public scrutiny that he or she may receive and the fishbowl environment that confronts the government agency CISO.

Within the federal government two different audit organizations are involved in the investigation and oversight of federal agency information security programs. These are the Government Accountability Office (GAO) and the various agencies of the Inspector General (IG).[14,15] The GAO is an arm of the Congress that has the responsibility for conducting program review and investigations on behalf of the Congress. Tasking for GAO reviews usually come from the various committees of the Congress, with the results used to frame subsequent public hearings held by the sponsoring committee. Over the past years various issues related to the status of federal agency information security programs has been a frequent subject of GAO investigations. The cumulative impact of years of GAO findings in this field probably led to the adoption of the FISMA legislation and its predecessor, the Computer Security Act of 1987. Once an audit or investigation is completed, the report documenting the findings and recommendations of the GAO examination are public documents available from the GAO website. GAO personnel also frequently testify before congressional committees on the findings of their reviews.

Agency IGs are also a part of the oversight matrix in which federal agency information security programs operate. As discussed in a previous section of this chapter, IG organizations play a major role in the annual FISMA reporting process. However, they also conduct independent evaluations of agency IT security programs and report their findings to the agency head.[16] Many of their reports are also publicly available through the Internet. IGs also have a criminal investigation responsibility. Increasingly these organizations are adding qualified computer crime investigators and digital forensics specialists to their staffs.

Congressional oversight can be especially rigorous in the event of a major information security compromise, which in turn can spark significant press discussion of the information security posture of a given agency. The recent loss of a Department of Veterans Affairs (DVA) laptop that held millions of records on military veterans provides a good example of the public oversight environment that confronts federal agency CIOs.[17] In the summer of 2006, a DVA employee took an agency laptop to his residence to do some work in the after-hours environment. This laptop contained information including Social Security numbers of 25 million veterans who had interacted with the department over the past 20 years. This device was subsequently stolen from the employee's home following a forced entry. The employee subsequently reported the loss of the laptop to his supervisor. In the days that followed this report, information about the data loss slowly worked its way through the DVA bureaucracy. Finally, the serious nature of the data loss was recognized and the matter was brought to the attention of senior DVA management about seven days after the initial report was received within the agency. Approximately ten days after the initial report of the loss of the laptop, a White House press briefing was held to disclose the loss and announce the plans for informing veterans about the loss of this information.

The public was stunned by both the circumstances of the loss of this laptop and the magnitude of the amount of information that had been potentially compromised. The story was featured on all of the television network nightly news programs and received significant coverage in the print media. Shortly after the story broke, several congressional committees announced public hearings on the lost laptop. Senior officials appeared before several committees in public hearings that were also covered by the major networks and newspapers.[18] These individuals were asked some very tough questions about the state on information security at the DVA and what plans they had to prevent such a similar scenario from reoccurring. The Congress also passed legislation that reorganized the CIO office with DVA, giving much more authority to the departmental CIO at the expense of the major subordinate components of DVA — medical and benefits. Several personnel changes also resulted from this incident. DVA now has a new CIO and has reorganized its information security program.

Different Threat Environments

A final difference between the public and private sector CISO is the different threat environments that confront information security professionals in these two sectors. In some respects it is difficult to distinguish between the threats to government systems and those to some companies, especially those that operate in the financial or critical infrastructure segments of the economy. However, many federal government CISOs must factor the national state-sponsored intruder threat into their risk management program.[19] Although some components of the private sector must address the issue of sophisticated criminal enterprises attempting to gain access to their systems, the government CISO must ultimately confront threats posed by a foreign intelligence agency or component of a military organization.

Over the past few years, there have been several reports of very sophisticated entries into many government systems, particularly those operated by DOD components,

Department of Energy laboratories, NASA, and other national security or high-technology government agencies. There is a growing consensus among responsible officials that foreign governments are specifically targeting U.S. government systems for reconnaissance and intrusion operations.

The problem for the federal agency CISO is to develop and implement an information systems security program that must ultimately address this sophisticated and well-resourced threat. It turns out that, in such a threat environment, "best practices" are not good enough. This is an evolving issue, and it will be interesting to follow the impact of the threats to government systems.

Conclusion

- The public and private sector CISOs share many common issues and challenges.
- However, there are some significant challenges that confront the government CISO which do not represent major concerns for his or her private sector counterpart.
- The majority of these result from the public nature of government operations. In this environment, information security is not exempt from discussion in the public domain.
- The public sector CISO also operates in a complex policy environment. In some instances there are multiple sources of policy that must be addressed when implementing the agency information security program.
- Oversight is also conducted in the public spotlight by legislative entities that have the authority to obtain access to sensitive internal agency documents and discuss these in a public forum.
- Finally, federal government CISOs operate across a threat spectrum that covers the unsophisticated teenage hacker to the highly skilled agent of a foreign intelligence service.

Public and private sector CISOs share a sense of dedication to protect the information resources of their respective enterprises. They seek to accomplish their missions in resource-constrained environments over which they have little authority. They are united in seeking to manage security risks so that their respective organizations can utilize information and telecommunications technologies to enable electronic commerce and government programs that benefit our society.

Notes

1. http://csrc.nist.gov/publications/history. History of Computer Security: Early Computer Papers, Part 1.

2. National Research Council, "Computers at Risk," National Academy Press: Washington, D.C., 1991, page 200.

3. Title III, The Federal Information Security Management Act, PL 107-347, December 17, 2002.

4. See: http://www.whitehouse.gov/omb/inforeg/infopoltech.html#cs for copies of annual FISMA reports prepared by the Office of Management and Budget.

5. See: http://www.gcn.com/online/vol1_no1/40146-1.html.

6. See: http://govexec.com/story_page.cfm?articleid=33811&printerfriendlyVers=1&; and http://scmagazine.com/uk/news/article/547286/has-fisma-helped/; and http://www.gcn.com/online/vol1_no1/43103-1.html.

7. http://www.opm.gov/fedclass/gs2200a.pdf.

8. http://www.whitehouse.gov/omb/inforeg/reports/2005_fisma_report_to_congress.pdf, page 5.

9. Ibid.

10. http://www.nascio.org/publications/documents/NASCIO-CISOsurveyReport.pdf, page 11.

11. *New York Times,* "In Washington, Contractors Take on Biggest Role Ever," February 4, 2007, page 1.

12. See: http://iase.disa.mil/8570FAQAug05FINAL.doc.

13. See: https://www.sfs.opm.gov/StudFAQ.asp.

14. See: http://searching.gao.gov/query.html?dt=&amo=1&ayr=2002&bmo=1&byr=2007&qt=computer+security&col=audprod&col=legal&charset=iso-8859-1. (Enter keyword into search field: computer security.)

15. See: http://www.gcn.com/online/vol1_no1/43107-1.html and http://www.dodig.osd.mil/Audit/reports/FY06/06-110.pdf as representative examples of agency IG activities in the information security field.

16. See: http://www.doioig.gov/upload/FINALInternetreport1.pdf.

17. See: http://www.cbsnews.com/stories/2006/05/22/national/main1640255.shtml.

18. See: http://www.govexec.com/dailyfed/0606/062706p1.htm.

19. See: http://www.washingtonpost.com/wp-dyn/content/article/2005/08/24/AR2005-082402318.html, and http://www.fcw.com/article97658-02-13-07-Web&print Layout, and http://www.fas.org/irp/wwwinfo.html.

A LEADERSHIP
EVOLUTION

Chapter 8

A CISO Introspection

Howard A. Schmidt

The following is an interview with Howard, which captures some of his thoughts about the security career and what he has done to contribute to his own success. What he shares here may help others succeed in this profession.

Why Did You Enter the Security Field?

I started building computers in the mid-seventies, and was also a ham radio operator. While enjoying these hobbies, it became evident that some individuals were abusing the technology by interfering with radio communications and spreading viruses and hacking. Also, while working for the police department, any crimes that were encountered using high technology methods were referred to me. As a result, I started developing methods for investigating technology-related crimes, as well as methodologies for protecting computer systems.

What Personal Experiences Can You Share to Help Our Readers?

- The most enlightening thing for me was when I realized what a struggle it is for non-security people to understand what security is, and how to implement it. In my career, I've worked with very smart people — bright, intelligent, and effective people, who struggle with why and how to safeguard information.

It's not feasible to believe that we can train or educate end users to think and act like security professionals when they're not. Thus we must design and implement a system that provides a secure environment for them.

■ The recognition that security is an ongoing process. Security is not a destination; it's a journey. It's a means to accomplishing a goal, e.g., protecting privacy, safeguarding intellectual property, and building a business. Thinking about security this way goes a long way to doing security successfully.

What Skills Are Required for a Successful Chief Security Officer?

Looking back at my career, there are four important characteristics that helped me achieve success:

1. An understanding of the technology — not necessarily the nuts and bolts, but its capabilities — and more importantly what someone can do to disrupt one's use of the technology.
2. The ability to anticipate future needs so one can strategize how to build security controls into new technologies as they evolve.
3. An appreciation of the legal and ethical ramifications of what is done in the security space.
4. A business acumen — having experience and education in business puts the entire package together that gives one the ability to succeed as a chief security officer.

How Does a CISO Acquire Business Acumen? Especially if He or She Grew up in the Technology Field?

There are two good ways:

1. Use security as a business process or a service. When you provide a service, you must understand the needs of your customer. Go to the business people and ask them: "What do you need to do and how can I help you do it securely?" Insert yourself into the process to see how you can make the business successful.
2. Look at security, not as an adjunct to some other thing that you're doing such as a new technology, but as a business. Identify the things you need to do to run a successful business:
   - Determine the business goals and the methods to achieve them.
   - Develop policies to implement controls and make them more understandable.
   - Manage costs.
   - Reduce risks.

What Can the CISO Do to Improve Working Relations with the Business? How Do We Get the Business Receptive to Security?

There's good news here. The process has evolved. I remember years ago trying to talk to the IT organization about security and it was a continuing struggle just to talk to IT, let alone talking to somebody in the business unit. The world is changing. Today, businesses are so much more aware of security risks. For example, look at how widely identity theft is publicized. Businesses are becoming very aware of the threats to the information they are responsible for and they are coming to security officers, asking how they can make the business secure.

As I continue to say: "Data is the currency of the business; it's the diamond, the gold, the silver of the Information Age." I see businesses going increasingly to the security department to seek out expertise and solutions for safeguarding their assets. More and more, they see security as a value-add. Our challenge is not so much to figure out how we get the business to pay attention to security; now it's a matter of how security can help the business and recommend solutions in a manner that will not introduce a negative impact on the way they conduct their business.

How Do You Sell Security to an Organization?

First, identify the core business product and describe ways security can enhance it. For example, if a company has an Internet presence with an online order system, the advertisement of strong security of personal information could be a market differentiator. If the business product is intellectual property, then keeping the IP from competitors will be critical to the business.

Create a security council or business risk council that includes the stakeholders and agree on policies, identify the ramifications of the policies, and create a cohesive strategy that incorporates security into the business processes.

At What Level in the Organization Should a CISO Report?

The most successful ones I've seen are at the most senior levels. I believe the higher in the organization, the more potential for success. Ideally, the CISO should report to the chief executive officer. However, in many instances, that may not be practical for one reason or another. But I think the lowest reporting level should be to the chief operating officer. Some may ask: "Why not to the CIO?" At one point, security was viewed as an IT issue, which I believe is incorrect. Security is much, much broader than IT and needs to be addressed in that manner. However, where we've seen failures in the past is when a security officer is taken out of an IT organization and put in a different function without the skills necessary to be successful. It sets someone up for failure and it's counterproductive for the CISO to have a mind-set of firewalls and intrusion detection and continue to techno-babble when they interface with business constituents. If the decision is made to move the CISO out of the IT organization, it is critical to make sure that he or she has the appropriate business, legal, and risk management competencies, or it will be difficult for him or her to succeed.

Skills, Competencies, Information to Successfully Present to the Board?

Look at the day-to-day goals of the business and identify how these goals can be furthered using good risk management. Evaluate appropriateness and adequacy of the security policies as they relate to the business objectives. If there are nonconformance issues, advise the board that there are risks that are not being addressed, and put the risk in business terms, with robust recommendations and concrete actions that the board can approve or disapprove.

If You Were to Groom a New CISO, What Type of Individual Would You Be Looking at?

I wouldn't want someone who looks at things in black and white only, but rather someone who uses good judgment to make decisions. I'd look for someone with technology know-how, experience in auditing, business processes, and systems, and an understanding of legal, criminal prosecution, and privacy issues. It's also important that one have the ability to communicate with executives, which is an art, not a science. I'd look for someone with public speaking skills, and the ability to present himself as an executive who specializes in security.

What Do You See as the Toughest Challenges Facing Today's CISO?

1. The many vulnerabilities that exist in software applications today that are outside the control of the CISO. This is one of the biggest challenges we see because we are forced to deploy software solutions, e.g., client software, voice-over-IP, and even security software tools, and many increasingly come with inherent vulnerabilities right out of the box. People spend more and more

time looking for and remediating those vulnerabilities. And worse yet, the vulnerabilities are exploitable and increasingly being exploited.

2. The proliferation of uncontrolled mobile devices such as laptops and PDAs that become company network-entry points, and places where company information goes outside the company's borders.

3. Wireless devices, where wireless is becoming ubiquitous and expected, such as the local coffee house. Unmanaged, unsecured networks that end users connect to.

4. Getting better control over the data. The identification of where the data is and how we classify the data. If you don't know where the data is, how can you manage it? If you can't manage it, you can't ascertain the priorities for managing and mitigating risk.

How Do Organizational Cultures Impact Security?

The level of security that is appropriate depends on what is being secured and the environment in which it resides. Systems involving law enforcement, national security, and defense must have stricter security controls than what might be expected in the private sector. As a result, defense, national security, and law enforcement organizations traditionally have a greater focus on limited access to information while widespread access to information is the more common culture in many private sector organizations. In either environment there will be people who do not have the good of the organization in mind, so the implementation of controls is necessary. There has been a transition toward openness, but with structure and an evolution toward a common, cohesive way of looking at security, be it in the public or private sector.

What Is the Value of Certifications?

I see professional certifications as (1) proof of a baseline of knowledge and competency where the professional with the certification has demonstrated experience or knowledge in a particular field, and (2) an employment differentiator. All other things being equal, the person with a certification will have an advantage over someone who does not, when a hiring or promotion decision is being made.

How Does a CISO Know He or She Is Successful?

It is difficult to use traditional metrics to measure if security procedures are effective. In essence, if the organization runs smoothly and efficiently with security controls that meet all regulatory (HIPAA, SOX, GLBA, etc.) and business requirements and there are no security incidents that impact business operations, the CISO might be considered successful.

When Is It Time to Leave a Security Job?

Know your strengths and leverage those strengths and abilities. If you're a builder, you would do well building a security program; if you're a maintainer and your strengths are fine-tuning, you would do well working long-term in this type of organization.

How to Survive Crises?

Good planning on how to deal with the unexpected, and having a good disaster recovery plan in place and implementing it. Anticipate, react, recover, learn from experience, and improve the process.

What's Next for the CISO?

An evolution to a hybrid of everything that we've spoken of — moving to a position such as chief risk officer, risk management officer. Essentially, it's all about the information. The biggest challenges: where is the data; how to classify the data; how to manage the data so it's accessible while being protected.

Chapter 9

How Savvy Are You? Can You Get What You Want?

Billi Lee

Back in the frontier days of the old American West, many people spoke a border patois, "Spanglish," introducing many words into our current version of American English. The word "savvy" derives from the Spanish verb *saber*, which means to know. The phrase spoken in those times, "Do you savé?" meant "Do you know or understand?" In the fast paced, ever-changing corporate world of today, "Do you savvy?" still means "Do you know?" but it also means "Do you get it?"

Do you?

Do you get what is happening around you or even to you? Do you pick up on subtle undercurrents swirling around the organization? Can you navigate the political waters to get what you want? Or are you one of the clueless multitudes wandering corporate halls in a perpetual state of naïveté, unawareness, frustration, and even anger?

The Un-Savvy

Do you recognize that more than hard work and talent are required to succeed, but protest this fact of life? Do you pride yourself on not being "political?" If so, this chapter is for you!

In spite of the un-savvys' desire that the world operate differently, that it should be more fair, and that no one should have to play any games to get their just rewards, the world is made up of imperfect human beings operating with imperfect human nature. People act in certain predictable ways and have done so across generations and across cultures since the whole thing started. When people group together, whether in churches, armies, governments, guilds, or in modern corporations, certain behaviors naturally arise.

A "political" climate emerges as people struggle for influence, power, and position. People want to contribute, to be included, to be heard, and to make a difference. Even people in agreement compete for the timing, means, and methods of accomplishment. Inherent in any group of people working to achieve goals are some small and large, covert and overt, tussles of influence. Un-savvy people, sensing they are poorly equipped, shun the struggle, keep themselves out of the game and away from the prizes, but often end up as collateral damage.

When the un-savvy stumble over obvious organizational pitfalls, they are often dismissed as "hardworking, or nice, or smart . . . but . . . ," indicating they lack something essential to be considered trustworthy for inclusion or assignment. This "but" reputation plateaus them.

The Savvy

This chapter is also for the savvy, people who do "get it," the enlightened ones who take for granted a corporate common sense, and expect others to possess it. These people seem to have a type of radar that picks up automatically on clues from the environment, enabling them to read people, situations, and even entire systems accurately, and then choose appropriate behaviors and responses. They would rarely consider this connecting-the-dots and strategically responding as "playing the game" or being "political." It is "just the way life is." Because the un-savvy can be dangerous in their simple naïveté, savvy people protect themselves by limiting their exposure to those less corporately mature. They choose their battles and their allies wisely. A mistake savvy people can make, however, is not knowing how to discuss and coach savvy to those they need, failing to develop more useful and more effective allies.

The Savvy Seekers

And of course, this chapter is also for the vast majority of people somewhere between the two extremes of the savvy continuum. These seekers often lament their lack of savvy, wish they had more of it, know it is useful, but don't know how to get it. They would love to play the game, if someone would only explain it to them, and they wouldn't mind adding "politically astute" to their résumé, but don't know where or how to acquire it.

There are no academic degrees in savvy. Far from being promoted in professional development circles, savvy behaviors are often degraded as corporate evils to be avoided and extinguished, while those possessing savvy quietly and efficiently use it to accomplish their objectives more elegantly. The seekers would love to have a more fully developed professional toolbox, too, so they could also work smarter and not just harder.

What Is Savvy?

Ask people if they know someone who is savvy or un-savvy, and they will answer. Ask someone to define what savvy is and they struggle. Is it know-how, expertise, insight, shrewdness, and sagacity? Or is it something sleazy? Is it a variety of behaviors, or is it a type of intelligence?

Knowing that savvy has been academically ignored and even scorned, and desiring to give savvy its due, the author put together a team within the Savvy Institute to define, study, and measure it. Results from The Savvy Profile™, a break-through psychometrically-sound instrument, are indeed confirming the author's original hypothesis: that savvy is an independent attribute, that people do possess different amounts of it naturally (inherent), and that they can acquire more (learned).

> Savvy is the combination of personality traits, innate abilities, and learned behaviors required to assess environments and situations, and to adjust behaviors to achieve goals.

Some people are born incredibly savvy, some acquire it easily over time, while others are woefully lacking in it either from inability, lack of desire, or instruction. Results from The Savvy Profile™ show that high scores correlate positively with age, income, and position.

At the end of this chapter, The Savvy Profile™ is described and made available to the reader.

Workplace Savvy

Respond with a yes or no to the statements in Table 9.1 as an introduction to some key workplace savvy behaviors.

Table 9.1   Workplace Savvy Checklist

	Yes	No	Workplace Savvy Checklist
1			I can back, support, and team with people I don't necessarily like.
2			I have allies who back, support, and protect me.
3			I'm in the information loop.
4			I consider my boss to be my personal customer.
5			I perform professional courtesies and favors, seeking possible paybacks.
6			I pay back.
7			I influence by giving something to get something, instead of by trying to convince.
8			I'm aware when the climate turns "political," and can respond productively.
9			I will spend time, energy, and money to get connected.
10			I can win some and lose some without taking it, or giving it, personally.
11			I know the company is not my family, and I don't expect it to take care of me emotionally or financially.
12			I can put work aside at the end of the day and can enjoy my personal life.

Savvy people are conscious. They distinguish between their personal and professional lives. They realize the workplace is an important game they signed on to play with a variety of players, teams, goals, obstacles, and referees. They focus on the goal, strategize around the obstacles, and are resilient to the ever-changing imperfect world. Far from naïve, they understand human nature and organizational politics. They choose which game they want to play, and don't get trapped playing someone else's. Their personal life is personal and separate from their work. They can roll with the punches and depersonalize at work. Their expectations are in line with reality.

Un-savvy people are fairly unconscious and quite naïve about the ways of the world. They don't know there is a difference between personal and professional systems, so they end up being easily hurt, victims of the systems they choose not to understand. Stubborn, often righteous, and unadaptable, they can't play even the game they signed up for. They impose their lack of resiliency and cooperation on others. Being poor influencers and strategists, they usually wait in vain for the rewards they want. They consider the workplace their family and expect to be taken care of, and feel betrayed when they are not. Instead of studying successful people and adopting similar behaviors, they cry "unfair."

Power and Influence

Ultimately, possessing savvy allows a person or an entire group to determine what is probable and possible, whom they may need, and what they have to do to get assistance. With this information they determine appropriate, timely, and strategically effective behaviors.

- Power is making decisions that other people decide to follow.
- Politics are the behaviors people use to get other people to decide to follow their decisions.
- Power, however situational, is an influencing act.
- Savvy gives you the ability to identify and use the appropriate behaviors to influence successfully.

The 12 Savvy Questions

The questions in Table 9.2 will help an individual or a group become and stay savvy in any situation.

Table 9.2 The 12 Savvy Questions

	Question	Response
1	What's the goal?	Clarify, clarify, clarify! Does everyone involved agree? Don't pick a strategy until the goal is precisely defined. Savvy begins here!
2	How much?	How will you know when you reach the desired goal? How much is enough?
3	What price?	There is no free lunch. What are the risks and rewards? Identify the true costs, both tangible and intangible, and prepare to pay.
4	Who can help?	Who has useful connections, information, and resources?
5	Who can hurt?	Who can pose problems, obstruct, or destroy?

Table 9.2 The 12 Savvy Questions (continued)

	Question	Response
6	Who is needed?	Who is essential?
7	What can be offered?	What incentives are available?
8	What's in it for them?	Before approaching anyone for assistance, determine how he or she would benefit.
9	What's in it for me?	Before agreeing to involvement, determine how you would benefit, negotiate your price if necessary, and assess and minimize any risks.
10	Who's allowing this? Why?	Determine why a situation is allowed to exist and who is condoning it before attempting to change it. Assess the feasibility and associated risks.
11	What's their agenda?	Discover the values, motivation, and any agenda, however hidden, that are driving another person or group. Use this information to design your approach, your avoidance, or your exit.
12	Who pays the price for the game I play?	Any decision you make will most likely affect others. Not wanting to play the game doesn't absolve you from consequences your action or inaction imposes on others. Be aware, be responsible, and be accountable. Ask questions 1 through 3 frequently.

Key Savvy Behaviors

■ *Be aware.* Scan and assess the environment. Pay attention. Get others' input and information. Notice changes. Determine the reasons.

■ *Establish your long-term and in-the-moment goals.* Always know what you want out of any situation or transaction, and then determine the price you are willing to pay.

■ *Develop allies.* Don't play by yourself. Identify savvy people whom you need and who may be useful. Discover their history, determine their values, motives, and agendas. Choose your allies based on need first, preference second. Seek out opportunities to expand your network. Keep the alliance mutually beneficial. Provide what they value to obtain their cooperation and contribution of resources. Barter, don't proselytize.

■ *Offer favors, pay back favors.* Providing information, making connections, lending expertise, furnishing skills, giving credit, taking blame, conferring status, protecting, and providing a reference are just a few of the favors that are traded among allies. Save some of your valuable time to do favors for others so you will have them to draw upon when you need a favor back. Keep track of who plays a mutually beneficial game and who doesn't. You can negotiate a payback ahead of time or when the chit is presented. Just make sure you pay back what they value. If you choose not to, understand the alliance will most probably be broken.

■ *Build an organization.* Make allies above, below, and around you. Identify who can help you or hurt you. Purposely mentor potential good allies.

■ *Be a good team player.* Support the goal, obey the coach, join rank publicly, disagree when necessary behind closed doors, know which role you are assigned to play, and sublimate your personal goal to the team goal. If you can't consistently support the goal, coach, or team, quit! You do not need a reputation for being difficult.

■ *Know your legend.* Find out what significant people think of you, not what you think they think of you, but what they really think of you … your legend. It may be even more positive than you deserve or it might be more negative than you deserve. Either way you need to know it. If it is negative, find out if they will let you change it. You may have to sit on the bench, do penance, or score big. But find out if it is changeable. Some people will never see you differently no matter what you do. You may need to change teams or organizations to establish a different, more beneficial legend.

■ *Be resilient.* If you can't change it, figure out how to use it.

■ *Have a "meeting before the meeting."* Be strategic. Orchestrate when possible. Lobby for support ahead of time. Develop contingencies and assign roles. Get invited to other "pre-meetings." Have a meeting after the meeting to strategize the next steps.

■ *Make your boss look good.* Treat your boss like your customer. Satisfy their needs and wants before you negotiate yours. Get known for helping others get what they want.

■ *Share the glory.* Even sports MVPs credit the team. Arrogance may be the number-one career killer, as it motivates other people to contribute to your fall. Do not seek a "golden boy" or "golden girl" status.

■ *Pick your battles wisely.* You will not win them all, so save your time energy and resources for the ones that count. Don't fight other people's battles unless there is a good reason to make them your own. Keep your eye on your career plan.

■ *Get a reputation.* You can't get asked to play if they don't know who you are. But get a reputation for what *they*, the people whom you need, value. Negotiate visibility, inclusion, and credit.

■ *Get in the information loop.* You need to know what is going on, so invite communication even if it verges on gossip. Be strategic with what you do with the information you receive; *you* don't want to be known as a gossiper. Keep significant others informed with information they need to make good decisions. Likewise, foster alliances who will keep you informed. This trade is at the heart of a good alliance.

■ *Don't confuse your company with your family.* Organizations are impersonal systems designed to achieve tasks, producing goods and services for those who will buy them. They will reorganize, downsize, and relocate to achieve their ends, expending people in the process. Families and friendships are personal systems designed to take care of the people within them. The culture, ethics, and rewarded behaviors are different for each system. You cannot expect an organization to act like a family and you don't want your family acting like an organization. Develop allies at work. Be friendly, but develop and keep your personal relationships and personal life at home.

■ *Depersonalize.* See above. What happens at work rarely has anything to do with you personally. Decisions are made in the best interest of the organization. They may or may not benefit you, and when they do, you can be sure they benefit the company first. You will play a more powerful, effective, and sane game if you depersonalize. Keep your emotions in check. Feel what you feel, but keep your behaviors professional. Treating the workplace as a game will help you depersonalize. You will have more fun and less frustration with this viewpoint. You will win some and lose some. You will have triumphs and defeats. But always keep in mind you are working to support your family and *that* is the most important part of your life!

The Savvy Profile™

The Savvy Profile™ is a new psychometrically-sound instrument from The Savvy Institute, Inc., being made available to you, the reader, online at www.billilee.com. After taking the profile assessment, you will receive your composite score, your Savvy Quotient™ (SQ™), and a separate score for each of the eight components that comprise the aggregate savvy attribute.

The Eight Components

1. Goalacity: The tendency to prioritize and choose a goal among multiple goals, and to use persistence, energy, and motivation to reach the goal.
   - This is the first component listed because it is the foundation for practical savvy. Don't choose a behavior or a response until you know what you want. This is harder than it sounds. Choosing among many possible goals requires closing some doors. Do I want the promotion or do I want to tell off my boss? You can't have both!
   - Many people fall in love with their strategies and fail to analyze if they are effective. Flexible strategies and well-chosen goals are keys to success.
   - Stick-to-it! Do what it takes. Pay the price. But first and foremost, know what you want in any given situation.
2. Intellectance: The tendency to accurately assess individuals, groups, and situations and to form effective responses to achieve a chosen objective.

- This is so important. The ability to get your radar up and to scan the environment to assess what is happening. The ability to connect the dots, to read between the lines. To get it! And then to be able to respond appropriately. Intellectance is what enables you to:
  - Know when someone wants the truth or just wants to hear what they want to hear.
  - To figure out who has power and who is just a figurehead.
  - And to detect if you are on the team or merely on the roster.

3. Reciprocity: The tendency to make mutually beneficial exchanges with others and to initiate or reciprocate favors, particularly with the goal of influencing others.
   - This is the art of influencing. Many people attempt to proselytize and convince to get others on board. Savvy people know that giving people what they want sets up and sustains a reciprocal response in others. Mutual benefit is also the key to establishing and maintaining a network of useful alliances.

4. Riskocity: The tendency to take risks.
   - This is the only component where you would want to score above average but not extremely high. Taking too many risks, or too big a risk too frequently, would hardly be savvy. But on the other hand, savvy people are calculated risk takers, assessing the up and down side of any proposed strategy, even a do-nothing one.

5. Self-Efficance: The tendency to take action to control one's environment rather than allowing the environment to control one's actions, thoughts, and feelings (similar to self-confidence).
   - Savvy people have an inner locus of control, believing they always have a measure of contol in any situation, no matter how small, and therefore seek ways to exert their desires upon the environment. Others have an external locus of control, believing external factors control their lives. Without self-efficance people routinely feel and act powerless.

6. Alliability: The tendency to enlist and use others as resources in the pursuit of one's goals.
   - Success is a joint venture. In spite of the sacred myth of self-reliance, success often comes through the concerted efforts of others. Whom you know and who is willing to help you really do matter. Savvy people expend time, money, and energy to make useful and mutually beneficial alliances, exchanging resources and favors. They do not limit their network to those with whom they could share a friendship, but seek to make even ad hoc allies based on need.

7. Compartmentance: The tendency to shift between relation- (people) or task-oriented roles and responses as needed and to be able to personalize and depersonalize situations and responses.

- Distinguishing what is personal and what is not is critical to choosing appropriate responses. Understanding, accepting and dealing with the fact that life offers us situations that are all about people (family, friends, school, church) and other ones that are all about the accomplishment of task (allies, associates, business, and war) require a maturity not found in un-savvy people.
- To be able to personalize and depersonalize allows savvy people to switch quickly and effectively between these two polar energies and activities, decreasing stress and frustration.

8. Resilience: The tendency to make effective use out of all situations, whether positive or negative.
   - Resilience is the hallmark of savvy people. When the constantly changing environment produces events or situations that cannot be stopped or changed, they can be used. Savvy people know they don't even have to like a situation to make it work for them. Resilience is more than a snappy attitude; it is what distinguishes progressive, creative, and successful people from those who get stuck and get sour.

For more information about The Savvy Institute, Billi Lee, The Success Savvy Materials, and The Savvy Profile, visit www.billilee.com.

Recap

- There are no academic degrees in savvy.
- Savvy is the combination of personality traits, innate abilities, and learned behaviors required to assess environments and situations, and to adjust behaviors to achieve goals.
- Be aware.
- Establish your long-term and in-the-moment goals.
- Develop allies.
- Offer favors, pay back favors.
- Build an organization.
- Be a good team player.
- Know your legend.
- Be resilient.
- Have a "meeting before the meeting."
- Make your boss look good.
- Share the glory.
- Pick your battles wisely.
- Get a reputation.

- Get in the information loop.
- Don't confuse your company with your family.
- Depersonalize.
- Take the Savvy Profile at www.billilee.com.

Chapter 10

Why and How Assessment of Organization Culture Should Shape Security Strategies

---

Don Saracco

Why Be Concerned with Organization Culture?

To answer this question, we must first answer another question: "How are security and culture linked?" The answer to that question lies not in what we know, but in what we don't know. Although we take it for granted that security is an indelible part of individual and organizational life, the definition and extent of that need varies greatly across any population of people and organizations. After all, if it is simply "common sense" to ensure security, of what use is the answer to the question? We should simply implement as much security as we possibly can and consider the job done. Of course, such a simplistic application of common sense could lead an organization into excessive spending and crippling constraints on employee productivity.

As it turns out every management practice in an organization will support or inhibit that organization in proportion to the extent that the practice is aligned with the culture. Failure to align with culture is the hallmark of "programs of the month" that come and go and end up on the trash heap of good intentions badly executed. Effective alignment enables security managers to design and implement necessary and sufficient security and the provision of no more and no less than that is the security manager's job.

The purpose of this chapter is twofold. First it is necessary to explain why you must understand the link between culture and security practices. Secondly it will describe how you can go about assessing your organization culture and linking that assessment to security strategies.

Learning to Be Secure: Some Theory

Security needs in people begin with what are apparently instinctive reactions to perceived threats. Humans seem to have a survival instinct hard-wired into the organism, and it is initially visible in the form of reflexes and later becomes more sophisticated. An infant reacts to loud noises or jerky motions with alarm. As the child grows and develops more sophisticated perceptions, reflexes are augmented by thinking processes. Reactions to threats include not only simple perception, but also analysis of the threat and the choice of an appropriate response.

As learning continues, the proactive process of consciously choosing a response can come to appear reflexive as the processing of information regarding familiar stimuli becomes "automated" in the brain. Familiar threats begin to produce what appear to be reflexive reactions, which are actually learned responses that bypass conscious analysis as an unnecessary step in dealing with that stimulus. Essentially, a person forms an "association macro" that runs an automatic analysis of the stimulus and then runs a programmed response. The person who hears footsteps approached from behind while walking down a dark street may not have thought about the danger, but experiences psychological arousal nonetheless. In fact the physical feelings were probably felt before any conscious thought occurred. Thus the foundation is laid for the person's tendencies throughout life to approach or avoid various stimuli.

In a sense the processes comes full circle from reflex to conscious thought and back to what appears as reflex again (see Figure 10.1).Such learned automatic behavior is even called "knee-jerk" in popular literature. The allusion to what happens when the doctor taps a person's knee to test reflexes is not without foundation. For all intents and purposes, it is the same thing. The only meaningful difference between the two responses is that the latter learned response could be altered by conscious cognitive intervention.

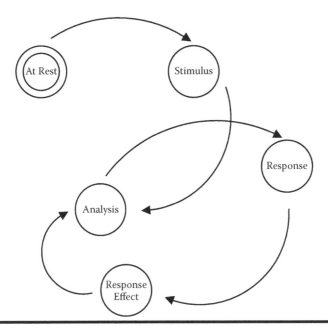

Figure 10.1   Response-learning process.

So What?

By now you are probably asking yourself why we began this discussion of assessing culture with a walk through Developmental Psych 101. It is important because this "biological inertia" to survive and to use programmed responses is also true for other organic forms in our world, including human organizations, and it finds its expression in the patterns that we call organization culture. That which is born does not normally want to die, and there is a will to live apparent in all viable organizations as well as in viable people. In fact managers in organizations accept their accountability for the protection of the organization's continued growth and survival unquestioningly. I have not seen a position description (except at the CEO level) that spells out this accountability for managers, but I doubt that any would deny that it exists. It could be argued that this reflexive will to survive is hard-wired into the organization or is at least automated in management practices.

The problem is that reflexes are not enough and reactions to risk must become anticipation of risk. Rapid discovery of a security breach must be secondary to effective reduction of a security risk. The design of the process of reducing risk is the point at which all organisms and organizations differ, and that difference follows from either personality in the individual or culture in an organization. So, just as we would need to understand the personality of an individual to understand his or her needs for security, so must we understand the culture of an organization to design an appropriate security program. Different personalities are likely to perceive personal risk differently, and different organizational cultures will also differ in their perceptions of what is most important to their survival. As we will see, culture can trump good common sense when it comes to management and security practices, and this is the compelling driver for including a useful assessment of culture in the development of a security program.

The Requirements of Assessment

- The first requirement of cultural assessment is support from the most senior levels of management for the conduct of such an assessment. It cannot be assumed that owners and other top managers of organizations want any such assessment to be performed, so we will devote a portion of this treatise to selling the idea of assessment.
- So, the next requirement for assessment of organization culture is a classification system. We use a fairly simple system that provides adequate direction without unnecessarily complicating our work.
- The next requirement is a method of assessment. The method must provide sufficient information to differentiate among organizations and be compatible with practices in the organization. We use both survey and interview methods. Both can be valid and can be used independently or together.
- The next requirement is a logical connection between the classification and specific security strategies. This requirement is partially met by the use of a robust classification system that is founded in valid and reliable principles of human and organizational behavior. It also calls for openness to changes in management practices where such changes will enable or enhance the effectiveness of strategies.
- The final requirement is effective presentation of the assessment results and recommendations to organization decision makers without whose support no effective program can be implemented. Both new or enhanced security strategies and changes to management practices are likely to include costs of some kind, so this step is crucial to getting the right program in place. Without appropriate management support many security personnel are relegated to the role of "virus and porn police" with no strategic impact on the business.

There are a number of definitions of assessment. For our purposes we will use the one that refers to assessment as a categorization, sorting, or classification. If we can provide a useful classification system for organization cultures, we can identify security strategies most appropriate for each class.

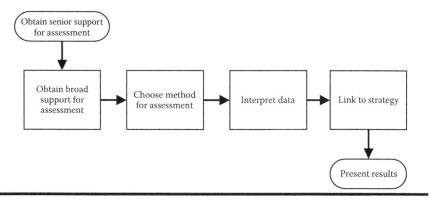

Figure 10.2   Assessment process.

Selling the Assessment

Selling the assessment may be the most important part of the entire process, for without it the assessment is not likely to move forward. The process is fairly simple, as shown in Figure 10.2.

Selling Yourself

It all begins with the ability of security professionals to be perceived as competent and trustworthy partners in the pursuit of business goals. If you don't really know how you are perceived, you will have to find a way to ask people. This is the first necessary step toward ensuring the value of your security program as well as your own influence in the organization.

Of course the first source to use should be your direct supervisor. He or she may be willing to give you some unvarnished feedback about your perceived effectiveness and can also help you to plan the reinvention of yourself in your role. If your supervisor lacks the skills or willingness to give you useful feedback and developmental support, you will have to go to your peers and customers. Frankly, you should never spend any significant length of time in a staff position without getting feedback from your customers anyway.

Soliciting Feedback

Soliciting feedback can be a dicey process. People who are asked face-to-face to assess your effectiveness are just as likely to tell you what they think you want to hear as to give you an honest appraisal of your relationship with them. An anonymous method is probably better. There are two ways to get anonymous feedback:

1. You can develop a valid questionnaire and distribute it to as large as possible a sample of your peers and your customers at every level of the organization.
2. You can have a surrogate interview people on your behalf, using a structured interview protocol that you have helped to design.

The former is faster and probably less expensive. It will also be statistically defensible. The latter method will get you nuances of perception and a richer pool of information, but will take longer, cost more, and lack statistical power. In either case, you should enlist the aid of a skilled assessment professional to help interpret the results of your data collection and help you to make specific plans for improvement.

If the current security staff already enjoys the confidence of peer and superior customers, selling the idea of culture assessment should be relatively easy, but it will not necessarily be a "slam dunk." In years past when we were first developing our assessment methods, we had the experience of getting agreement from a senior management sponsor to do the assessment, only to find that when we tried to roll out the method there were others who objected to it. We quickly learned that an assessment of culture would succeed only if there were broad management support for doing it. At a minimum this support should include the senior business operations managers, HR, risk management, audit, the CIO, the CAO, and a significant sample of middle managers throughout the organization.

Selling the Organization

We and our clients have found that a well-designed and planned "road show" can be a very effective method of gaining the broad base of support that you will need. A road show has two central elements. It contains factual information and it succeeds in generating dialogue. The factual information is necessary because people want to know exactly what they are being asked to support (or at least not object to) and how it will help them to reach their goals. The dialogue is necessary because you will need to know what those goals are before you can position the assessment as helpful.

In most cases this selling process involves multiple iterations of face-to-face meetings with key people. Initial meetings can be exploratory for the purpose of exchanging general security program and business unit goals. One of the most common mistakes that we have seen people make is to assume that they have the support or agreement of someone as a result of a single conversation. Support and agreement must be treated like living things that require constant nurturing and renewal. Organization life today is much too dynamic to assume that any relationship is permanent.

A skilled security manager will do much more listening in these meetings than talking. He or she should be certain about the strategic goals that provide the direction for the program in case peers and superiors want to know, but there is little or no value in long-winded speeches filled with technical jargon intended to impress people with your brilliance. There is tremendous value in sincere inquiry about the things that are important to business operations. So, if you are asked to describe your program, respond with a brief but complete statement of your strategic goals, followed by a question such as, "What can we do that will best support your business goals?"

For example, you may see that an assessment of the culture can be incorporated into any analysis of readiness for organizational change as well as into actual change initiatives. If the organization plans to leverage the cost of the assessment by using the information for more than security program development, that fact must be shared with people in the beginning.

Of course the people with whom you are meeting will be curious and perhaps even suspicious about what you want from them. We have found that it is always best to be brief and honest about that. You will be asking for support in the conduct of an assessment of the organization's culture. It is important to formulate a succinct statement that says what you want and what it is likely to cost the other person, if anything. Your purpose in assessing the culture is not to try to change it or be critical of it, but to understand it so that your program will be appropriately aligned with it. You should operate under the assumption that the culture is what it is and represents part of what makes the company successful. Unless the company is in the toilet, this is usually a safe assumption.

If you are asked for details, focus on providing "minimal truth." Avoid technical jargon and be prepared to give a simple example of how you will use the information. Such an example might be that you need to develop security policies that are consistent with the culture, because to do otherwise puts you in danger of being either overly restrictive or not sufficiently diligent.

Security policies and practices must blend with the culture rather than attempt to change it — unless such a change is necessary to reduce or eliminate a legitimate risk.

Choosing Assessment Methods

The choice of assessment methods is critical to the success of the process. Organizational activities associated with programs and initiatives must gain fairly wide acceptance so as not to be disruptive or face resistance.

Potential Barriers

- *Disruption can come from poor understanding of the motives for the assessment.* In these times when people are increasingly likely to distrust employers' actions, any assessment may be viewed as a step toward restructuring or rightsizing with the consequences of reduced productivity and malicious compliance.

■ *Resistance, both open and passive, can also derail an assessment.* As people become successfully socialized into their organizations, they learn how not to do things as well as how to get things done. Research tells us that when they are threatened, people will often plead lack of time or insufficient priority to avoid engaging in a mandated activity without clear purpose. Passive resistance is very difficult to identify, as people will invoke reasons for not doing their part, apparently rooted in a focus on central organizational goals. Senior managers are unlikely to be critical of people who appear to be supporting management's primary reasons for being. You might be persuaded to think that obtaining senior management support for an assessment would be sufficient to overcome resistance, and for some percentage of the population in some organizations that would be true. There is, however, no substitute for gaining broad support from all levels of management as well as from the rank and file of employees.

■ *There will always be those who suspect the information will be somehow used against them in administrative proceedings.* Of course to do so would be both unethical and in some states illegal. It is necessary to guarantee anonymity for individuals. Verbal assurances may not be enough to support a guarantee of anonymity. You may need to share an explicit description of how that anonymity is going to be protected and make the process open to inspection.

Interviewing

Effective interviewing is an art. It requires both discipline and sensitivity to what is not being said. The discipline can be rooted in the interview protocol, but even skilled interviewers can succumb to the temptation to stray from the protocol just for the sake of variety. Reliance on the protocol should be absolute as a consistent framework for interviews. Properly done interviews can provide a very rich body of data from a relatively small sample of subjects, but interpretation must be done with the highest standards of professional discipline to avoid overly subjective interpretation of results. Having the data collection and the interpretation done by different people can overcome this pitfall and help to ensure that conclusions about the culture can be supported.

Sensitivity to what is not being said enables an interviewer to demonstrate that he or she is sincerely listening, makes the interview more conversational, and allows the interviewer to probe beneath the surface for foundation beliefs about the culture and experiences within it. This is the part of interviewing that is the most artful and which takes significant experience to learn. We do not recommend that inexperienced people use interview methods. An unskilled interviewer can come across as an interrogator and that will do nothing less than confirm any negative suspicions about the purpose of the interview that the subjects may have had at the outset. We do recommend that anyone hoping to be successful in staff roles learn effective interviewing skills. They will serve you well throughout your career.

Interview Protocol

The interview protocol is the essential structure of the interview process as well as the list of questions you intend to ask. The core questions must be asked of all subjects to ensure accurate interpretation of results. It should consist of enough questions to develop sufficient information for analysis, but not so many as to cause you to be rushed near the end of the scheduled time. We have found that somewhere in the neighborhood of ten to fifteen open-ended questions fit fairly well into a one-hour time slot. This allows you to get enough information to contribute to a classification of the culture archetype and enough time to maintain a friendly, conversational tone to the interview.

Selecting Interview Subjects

The selection of interview subjects should be done with input from stakeholders or neutral parties. We have found input from senior managers as well as from senior administrative assistants to be very useful in selecting a good cross-section of the population. The subjects should include managers at several levels as well as rank-and-file staff of all types (e.g., exempt and nonexempt). Include people both with significant tenure and those that have less than 18 months with the organization. Most people should be able to provide enough information to help with classification of the culture after they have been on board for about 90 days, but a little longer is probably better. Frankly, it depends on things like the actual age of the organization. It is important to get a good cross-sectional representation of organizational functions to ensure that you account for internal differences in departments. A large organization with rigid silos can have important differences across departments and these differences can influence how you implement security measures.

We have done an analysis in an organization where more than half the personnel had been with the organization for less than a year and were still able to make an accurate assessment. The rapid growth of the company called for people to truly "hit the ground running," and the recruitment process aimed at fully informing new hires about how things were done in the company. We were able to get a very good representative sample of the various functions and thus to understand the differences with which the program would have to cope.

Interview Structure

The overall structure of the interview should help to ensure an appropriate tone and that you get the information that you need. The general process structure should look something like this:

- Introduction
  - Purpose and affirmation of anonymity
  - Process description
  - Check for understanding
- Opening questions (ask about the subject's role in the organization, tenure with the organization, experience with security, etc., to establish a conversational tone)
- Core questions (start with the most general and unrelated to the person's own experience and work toward more specific examples of subject's personal experiences)
- Finish by giving the subject an opportunity to ask questions of you, offering thanks, and by sharing what the next steps in the process will be

Case Study

In a land development organization where we conducted the assessment, we repeatedly heard that decisions were seldom made below the executive level. In our classification system this theme clearly points to a vertical archetype. Other information that supported this conclusion appeared in stories of a sort of "bipolar" way of doing things. It either took "forever" to get anything done or things had to be done immediately so as to not suffer the disfavor of a senior manager. This is another clear indication of the vertical archetype that is described in the section on the classification system.

Assessment by Way of Surveys

Assessment by survey is more about science than about art, though the artful preparation of the survey is still necessary. You may even find that some people are more suspicious of surveys than of interviews. Any survey that smacks of psychology or social research can provoke hostile reactions in some people. People sometimes have bad experiences with surveys badly done, so that they will never greet one without deep suspicion or resentment. You can protect against hostile reactions by sufficiently and honestly communicating the purpose of the survey, affirming the anonymity of respondents, and fully describing how the data will be handled and processed.

A survey is more science than art because it can avoid any tendencies for the data collection process to be biased by subjective interpretation of data. It provides an objective measure of opinions and usually allows for a much larger sample of organization members to be included in the data collection process. On the other hand, science calls for a certain level of rigor in the creation of the survey instrument and the treatment of results.

The Survey Instrument

At the time of this publication, we have not been able to find a standard instrument designed to be used in the design of a security program. There are several that have been developed to assess cultures with regard to safety issues as well as tools intended for use in general assessments of organizational climate. There are apparently none based on a classification system that can be related to security strategies. This is not particularly surprising when one considers the fact that most security experts avoid the subject of culture as a factor in the program, preferring to focus on the power of technology and policy to achieve security program goals.

Developing Your Own Survey Instrument

There are two major concerns when it comes to using survey instruments:

1. Validity: The instrument must measure what it intends to measure.
2. Reliability: Produce similar results with repeated use.

We have been using a survey instrument of our own design for culture assessment for the past decade. It is based on a classification system that readily provides guidance for a wide variety of organizational development activities and initiatives. Although the instrument has not yet been statistically validated, it consistently returns internal reliability coefficients above 0.90 (above 0.80 is considered fairly reliable and above 0.60 is often considered acceptable in social research). Essentially, this suggests that the instrument is essentially coherent and is measuring something consistently. We believe that it is measuring the factors that we assume characterize the major archetypes of culture that we believe exist, but we have not yet secured a research partner to help us to validate our assumption.[1]

Tutorial on Developing and Interpreting Survey Items

The instrument items are usually written in the form of statements with which people are asked to agree or disagree on a scale from "strongly disagree" to "strongly agree" because what we are looking for is where on a continuous scale the person's perception falls. For example, if, as the first item below states, leadership is emphasized more than control, we get an indication that the organization culture archetype is more horizontal than vertical. There must be multiple items in the instrument that seek the same determination until a single item is validated statistically to provide the information alone. In our instrument we use 36 items to identify placement in three categories. That gives us 12 items for each archetype looking at six different factors, so each factor is measured two times.

1. Leadership (inspiration) is emphasized and rewarded much more than is management (control).
2. My primary customer (the person I must please) is my supervisor.
3. People are rewarded and recognized primarily because of their individual accomplishments.
4. There are things that are not "discussible," i.e., things that everyone knows, but it is not OK to talk about.
5. Innovation is highly valued despite the risk of failure.
6. People must get permission to do anything new or different.

The Survey Protocol

There is a standard general protocol for the use of social research tools. It is designed to avoid contamination of survey results that can come from conscious or unconscious bias. The following steps are an adaptation of the protocol for the use of individual assessment instruments:

1. Administer the instrument.
2. Score the instrument and collect relevant statistical results.
3. Interpret the results in terms of the classification system and implications for strategy.
4. Report the results to stakeholders, including implications for security strategies.

The critical part of this protocol is administration before the classification system model is discussed with any of the participants in the survey. Results can be skewed by knowledge of the model unless the survey includes enough items of the right kind to identify deliberate bias in the responses. For custom-designed tools and most others that are commercially available, this kind of robust instrument design is seldom available.

Interpreting Results

Interpretation of interview and survey results calls for intimate familiarity with the culture classification system that you use and the implications of each class for security strategies.

The process for drawing information from interview data is called "thematic analysis" because what you are doing is identifying relevant themes that appear across interviews. These themes lend support to your conclusions about the classification of the culture and subsequent application to your program. A theme is a response to your core interview questions that appears more than two or three times in as many separate interviews. We have found that in an organization of medium to large size, between 20 and 40 interviews should be sufficient.

Interpreting the results of a survey is dependent upon understanding what the raw scores mean and how the application of basic descriptive statistics can add to that meaning. Raw scores generally tell us very little because the values assigned to survey items are artificial and not absolute. They also do not describe any consistencies or differences across the population of respondents. Simply put, they are data and not information. We use descriptive and analytical statistics to convert the data to information. In fact, looking at individual item raw scores can be very misleading and urge conclusions that are simply not true. This is called a "Type 1 Error" in research.

Descriptive statistics are usually sufficient for this sort of survey analysis. Descriptive statistics consist of means (average scores for items or groups of items, called scales), medians (the scores midway between the highest and lowest scores), modes (groupings of the most frequent scores), and standard deviations (the variance from the mean scores for items or scales). These numbers tell us how the overall population of respondents feels as a single organism about an item or scale. They provide information about the population and not merely single anecdotes about individual responses. Statistics achieve with impersonal numbers what thematic analysis achieves with rigorous discipline.

A Classification System for Organizational Cultures

Cultural analysis is defined in the organizational psychology literature as a stream of investigation that seeks to understand and map trends, influences, effects, and affects within cultures. Standard analysis of culture is based upon an idiosyncratic array of symbols, norms, myths, legends, and character archetypes. The analysis and classification framework that we use is derived from research and practice concerned with psychological contracts and core relationship dynamics within organizations. Psychological contracts are the operant agreements regarding the understood exchange of value between employees and their organizations. The exchange of value generally calls for employees to give things like their attendance,

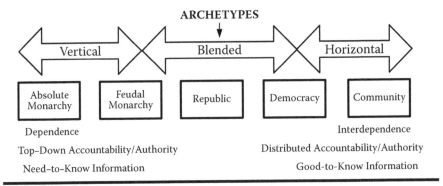

Figure 10.3 Archetypes governance model.

their best efforts, loyalty, and adherence to organization values in exchange for adequate compensation, benefits, opportunity, and quality of relationships, etc. These contracts tend to be very unique on an individual level, owing to the unique psychology of individual people. At the level of organization archetype, the contract is a normative one that is shared by all employees with the organization. Research over the past two decades by MLC & Associates, Inc., a management consulting firm, has shown organizational archetypes which are characterized by certain underlying beliefs, practices, and elements of the psychosocial contract that are common across the vast majority of relationships between the organization and its members. These archetypes can be described as analogous to fundamental models of governance ranging from absolute control by an individual to widely distributed control as may be seen in a community, as shown in Figure 10.3.

The Organization Imperative

Humans will organize. Whenever people commit to work toward shared goals, they will organize to reach those goals. Granted, the organization may not always be elegant or functionally effective, but it will exist. It appears that people will organize because there is a need to know how we relate to others with whom we work and an organization can define relationships according to commonly accepted definitions of roles.

Organization relationships are most significantly influenced by the distribution of authority and accountability (A&A). This distribution informs people about how they can learn what is important and how things get done in the organization. It also defines formal freedom to act, which is a de facto control on the extent to which people can be creative.

The Psychological Contract: The Heart of the Culture

Psychological contracts are both individual and collective (normative). Each organization has a normative contract in place that can serve as a basis for the classification of the culture. Many elements or clauses are included in the contract (see Figure 10.4), but there are some that represent a core of critical factors. These revolve around the distribution of A&A and include how information is managed, and how much dependence is expected from people. Such a classification system allows us to make the connection between the culture and how we must design the organization's policies and practices, because each archetype calls for specific patterns of behavior and belief, as depicted in Figure 10.4.

The distribution of A&A is primarily governed by the formal structure of the organization, but one must be aware of the informal structure as well because it can provide useful nuance information about how people both use and circumvent the formal system.

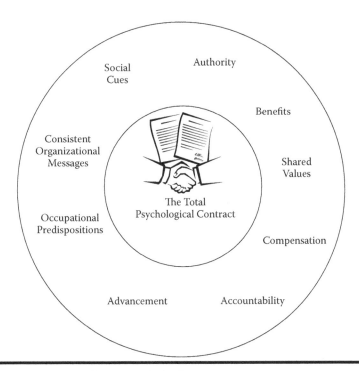

Figure 10.4 Inputs to the psychological contract.

Case Study

In every one of the hundreds of organizations with which we have worked over the past two decades, there have been people whose influence far outstripped their formal authority. Sometimes that influence has positive effects on policies and practices, and sometimes not. One example can be seen in a client of ours. This manufacturing organization implemented a wireless RF system in support of its logistics control and communication functions. A single individual from outside the IT Department held sway over what was done with the system, including the extent to which it was made secure — or not secure. Despite our urging that the system "ownership" be shifted to IT to ensure adequate support and security, management was unwilling to confront the current owner to affect the change because it might call into question the need for his role and pay grade. We had to resort to having one of our consultants gain access to the organization's network from a laptop in a car in the headquarters parking lot to demonstrate the extent to which the organization was in jeopardy. Remember this example as we look at the vertical archetype which follows, as we will return to it as an example of the predictable patterns of behavior in the archetypes.

Vertical, Horizontal, and Blended Cultural Archetypes

Generally an archetype is defined as "the original model of which all other similar persons, objects, or concepts are merely derivative, copied, patterned, or emulated." In psychology, it is often described as an unconscious predisposition to perceive in categories, though not to be confused with stereotypes. Archetypes are more fundamental and tend to endure over time and social system changes. The archetypes in our model reflect commonly understood models of relationship that can be traced to the beginnings of human organizations such as families and military/religious organizations.

The Vertical Archetype

The vertical archetype is based on a fundamental model for organization relationships — the hierarchy. Although it may be argued that there is some degree of hierarchy in all organizations, there are significant differences in culture tied to the depth and rigidity of that hierarchy.

In a family, an army, a church, or a business organization, position in the hierarchy defines formal authority and accountability. Of course there are those in the lower levels of the hierarchy that wield power beyond that vested in their formal roles; that is a subject for another treatise. Here we are concerned with the expected characteristics of the formal organization.

Let's look at the characteristics of a well-run vertical organization:

■ Membership comes from actual or virtual belonging to a familial system. For example the owner's relatives may be employed by the company and others are told that they are joining a virtual family when they are recruited or interviewed for employment.

■ Continuation of membership depends upon compliance and loyalty to leaders. More than a few people have been let go from organizations for violating the expectation of loyalty.

■ The ideal vertical leader is a strong, caring parent figure.

■ Leadership roles are assigned along with legitimate status and authority to positions in the hierarchy. If one has subordinates, one is expected to lead.

■ The ideal member is a dependent, well-adjusted child.

■ Authority and accountability are distributed in direct proportion to vertical position.

■ Superiors are the primary source of direction, feedback, and recognition/reward.

■ Information is handled on a strict need-to-know basis.

■ Permission is generally required before acting.

■ Members relate to one another as parent to child (leader to follower) or as siblings (peers).

■ Work and people are organized along department or functional lines.

■ Change initiatives such as program or system implementations can be propelled to success by directives from respected (or feared) senior people who can compel compliance.

The Horizontal Archetypes

Still fairly rare but visible on the horizon of organizational evolution is the horizontal organization, which claims maximum versatility, resilience, and speed of both operations and adaptation. A well-run horizontal culture looks like this:

- It is based upon a "community of well-adjusted adults" with minimal hierarchy as the model for organization (flat structure).
- Emerging as an organizational model along with the spread of technology. The nature of emerging information technology urges the work surrounding it to be more team-based and customer-driven.
- Membership hinges on effectiveness in adult-to-adult relationships. Single superior–subordinate relationships are not the key to personal effectiveness. People must be able to function effectively in teams and often in multiple teams.
- People are organized in teams responsible for projects (long and short term).
- Leadership is a more distributed function.
- Information is handled on a good-to-know basis. It is pushed at people, requiring them to be able to select the important from the unimportant.
- Permission from superiors before acting is seldom required, though assent from affected members may be commonly required.
- Customer's needs and team culture rather than superiors primarily provide direction.
- Feedback comes from customers and teammates as well as directly from the work.
- Authority and accountability are widely distributed and sought by those in a position to impact customer satisfaction, revenue, and organizational continuity.
- Change initiatives such as program or system implementations will normally require significant investments of time, effort, and materials to educate and enlist the cooperation of organization members.

Archetypes in the Middle

The vast majority of organizations today have a culture that is a blend of vertical and horizontal elements in the contract. Such an organization may be more complex to manage, but it can run well so long as everyone is aware of the contract requirements, such as:

- Fundamental hierarchy that includes elements of a horizontal archetype. People are primarily accountable to a superior, but get significant direction from customer needs.
- Probably the most common type found today. As organizations evolve along with the spread and development of technology, pure verticality is disappearing.
- People are organized by function, and work may be organized by function or by project.

- Direction may come from superiors or customers, but evaluation of performance is primarily by superiors.
- Authority and accountability tend to flow upward, but may be temporarily distributed to teams working on key projects.
- Management is significantly more complex, owing to the blending of vertical and horizontal archetype characteristics.
- Permission to act is generally necessary, but successful risk taking will be rewarded.
- Leadership in functions is vertical and in project teams may be distributed.
- Accommodates the widest variety of psychosocial contracts because messages about organizational expectations will contain emphasis from both ends of the continuum from vertical to horizontal.
- Reference to both vertical and horizontal systems produces a highly political climate where power, the trappings of power, and the pursuit of power are constantly visible as features in day-to-day dynamics.
- Both formal/public and behind closed doors are important methods of communication.
- Change initiatives such as program or system implementations are dependent upon top management commitment and support as well as successful engagement of affected organization members.

The key feature that changes among archetypes across the continuum is the distribution of ownership, both felt and actual. It is this feature that most strongly influences the array of characteristics in any organization culture.

Not Only What, But How Well

The key reason that it takes some skill to interpret the results of an assessment of culture is that it is not quite enough to know what archetype is operant in an organization. It is also necessary to have some insights into how well that archetype is being expressed. For example, a pure vertical organization can be very effective, but only if there is strong, competent, and caring leadership at the top as the model for other leaders in the organization. The absence of proper leadership will result in political infighting, poorly founded decisions, wasted resources, and fearful people. Security policies and practices will reflect this lack of leadership in both policy and practices, as shown in Figure 10.5.

To understand the impact of management effectiveness, it is necessary to look at the stable characteristics of the organization and make an educated assessment of how well they are being expressed. For example, in a blended archetype organization information will be managed essentially on a need-to-know basis, but there must also be a strong internal communications function that can push necessary and sufficient information to the population so that people can adequately serve

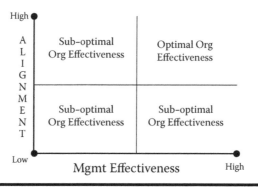

Figure 10.5 Optimal culture–management alignment.

customers and represent the organization. Drawing the links between culture and strategy demands a profile that identifies the archetype and assesses its effectiveness, but of the two factors the archetype will always be the more powerful.

Linking Strategy to Culture

By now you may have begun to see how the classification system based on vertical, horizontal, and blended archetypes can inform the design and implementation of security policies and practices. The linking process is shown in Figure 10.6.

The more vertical the organization, the more top-down its dynamics and the more employee behavior can be influenced by demands for compliance.

As organizations become more flat and horizontal, the drivers of behavior are more varied and include customer and peer influences. The business case for behavior becomes more important than compliance when change is implemented in flatter organizations. How people define value is more driven by customer needs and actual impact on operations than by how much superiors approve.

If the contract that an individual accepted along with employment calls for appropriate dependence (vertical archetype), people are less likely to resist security controls. If a truly caring leader leads the vertical organization, resistance is even less likely because such a person will be assumed to have the best interests of the business and of people in mind when creating and applying policy.

In flatter organizations people feel effective because the feedback they get tells them that they are having the desired impact on customer satisfaction and are working well with teammates. These are nothing more or less than different definitions of competence. The strategies that a security program chooses must recognize this sort of fact. Consider this example of how different types of organizations can respond to a common threat to security — social engineering.

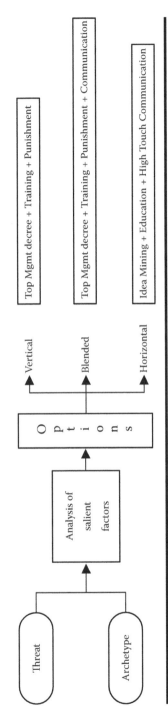

Figure 10.6 Linking culture to strategy.

Recognition of the social engineering threat includes acceptance of the fact that this is one of the most difficult threats to reduce because both the threat and the solutions involve influencing human behavior. Let's assume that the cultural archetype in this organization is blended, so we may infer that behavior is influenced both by strong leadership and customer needs. The archetype also suggests that our efforts will be positively influenced by effective performance management and employee relations practices. Let's say that our organization is fairly typical in that performance evaluations are done on an annual basis by direct supervisors who may or may not have input from customers and peers of subordinates. Further let's assume that our employee relations practices are focused on reducing risk to the organization, as is the case in most organizations today. Of course there are likely to be other factors, but let's focus on these for purposes of explanation.

Formal written policy is organization law. For our security policy with regard to social engineering to have weight, it will have to be visibly blessed by top management. The policy should also define infractions as well as include a general description of administrative consequences for violations of the policy, so its language must be coordinated with Human Resources as well as legal counsel.

If there are administrative consequences for infractions there must be some methods of enforcement implemented and publicized to deter policy violations. If we believe that our perimeter security is weak because people are frequently allowing "tailgating" by strangers, we might install video surveillance at the entrances both as a deterrent and to capture a record of infractions.

We might also implement training to ensure that everyone in the organization understands both the nature and the threat of social engineering because the phrase is not self-explanatory. Initially this training will have to be done across the population, and the best method might be a video or computer-based approach that ensures access to the information, but does not place great demand on people's time. Media materials in support of this policy should include the image and voice of top management to lend credibility to the messages. In our organization, policy and training language should also include information about impact on the customer experience and company profitability (especially important if employees have an ownership stake in the company). For ongoing training, the introduction to security policy and practices should be a part of formal and informal new-hire orientation.

If we were addressing this threat in a horizontal organization, our approach would be different. Our focus at the outset would be on developing ideas from among the employee population about how the threat can be addressed by policy and practices. The responsibility for enforcement would be distributed among the population and education about this part of role expectations would be "high touch" rather than "high tech," and directly involve the most senior managers in the organization. Discussion of security threats of all kinds would include metrics that describe the impact of breaches in business terms.

You may be able to see from our example that understanding the culture in terms of the most positive aspects of the archetype logically leads to workable strategy.

Presenting Assessment Results

Focus on Strategy

It is not necessarily required that the results of an assessment of culture need to be presented to anyone per se. This is truer if the organization is more vertical. What matters to people are the strategies because the strategies will impact operations and behavior. So, it can be enough to say that an assessment of organization needs with regard to security policies and practices has led to a set of strategies that are aligned with the current culture and business needs. Thus it is the strategies that are presented, not the direct results of the assessment.

If They Really Need to Know

If there is an organizational interest in what drove the creation of strategies, choose the briefest description of the assessment process that you can. You may want to dazzle people with your brilliance, but we have learned that there is little value in over-informing senior people. Lead with results (strategies suggested or implemented) even if you have been asked to talk about methods, and then describe methods briefly. Finish with how the strategies are expected to support organizational goals. Remember to give credit to your steering committee or your program management team or whoever supported your efforts in developing the strategic direction of the security program.

Some Final Thoughts on Culture

Is there an ideal culture for optimal security? Given the conventional wisdom about what culture is and how to understand it, this could be a reasonable question. Actually the answer is "no" if we are talking about an ideal archetype. There certainly can be a well-executed cultural archetype combined with strategies that are appropriately aligned with that archetype.

The social influence of leadership is one of the most powerful forces available to ensure the security of people and property. As a security professional, you have an obligation to provide leadership by aligning your program with the cultural reality in your organization. If it walks like a duck and it quacks like a duck and it waddles like a duck, there is a fairly good chance that it is a duck. Your job is to help it be the absolute best duck that it can be. Excellent alignment of programs with culture fosters faith in leaders. Faith in leaders encourages trust in policies and practices. Faith and trust within the organization makes your job much simpler in that you can focus on the threats from outside and on helping business operations to have necessary and sufficient security without it having to be an inhibiting influence. Rest assured that if your security measures are not aligned with the culture and with the needs of business units, they will be ignored eventually by your own people. As a staff professional, you do not want enemies within the management ranks of your organization. You want to be perceived as an ally in reaching the business goals of the organization, and it is your job to align your program with those goals, not the other way around.

Can culture be changed? Most certainly. There are numerous examples of cultural change in management history. Most rapid and dramatic changes, though, have come about because organizations are in serious trouble. Under those conditions change is both possible and relatively easy, though not painless. A much more productive path to change is found in accepting the archetype for what it is and optimizing the way that it works.

In one organization with which we have worked, there was a deep crisis period that caused extensive force reduction and broad financial restructuring. One of the most powerful changes that helped the company to bounce back was to change the work schedule. They lengthened the work day slightly Monday through Thursday and ended the formal work week at noon on Friday. The changes that the remaining people were being asked to accept would certainly have been resisted more if not for the enormous morale boost that came from giving employees Friday afternoons off. In fact, informal measures of attendance some months after the change showed that a significant number of employees were working into Friday afternoon anyway.

Should culture be changed? Not necessarily. Just because a thing can be done does not mean that it should be done. In cases where real change has been successful, it was led by a visionary manager who could see decades into the future and was willing to do the hard work of sticking to the path that he or she set. Strong leadership opened up opportunities for people to become more accountable and able to have more direct impact on how things got done within the company. Usually, the growth that the company experiences during the deliberate change process is testimony to the wisdom of pursuing it.

By contrast, during the late-20th century a number of companies quickly embraced the bright promise of Total Quality Management without understanding that full implementation would require changes in culture to accompany the implementation of quality tools. Essentially the full value of TQM required that work become designed around teams, that structures become more flat, and that more information be made available to more people. Organizations that were unwilling or unable to make that sort of radical change got little benefit from quality tools and practices.

This treatise was intended to provide some practical instruction as well as to demystify the question of aligning culture with security program design. Our experience tells us that if you apply the information thoughtfully, you will increase the likelihood of your program's being successful. If you apply this knowledge, let us know how it worked for you.

Recap

■ The social influence of leadership is one of the most powerful forces available to ensure the security of people and property. As a security professional you have an obligation to provide leadership by aligning your program with the cultural reality in your organization.

■ Every management practice in an organization will support or inhibit that organization in proportion to the extent that the practice is aligned with the culture. Failure to align with culture is the hallmark of "programs of the month" that come and go and end up on the trash heap of good intentions badly executed.

■ Just as we would need to understand the personality of individuals so as to understand their needs for security, so must we understand the culture of an organization to be able to design an appropriate security program.

■ The purpose in assessing the culture is not to try to change it or be critical of it, but to understand it so that your security program will be appropriately aligned with it.

■ Effective alignment enables security managers to design and implement necessary and sufficient security and the provision of no more and no less than that is the security manager's job.

■ Culture can trump good common sense when it comes to management and security practices, and this is the compelling driver for including a useful assessment of culture in the development of a security program.

■ A successful cultural assessment requires:
  − Support from the most senior levels of the organization.
  − A method for classifying organizational cultures.
  − A comprehensive survey or interview methodology.
  − A logical connection between the classification system and the specific security strategies.
  − An effective presentation of the assessment results and recommendations.

Note

1. The information above is not included as an advertisement, but to demonstrate that developing your own instrument can be difficult and requires adherence to rigorous research rules. We are willing neither to offer our tool on the market nor suggest to clients that it is more than it is because it does not yet meet the standard for a research tool. Neither should you pretend that your homegrown survey is valid and reliable without appropriate statistical evidence. Questionnaires are fairly easy to write, but scientific instruments take years to develop and require a solid theoretical basis. Perhaps some of the purveyors of security technology and program support will be willing to invest in the development of useful culture assessment tools as they learn about the need to align programs and technology with culture. That does not

mean that you cannot design your own survey instrument and use it. It only means that you will need a robust classification model upon which to base your questionnaire and that you must include the limitations of your tool in any report of results that you produce.

References

Aronson, E. (1995). *The Social Animal.* New York: W. H. Freeman and Company.

Barron, R. A. and Neuman, J. H. (1996). Workplace violence and workplace aggression: Evidence on their relative frequency and potential causes. *Aggressive Behavior*, Vol. 22, pp. 161–173.

Baxter, V. and Margavio, A. (1996, August). Assaultive violence in the U.S. post office. *Work & Occupations*, Vol. 23, pp. 277–296.

Biddle, B. J. (1979). *Role Theory: Expectations, Identities and Behaviors.* New York: Academic Press.

Burke, W. W. (1997). The new agenda for organization development. *Organizational Dynamics*, 26, 1, 7–20.

Chilton, K. and Orlando, M. (1996, Winter). A new social contract for the American worker. *Business and Society Review*, No. 96, pp. 23–26.

Culture Assessment Survey, http://www.employeedevelopmentsolutions.com/cultureassess. htm. The Culture Assessment Survey focuses on a few key areas of the culture: Are relationships healthy throughout the organization? Does feedback flow smoothly?

Herriot, P. and Pemberton, C. (1996, June). Contracting careers. *Human Relations*, Vol. 49, pp. 757–790.

Kuttner, R. (1995, July 10). Needed: A two-way social contract in the workplace. *Business Week*, p. 22.

Laker, D. R. and Steffy, B. D. (1995, September). The impact of alternative socialization tactics on self-managing behavior and organizational commitment. *Journal of Social Behavior and Personality*, Vol. 10, pp. 645–660.

Levinson, M. (2006, June). *CIO Magazine*, CXO Media, Inc. http://www.cio.com/ archive/060106/ag_edwards.html.

Mills, D. Q. (1996, October). The changing social contract in American business. *European Management Journal*, Vol. 14, No. 5, p. 451.

Mingery, J. T. and Rubin, R. B. (1995, February). Organizational entry: An investigation of newcomer communication behavior and uncertainty. *Communication Research*, Vol. 22, pp. 54–85.

Morrison, E. W. (1993, April). Longitudinal study of the effects of information seeking on newcomer socialization. *Journal of Applied Psychology*, Vol. 78, pp. 173–183.

Morrison, E. W. and Robinson, S. L. (1997). When employees feel betrayed: A model of how psychological contract violation develops. *Academy of Management Review*, Vol. 22, No. 1, pp. 226–256.

Nelson, D. L., Quick, J. C., and Joplin, J. R. (1991). Psychological contracting and newcomer socialization: An attachment theory foundation. Special issue: Handbook on job stress. *Journal of Social Behavior & Personality*, Vol. 6, pp. 55–72.

Organizational Cultural Competence Survey, http://www.aucd.org/councils/multicultural/Cultural_Competence_Survey.htm.

Patient safety culture assessment in the nursing home – Handler, http://qshc.bmj.com/cgi/content/full/15/6/400.

Rousseau, D. M. (1990). New-hire perceptions of their own and their employer's obligations: A study of psychological contracts. *Journal of Organizational Behavior*, Vol. 11, pp. 389–400.

Rousseau, D. M. (1989). Psychological and implied contracts in organizations. *Employee Responsibilities and Rights Journal*, Vol. 2, pp. 121–139.

Rousseau, D. M. and Mclean Parks, J. (1993). The contracts of individuals and organizations. In L. L. Cummings and B. M. Stow (Eds.), *Research in Organizational Behavior*, Vol. 15, pp. 1–47, Greenwich, CT: JAI Press.

Safety Performance Solutions — Safety Culture Assessment. http://www.safetyperformance.com/Services/SafetyCultureAssessment.asp

Shafritz, J. M. and Ott, J.S. (1996). *Classics of Organization Theory*. New York: Harcourt Brace & Company.

Sims, R. R. (1994). Human resource management's role in clarifying the new psychological contract. *Human Resource Management*, Vol. 33, p. 373.

Vulnerability Assessment and Survey Program Lessons Learned, http://www.esisac.com/publicdocs/assessment_methods/OEA_VA_Lessons_Learned_B.

Weidenbaum, M. (1995, Jan–Feb). A new social contract for the American workplace. *Challenge*, Vol. 38, p. 51.

Wheatley, M.J. (1992). *Leadership and the New Science*, San Francisco: Berrett-Koehler Publishers, Inc.

Chapter 11

Selling Information Security

James S. Christiansen

What Is a Chief Information Security Officer (CISO)?

The CISO is a salesman for security; it is as simple as that. OK, maybe there is a bit more to it than that, but the primary role is to drive investment into the security organization to meet the goals of the business.

The key role of the CISO is to:

- Find the balance of risk from information technology and the cost of implementing the additional controls.
- Provide the means for the business to share information with business partners meeting the need for confidentiality and privacy.
- Enable the business by focusing on how it can achieve its goals with the proper amount of security.

Successful CISOs have some key qualities and strengths. In this chapter we will explore:

- *The misconception of the primary role of the CISO.* You may think the primary job of the CISO is vision, leadership, and strategy, but the real job of the

CISO is to sell security to the organization. Of course, the CISO will have to be the leader, set the strategy, and guide the organization through the execution, but in the end it is the CISO's main mission to drive investment into security, and to accomplish that requires a good salesperson with a great product.

■ *How to gain visibility in the organization.* More successful CISOs are those that stay visible in the organization. If CISOs are in their office, they are not doing their job! They must invite themselves to divisional meetings, schedule meetings with the key leaders to discuss the security program, and ask what their goals are and how the security program can contribute to their success.

■ *How to gain the trust of the executive team.* Effective CISOs have learned how to gain the trust and confidence of the executive team. How does an effective CISO approach this problem and what are the "tricks of the trade"? Like any other management role, the CISO must begin by surrounding him- or herself with brilliant staff. Having a strong security management team is essential in building credibility with the executive team.

■ *How different organizational structures affect the role of the CISO.* There are a number of ways the security program can be organized in either direct reporting relationships or matrix management organizations. My advice: Instead of asking, "Where should information security report?", the smart CISO asks "Who can I look to for support in the organization?"

■ *Other key areas of concern for the CISO.* The CISO must:
  – Be cognizant of the legal and regulatory environment in which the organization plays, and the security implications of compliance.
  – Be aware of any international management challenges.
  – Be on top of issues of third party risk management.

Believe in Your Product!

If you believe in your product, you can sell it to anyone. The CISO is head of sales for the internal security product. His or her key role is to convince business leaders to invest in the security program. First, the CISO must understand what he or she is selling — not the biggest and best technical whiz bang, but the business value of the security solution. Of course, to be able to speak in business terms, the CISO must understand and acknowledge the business drivers for security. Next, the CISO has to be able to link security to the business needs. To do this, look for security articles that discuss how a security project enabled a new application or allowed a business to expand into new markets. Share that knowledge with the executive team, line managers, anyone who has a stake in the business' success. Security is easy to sell if the CISO focuses on the benefits to the company: create a talk track and communicate the key messages to all applicable audiences in as many formats as necessary to get your points across.

A wise man once told me that a message must be heard seven times to be fully comprehended. I don't know if that is true, but an effective CISO finds more than one way to keep the message fresh and relevant to the business. Believe in your product, get excited, and you will generate excitement around you.

In times of desperation, CISOs may resort to FUD (fear, uncertainty, and doubt). Effective CISOs resist that temptation. Learn how to communicate the value of information security in terms appropriate to the audience. That does not mean that CISOs do not discuss the impacts of a new vulnerability or what can happen if intrusion detection is not installed, but those conversations are best kept brief and not the focus of the overall message. There is the right audience for those conversations, e.g., operations managers, but it is not the executive team.

Stay Visible!

A few years ago I was given the "Experian Elite" award by Experian executive management. The Experian Elite award is given to the top salesperson in each of the different business lines of Experian. How does a CISO win a sales award? By staying engaged in the business, understanding the needs of the organization, and supporting the goals of the business line presidents. Stay in tune with the organization priorities and tie your message to those priorities. Meet with potential and existing customers and help them not only understand what the company security practices are, but also help them to better understand the risks their own company faces and how they can overcome them. Customers appreciate the unexpected added value of gaining insight from an expert in one of the most pressing issues facing their company — risk management.

After the award ceremonies the chief executive officer from Europe asked me, "To what do you contribute your success?" With some additional time, I probably could have come up with a more eloquent answer, but in the heat of the moment I responded, "I find a way to say yes … yes, but…." It was probably not the best answer, but it was the most honest. It is the security organization's responsibility to watch for inappropriate activities that expose the company to unnecessary risk. Successful CISOs find a way to help the business achieve its goals while providing the right level of protection for the information. "Yes, but…" may result in additional cost to provide the potential business transaction. The additional cost may make the new project unprofitable, but at that point, it's the business' decision to proceed or not. It is not the security group saying they cannot move forward. This is a key success concept for CISOs. Find a way to say yes. Make the decision to proceed or not proceed a business decision based on profit and loss.

Communicate at the Executive Level

For a CISO to be taken seriously at the executive level, it is important to learn to communicate to executives in ways that make sense to them. Winning CISOs understand that they must show confidence and integrity when communicating to the executives. Never apologize for doing the job and never shirk the responsibilities. Like any other sales job, it is important to point out the benefits of the service in terms that the receiving party can understand, terms relevant to their concerns.

Additionally, building the support structure for the security initiatives is essential to developing a strong security program. Identify those executives that have a broad and vested interest in the organization, and begin to build strong relationships. Point out those areas where your organizations have synergies and explain how you can help them be more successful.

Starting at the Top: The Chief Executive Officer

The CEO is responsible to the board of directors and shareholders to drive increasing revenue. Attempting to convince a CEO to invest in security by pointing out the potential "bad things that will happen" is not very successful over time. Effective CISOs are sensitive to the fact that, although the CEO is concerned about risk, operational security risks are just some of the many issues on the CEO's mind. For example, before meeting with the CISO, a CEO may have been discussing the recent filing of a million-dollar lawsuit, or a budget overrun for a project that is going to delay implementation of a new product. Although the risks are significant to the CISO, they may not be the CEO's top priority.

How is the security organization helping to drive revenue? Depending on the industry you are in, the answer can be simple. Ask yourself the following:

- Do I have clients, investors, etc., that are depending on the company's good name?
- Did I meet with a client, do a briefing at a forum where clients are present, or help negotiate the security requirements in a new contract?
- Did the security organization assist in a review or answer a question from the legal team?
- Was the information technology group able to implement a new system to provide customers with new, timely information that without the security solution could not have been done?

Effective CISOs look for ways to become directly involved in the revenue stream. Meet with the head of sales, understand the business imperatives, and seek ways to assist them. These successes will help create a relevant message for the security organization. Maybe it is trust, security, brand name, or something else, but in every company there is something that is important in driving revenue that smart CISOs can use to get directly involved.

How Can I Possibly Influence the Chief Financial Officer?

How does a CISO understand what is motivating the CFO? What are their priorities, and how can the CISO help them achieve their goals? When talking with the CFO, discuss ways to reduce overall cost or how to avoid future costs. Better CISOs focus on cost savings rather than cost avoidance; this strategy may very well garner the CFO as an ally. Consider: did the security organization implement anything that would reduce overall cost? Achieving cost reduction is more difficult for security than most business functions, but there are opportunities, e.g., reducing the cost of password resets, streamlining contract negotiations, and reduction or redeployment of staff due to automation of the access administration team. Even if you have not reduced overall cost, a good CISO focuses on the message that they are constantly looking for ways to reduce the total expense. Did you ever say, "I spend the money as if it was my own!" Unlike the CEO, the CFO is oftentimes less motivated by brand damage, focusing more on the strategic objectives of the overall corporation. A good CISO finds ways to provide direct customer support, sales team support, or even help remove existing barriers to the business.

The Business Line President: A Must-Have Ally

Winning CISOs understand that having the support of the business line president is a must. Better CISOs focus their message when speaking with the business line president on the needs of the business unit and not on generalizations. Show them that you understand *their* business needs and are willing to adapt the security program to those needs. Be willing to demonstrate that the security program will not place an undue burden on the cost structure of the business line. Ask yourself:

- Is the security program adaptable?
- Am I going to put unnecessary controls into the business unit?
- Can I talk about how I can help build the business?
- How do I convince the president that I won't add unnecessary controls that will burden his organization?

A CISO must understand that the business line president is responsible for the profitability of the business line and, as referenced prior, when working with the CEO, the message has to be focused on the business drivers, such as how the security program will help them win new customers and retain existing customers.

General Counsel: Can This Be a Win?

General counsel can be one of the biggest supporters of the CISO on the executive team. The primary role of the general counsel is to protect the company against the cost of legal actions and the resulting brand damage. To perform effectively, the CISO must not only understand the regulatory requirements that mandate safeguard provisions for the specific industry (e.g., Sarbanes–Oxley, GLBA, HIPAA, etc.), he or she must also understand how a comprehensive security program can help to ensure that the company has met the obligations under these laws and regulations.

CISOs should take the opportunity to reassure the general counsel that they understand the security implications of the regulatory requirements and can partner with the Legal Department to help reach a level of due care. Thus, the CISO can leverage the legal ramifications of the security program and gain general counsel as an ally on the executive team. Please note that it is important to absolutely avoid technical talk; general counsels typically speak in "legalese" and are most likely not familiar with "techno-babble." So, stay away from technical jargon. A key thing to remember: legal counselors do not run projects or implement new systems. So it may be second nature to the CISO, but legal counselors have not been in a position where they need to "socialize" a new idea. Understand their needs, motivations, and what is keeping them up at night. The smart CISOs position themselves to relieve the burden of the general counsel, or at the very least, give the impression that they are also shouldering the concern.

Chief Information Officer: A Natural Ally?

It's been my experience that the most comfortable executive to communicate with is the CIO. The CIO has similar backgrounds and concerns that make the CIO a natural ally. But the CIO is under constant pressure to reduce costs, and one of the easiest targets is the security program. The CISO's message to the CIO should focus on the effectiveness of the program. Think through these questions:

- Is the anti-virus product providing a reliable and useful service?
- How about spam protection? Is it saving resources and outages?
- Are there any new integrated products that reduce the cost and make the implementation more efficient?

The CIO has three primary concerns: cost control, system reliability, and new services to meet the internal customer demands. Successful CISOs seek out opportunities to help the CIO meet his or her goals. Can you speed up the encryption program for the customer deliveries and improve the delivery times? If there is a breach in security, have you helped prepare the reaction program (e.g., a cyber-incident response team)? A good CISO understands that CIOs have to see you as an asset and a key resource to their extended team.

Internal Audit: A Symbiotic Relationship

There is not a more natural ally for the CISO than the head of internal audit. Both functions have the same goal — bringing the right level of controls to the organization. Further, both groups suffer from many of the same organizational challenges. Better CISOs align themselves with internal audit and use the relationship to assist in making sure any security audit findings are significant. Typically, internal audit reports directly to the audit committee of the board of directors, and thereby has a great deal of power at its disposal to drive change in the organization. Wise CISOs use their influence to assist the audit team in identifying the high-risk items, allowing the organization to focus on critical risks and avoid the distraction of trying to fix a less serious control failure. They use their relationship to gain another supporter on the executive team that can assist in explaining the value proposition of the security organization.

To summarize, the critical points are (1) look at each member of the executive team and customize the message to demonstrate the value of the security program in terms that assists them in reaching their specific goals, (2) stay visible, (3) communicate effectively, and (4) communicate often.

Manage through Influence

Good CISOs learn to manage through influence. At my former organization, the business units are managed geographically by separate presidents (e.g., United States, EU, Asia). Each of the presidents reports to their own board of directors. The head of security for this corporation lacks authority to convince the operating areas to implement the security program within their respective unit. To gain support of the program, the CISO must be able to show the business value and use his or her influence to gain support of the program. This lesson carries over into all aspects of being a better CISO. When dealing with direct line staff or with other organizations, influencing has a better chance in getting them to proceed in the direction the CISO wants. Telling them may result in short-term compliance, but over time compliance will erode quickly.

My advice: don't throw your weight around if you can avoid it. Never resort to authority to gain support of an idea. I often hear, "You need to do that because it is security policy." A smart CISO will never use that as justification for implementing a control. A policy is a method for the executive team to communicate its expectations on how things are done. Therefore, we don't implement a specific control because it is policy, but rather we implement the control because it is the direction of the executive team and the policy serves as the method of communicating that message.

Organizational Structure

Over the past 10 years, I have established security organizations for three major corporations. In 1998, one company did not have a formal security organization. Security responsibilities were divided into two functions: the technology departments (firewalls, virus control, etc.) reported to the information technology engineering organization and the access control function reported in information technology operations. We had the opportunity to establish a brand new division at this company, focused on information security.

There are many ways to organize the security function and they all have advantages and disadvantages. Better CISOs understand it is not as important how security is organized, or the hierarchical structure. The key to success is the support structure the CISO is able to build among the executive team.

However, the manner in which security is organized will change the methods and processes a CISO will use to be successful. Effective CISOs will adapt their approach to the most advantageous organizational structure. The two primary organization structures most common are (1) the matrix structure, in which the CISO is a corporate-level organization and the security staff report in the business lines, or (2) the CISO has direct responsibility for the implementation and operations of security.

It is smart for CISOs to understand that they do not need to have all the security staff in their direct reporting line. Be ready for decentralization. Being a powerful CISO is not about how many staff you manage; it's about how many staff you can influence. Drive the direction of security any way you can: through direct staff, matrix staff, and supporting staff, to reach the security program goals.

Matrix Organization

Be prepared to manage in a matrix organization. Large companies have already implemented a matrix organization or are seriously reviewing how to manage the business lines more effectively. Often this is achieved by making the business lines totally accountable for their business. In these organization structures, the security operations typically report directly in the business unit and corporate manages the overall security program.

Large corporations have many layers of matrix managers and a CISO must learn quickly how to survive having more than one boss as well as having staff that report to more than just the CISO. Mixed priorities are a daily occurrence and misconceptions about how the staff is doing on a particular project can be problematic.

Lacking proper processes and communication, it is easy for one to assume that staff is totally engaged on a priority of the CISO, when in reality the staff is working on another project that was entirely unknown to the CISO.

At a former company, the security leaders in the business units report directly to the chief information officer of that business line. As CISO, my direct reports included the leaders of each of the major business lines, e.g., manufacturing, credit, etc. The leaders of those business lines had matrix reports in each of the major business units. The manufacturing security officer would have matrix security staff that would be responsible for a sub-business unit such as North American manufacturing. The cycle continued down the organization until one of the subsidiaries has actual staff doing actual security work!

A good CISO must understand that managing in a matrix organization is very different than managing in a direct line management structure. Many of the best lessons learned in being an effective manager are those thrust upon the CISO as a matrix manager. Being able to communicate the value of an objective to the executive team or the matrix report is critical to success. The matrix report will be balancing objectives given by the CISO with those from their other matrix managers, so it's important to communicate formally, with milestones and delivery dates. Thus, the CISO must use his or her ability to influence the matrix staff leaders to gain their support to reach common objectives.

Communications in a Matrix Environment

In a direct line management organization, communication to a direct staff member can be informal, loose, and often incomplete. If communication is not effective the first time, just talk again! In a matrix environment, goals, objectives, projects, etc. must all be communicated in a formal method. One way to accomplish this is by establishing metrics to determine if progress is being made and to hold individuals accountable for their commitments.

Line Organization

We formed the first information security division at another company in 1998 consisting of four functional areas: information security service management (policies, training, etc.), information security engineering (technology implementations), information security investigations (CIRT, forensics, etc), information security operations (access control, encryption keys, etc.). Managing a direct line report structure requires excellent leadership skills. The CISO must develop the strategy, vision, and overall objectives, and must also have skills in managing direct staff. Performance monitoring and objective setting will take up more time in the line organization than in the matrix organization.

Managing in a direct line structure can be easier and allow for more flexibility and speed in implementing the security program. Without the need to influence as many different groups, the security program can be more nimble and able to change direction faster than one being implemented in a matrix organization.

Legal Responsibility

There is more to being a CISO than just understanding security. It's also important to stay apprised of new regulations that may impact the business.

As a CISO, expect about 20 percent of the time to be devoted to legal aspects of the company. Better CISOs are able to read a contract and understand the legal terms, references, and writing style. Many times, the CISO must guide the legal team on the risks that the organization faces if they proceed with a project. Are you prepared to advise on requirements that should be in an agreement or note change on requirements in the agreement that may add unnecessary expense to the organization?

There are two primary duties of the CISO relative to regulatory and legal requirements. Contracts are the lifeblood of every company, but if not carefully drafted, they can add unnecessary cost to the corporation, or even worse, may be ignored by the company. There are two times when everyone looks at a contract: the day it is signed and the day something goes wrong. The day a security breach impacts a customer, everyone will be looking at the contract to see what was committed and how well that has been implemented. Therefore, a CISO should understand the contractual requirements and work closely with the Legal Department on what needs to be done to comply with the requirements.

The CISO must also stay current with pending changes in regulations that have safeguard requirements or implications. CISOs do not only react to new demands on the company; they may also perform an impact analysis, allowing both the regulator and the organization to understand the impact new legislation may have.

International Management

If the CISO is employed by a multi-national organization, his or her job does not stop at the domestic border. Also, in many cases, the CISO will have an international management responsibility.

Many CISOs are faced with the need to manage an international team, coordinate efforts with international teams or even the responsibility for outsourced operations in another country. Managing across organizational borders is like solving a three-dimensional crossword puzzle. The answers are the same, but each problem has a different twist. Effective CISOs understand the local business culture and don't make mistakes like scheduling an 8:00 am meeting in a location that typically starts work at 9:30 am.

Communication is especially important in the international arena. The CISO must demonstrate knowledge of the business and demonstrate knowledge of the business culture. Depending on the region of the world the CISO is working in, the concerns and approaches will change, but one thing is constant. Take assumptions and leave them home. Better CISOs start with a fresh look at the problem and revalidate the things they "know."

Third-Party Risk Management

Oftentimes, the responsibility of the CISO does not stop at the company; it sometimes extends to partners' businesses. Managing the security of a major corporation can be a daunting task, there are so many things to think about, anticipate, plan, bargain, beg, and let's not forget, plead for resources. And after all that thought and work effort comes the satisfaction of knowing that there is proper protection for the company, employees, and investors. Then, just as you think everything is covered, the company decides to send the sensitive, valuable information to a third party. The nightmare starts all over again. Is the third party secure? Does it have the proper controls? Can it prevent a security breach? Can it react to a security breach? Does it understand the contractual requirements, and is it able to meet them? Will the CISO be notified that information has been breached before reading it in the newspaper?

The number of third parties receiving sensitive information from most large companies today reaches into the thousands. How can security or risk management departments possibly manage all of these relationships? The CISO must go back to basics. Review the basics of security and the domains that govern security, e.g., governance, vulnerability management, threat management, identity management, data protection, physical security. Establish a program that can measure and monitor the ability of the third party to meet or exceed the security requirements.

Establishing a process and system to assess and reassess on a regular basis the security level of a third party is not for the light of heart. Look for a business partner who can provide this service in a cost-effective and efficient way, using a standard methodology for measuring security maturity, e.g., the International Standards Organization (ISO) 17799/27001 standard.

CISOs have a significant responsibility to their companies, to the shareholders, and to those individual consumers that trust them to keep their personal information secure. It is a rewarding position and one that can help the CISO grow professionally in many ways. Good luck!

Recap

- The key roles of the CISO are to:
  - Find the balance of risk from information technology and the cost of implementing the additional controls.
  - Provide the means for the business to share information with business partners meeting the need for confidentiality and privacy.
  - Enable the business by focusing on how it can achieve its goals with the proper amount of security.
- More successful CISOs are those that stay visible in the organization.
- Effective CISOs have learned how to gain the trust and confidence of the executive team.
- There are a number of ways the security program can be organized and a number of different reporting structures.
- The CISO must be cognizant of the legal and regulatory environment in which the organization plays, and the security implications of compliance.
- Security is easy to sell if the CISO focuses on the benefits to the company.
- Winning CISOs understand that communicating to the executive must show confidence and integrity.
- Manage through influence. Identify those executives that have a broad and vested interest in the organization and begin to build strong relationships.

Chapter 12

The Importance of an IT Security Strategy

Randy Sanovic

Strategic IT Security

If you want to stay long-lived and progressive as an IT security manager, director, CSO, or CISO, you must eventually be capable of creating and marketing your company's IT security strategy. Most of us have gotten by through many seasons of tactical fire drills solving immediate IT security problems with technical projects, some process, and just-in-time policy. The decade of just-in-time IT security solutions is past; now is the time for strategic planning and actions. Yes, the executive buzzwords of vision, mission, goals, objectives, charters, etc. are important, but in too many cases they only serve to cloud the present approach to our IT security future. So what should an appropriate IT security strategy, which usually covers a one-to-five-year agenda, encompass? Several logical and key steps are important if you are to have a chance to embed your strategic plan in the business and IT processes and culture.

Planning is usually short term. Strategy development is medium to longer term. IT security strategy focuses on risk mitigation and often is based on a threat-based risk-management approach, which considers protecting, detecting, containing, and eradicating threats. Any useful IT security strategy must be reviewed annually and updated as appropriate to comprehend business (e.g., responding to

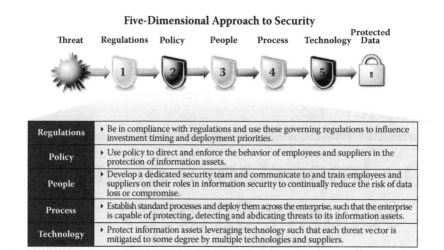

Figure 12.1 provides a visual representation of the Five-Dimensional Approach to Security, with the following table content:

Regulations	▸ Be in compliance with regulations and use these governing regulations to influence investment timing and deployment priorities.
Policy	▸ Use policy to direct and enforce the behavior of employees and suppliers in the protection of information assets.
People	▸ Develop a dedicated security team and communicate to and train employees and suppliers on their roles in information security to continually reduce the risk of data loss or compromise.
Process	▸ Establish standard processes and deploy them across the enterprise, such that the enterprise is capable of protecting, detecting and abdicating threats to its information assets.
Technology	▸ Protect information assets leveraging technology such that each threat vector is mitigated to some degree by multiple technologies and suppliers.

Figure 12.1 The five-dimensional approach to security is to protect assets through regulations, policy, people, processes, and technology.

changing legislation, regulations, and business requirement operations) and technology changes (e.g., IDS versus IPS). In developing an enterprise-scoped strategy, you should take into account the involvement of and impact relative to people, process, and technology, and to any related policy, regulations, and legislation, as shown in Figure 12.1.

Know Your Threats

Identify and prioritize the threats that pertain to your day-to-day business operations. All threat vectors are not created equal; security and threat potentials vary with respect to probability and impact. For example, viruses and worms may be more frequent; however, you may have already mitigated most of their impact, whereas denial of service and remote control may present serious challenges to your business operations. It's important to prioritize, classify, and analyze your current and emerging security threats as they may impact your business operations. Doing so should enable you to better define the necessary risk-mitigating actions you will need to take. Because you can't manage what you can't measure, you will also need to assess and develop performance metrics and or scorecards that reflect your ability to defend against the recognized threat vectors. However, metrics for metrics' sake is often a useless exercise full of meaningless data. To make metrics useful in management terms, you must move from data to information to knowledge to wisdom, and finally your analysis, diagnosis, and prognosis must produce a closed loop of appropriate

Some Types of Threat Vectors	Description of Threat Vectors
Worms and Viruses	▸ Program consisting of executable and replicatable code designed to distribute itself and cause operational problems.
Hack / Attack	▸ Unauthorized external person and/or computer that gain access to systems to plant worms/viruses to disrupt operations.
Denial of Service	▸ An attack designed to overload and/or stop the normal function of a system.
Remote Control	▸ User remote to access systems, applications and/or data via the Internet.
Annoyance	▸ Unsolicited and/or undesirable e-mail advertisements that are offensive and/or fraudulent.
Social Engineering	▸ Exploitation of natural human tendency to trust a seemingly appropriate request for sensitive and/or confidential information.
Malicious Use	▸ An internal attack focused on committing "fraud" and/or stealing confidential information.
Inappropriate Use	▸ Illegal, unauthorized, disruptive use of systems and equipment.

Figure 12.2   The threat-based risk management approach requires identifying and prioritizing current and emerging security threats as recognized by industry. These are known as "threat vectors." These threat vectors are classified and analyzed in regard to main causes and effects building the basis to define risk-mitigating actions.

actionable decisions; otherwise, you will lose management's interest and not accomplish the IT security strategy goals and objectives that you've developed.

Your overall assessment of the impacts to your business operations should be based on their probability of occurrence, the potential impact on the enterprise, and your ability to defend against the specific threats. An example of a threat matrix is noted in Figure 12.2.

You will need to determine what your overall approach to resolving your security threat vectors will be. Such approaches vary from multiple levels of defense to perimeter defenses. Related costs and the maturity of the various solutions will be factors you will need to consider in your risk mitigation strategy. Another issue to keep in mind is how you will consolidate, correlate, and interpret the inputs you will get from your detective, defensive, and protective measures and the appropriate actions you will take in response to threats.

Determine Your Vulnerabilities

Do so by arranging for a trusted and qualified third-party to do a broad-based security vulnerability assessment (SVA). Such assessment should include specific sample populations, i.e., areas of your IT and business infrastructure and operations (e.g., IT architecture, information transport, wireless, social engineering, Internet and intranet scanning, web applications, commercial off-the-shelf software, databases,

Elements of Annual Security Vulnerability Assessment

Executive Interviews	▸ Interview with Business Executives to understand business issues related to Information Risk.
Site Review – Physical Security	▸ On-site assessments to review physical measures in place to protect information Assets.
Wireless AP Detection/ Analysis	▸ Discover a site's wireless access points, and if appropriate security measures are in place.
Social Engineering	▸ Using human intelligence gathering techniques, assess how personnel react to requests for sensitive information.
Intranet Scanning	▸ Sampling of servers and workstations of the 'internal network' to assess their security protection compliance.
Internet Scanning	▸ Sampling of network perimeter devices, to discover security weaknesses that may be exploited by a Hacker.
IT Security Architecture	▸ Review of 'architectural' protection mechanisms related to Network Computing environments.
Web Applications, COTS, Database	▸ Assessment of COTS Database, Web Applications/Portals security protection mechanisms.
Dial-Up Assessment	▸ Review the security of all modems and touch-tone based systems connected to the Enterprise Network.
Information Transport	▸ Determine the protection provided sensitive information, to and from the Enterprise, and within the Enterprise's Networks.
Information Security Surveys	▸ Judge the understanding and effectiveness of Policies from a user and management view.
Policy and Procedure Review	▸ Evaluation of Policies and Technical Security Requirements related to the business, risk, and compliance to applicable laws.

Figure 12.3 Third-party IT security vulnerability assessment matrix. A third-party review of security vulnerabilities will be conducted annually to assess the effectiveness of the defense strategy.

field offices, policy and standards reviews, physical security, etc.). When doing this, use a holistic approach that examines the root causes and corrective actions (not only in the sample populations, but throughout your IT environments) and break down your recommendations for remediation into the five basic elements of people, policy, process, regulations, and technology. An example of an IT SVA matrix is noted in Figure 12.3.

It is essential to realize that tools and techniques for finding and eradicating vulnerabilities must evolve over time to keep up with the constant barrage of new and blended threat vectors.

Always keep in mind that true business risks can be accepted, remediated, or mitigated. In many cases your IT security strategy will be to mitigate or accept business risks rather than fully remediate the risk or vulnerability. You will need to determine where the enterprise stands related to security life-cycle choices. The results of your SVA will help determine what choices you make. Strategies utilized for mitigating controls are reflected in Figure 12.4.

Mitigating Controls Lifecycle Strategy

Protection	▸ When possible provide effective protection mechanisms.
	▸ The ability to do so may be limited by the maturity of Technology.
Detection	▸ To complement ***protection*** efforts or when you are not able to provide an effective protection mechanism, then provide an effective ***detection*** mechanism. – Detect threats you have protected against in the event that there is a breakdown in the protection mechanism. – All events that are detected will go to central monitoring/operations center.
Containment	▸ When threats materialize: Minimize their impact on the enterprise by providing means to contain their propagation.
Education	▸ Provide technology tools to remove materialized threats.
Enhancement	▸ Monitor and evaluate your solutions to assess their effectiveness. ▸ If a failure occurs, determine the best approach to prevent a repeat, and either implement a change or provide a new capability.

Figure 12.4   Use a life-cycle strategy to protect IT assets.

Avoid Techno-Babble: Talk in Business Terms

Keep in mind that business and IT management will react better if you govern your approach with the basic tenets of business risk management (e.g., low risk/ low investment, high risk/higher investment). Stay away from using IT security-focused terminology, which all too often resolves itself into techno-babble. This is not the language that upper-level business executives, who control the resources and expenditures, are comfortable with or react well to. If you don't do this right, you will lose their interest and support and be relegated to your history of fighting for a glacially progressive set of tactical, technical IT security fixes.

Many IT security programs have died in infancy because they focused on a narrow spectrum of short-lived technology fixes that had minimum or no real sustainable business risk reduction value.

Whose Plan Is IT?

To be successful in this process, you must create and market or sell an appropriate IT security strategy, a.k.a. strategic plan, which is tailored to your company's risk profile requirements and business operational needs. You may be pleasantly surprised that it is often easier to convene an appropriate IT and business management advisory council or committee to help you in this strategic planning process if you present them with a business risk management-based charter (or goals, objectives, etc.) that is couched in business terms, is measurable, and helps them achieve their business operational responsibilities.

One key aspect to keep in mind is your IT security strategy must integrate and evolve with your organization's operational business strategy. To ignore such integration and evolution is a quick path to loss of interest and support for your IT security strategy at the key level of executive management needed to initiate, drive, and sustain your IT security programs. If you do not directly link your IT security strategy to your organization's operational business strategy, then your best efforts may well become easily overwhelmed by the organization's natural tendency to resist change. To attain, maintain, and progressively evolve your IT security strategy to synchronize with very diverse and constantly changing operational business environments is a compelling and challenging aspect to sustaining an effective IT security strategy. In short, your IT security strategy must be able to demonstrate real and progressively measurable business value (e.g., return on investment) to the business and its operationally complex environments.

It is also very important to establish a broad base of IT and business management "ownership" (i.e., not just "support") of your company's IT security strategy. Lacking that support, the strategy will be nothing more than a random and disconnected set of IT security programs and projects. Although they may offer some level of protection, detection, and risk avoidance, it is highly unlikely that the business and IT will understand and buy-into the plan without measurable risk-reduction targets.

Implementing Your Strategy

When you plan to start implementing your strategy, consider that many of the related projects will span greater than one year. Many such projects have failed due to untimely planning and setting unreasonable time frames, which doom them to failure even before the projects start. To add realism to your projects, consider proofs of concept, prototypes, and limited pilots. This is especially true of emerging technology programs and projects. Especially when dealing with emerging technologies, you should consider measuring or benchmarking yourself against industry capabilities. It also is recommended that you continually review and measure your strategy against the appropriate security and controls standards such as ISO 17799/27001 or COBIT.

Recap

- The decade of just-in-time IT security solutions is past; now is the time for strategic planning and actions.
- Follow these steps to craft a strategy:
  - Identify and prioritize the threats to day-to-day business operations.

- Perform a vulnerability assessment to identify weaknesses in the business and IT infrastructure.
- Create and sell the strategic plan, tailored to your company's risk profile requirements and business needs.
- Establish a broad base of IT and business management ownership in the plan.
- Implement a realistic strategy with reasonable time frames.
- Consider small phased steps, e.g., proofs of concept or pilot projects
- Review the strategy against industry-accepted standards.
- Demonstrate and measure progress and ongoing business value.

Chapter 13

Extending the Enterprise's Governance Program to Information Risks

Rolf Moulton and Robert Coles

Background

Winds of change have been blowing through the corporate world since the Enron collapse. Corporate governance and accountability are now at the top of government and investor agendas — not just in the United States, but also throughout Europe and Asia. Chief executives' and corporate boards' responsibilities for control are increasingly demanding. The Sarbanes–Oxley Act will require all companies that are U.S. listed (this includes many of the UK's largest corporations) to include reporting on internal controls in their annual reports. The programs to achieve compliance with these and probable European-driven legislation are only just beginning. They will have a significant knock-on effect on technology, particularly security governance. And, financial institutions face the additional prospect of complying with the requirements of Basel II.

This may seem like a very dry subject, but the reality is that governance failures could mean damaged careers, and no chief executive wants to see serious failures on his or her watch. In this litigious age the result could be shareholder lawsuits or corporate collapse. Similarly for the IT director or head of security, failure to establish effective governance can have serious implications. On a personal level, security governance means making sure that you have applied sufficient rigor to safeguard your organization — and your career.

Security Governance

Despite the consequences of failure, security governance is still a mess. It is poorly understood and ill-defined, and therefore means different things to different people. So what is it? Is it a security policy, a framework, a security program — or all of these? If we take a lead from some of the experts in the field of corporate and IT governance, we can perhaps apply their principles to security.

The IT Governance Institute defines enterprise governance as the "set of responsibilities and practices exercised by the board and executive management with the goal of providing strategic direction, ensuring that objectives are achieved, ascertaining that risks are managed appropriately and verifying that the enterprise's resources are used responsibly." In this context, governance focuses on managing the organization and making the best use of its resources. Others have different views, such as the OECD, which focuses more on the maintenance of the balance of power between the managers of an organization and its investors.

If we accept that security governance is a subset of corporate or enterprise governance, then by extending the definitions above, it could include the following:

- Security responsibilities and practices
- Strategies/objectives for security
- Risk assessment and management
- Resource management for security
- Compliance with legislation, regulations, security policies, and rules
- Investor relations and communications activity (in relation to security)

This could end up as a never-ending list of activities that define anything and everything to do with security. It gets even more complicated when you look at what is the scope of security. Does it cover information security? IT security? Physical security? Fraud, internal audit, compliance, insurance, etc.?

So let's put a stake in the ground: Our definition of information security governance is "the establishment and maintenance of the control environment to manage the risks relating to the confidentiality, integrity, and availability of information and its supporting processes and systems." This is separate from:

- Audit (ensuring that governance processes have been properly established and are functioning)
- Security operations (day-to-day performance of security administrative activities)

- Security development (engineering of new IT or processes to meet security objectives)

Does any of this really matter? Until last year there was no such term as *security governance* and we got on with our jobs well enough without it, so why does it matter now? Well, it matters now for three reasons: it matters for enterprise risk management; it matters that we have a defensible position, one that allows us to have an intelligent discussion and defense with shareholders and regulators; and it matters for the continuing development of the information security profession.

As an expansion on why it matters:

- For risk management, the executive management of the enterprise (ENT$_{MGT}$): The board members, CEO, chief counsel, and chief auditor need to identify security risks that could have a significant negative impact on the enterprise. It then needs to ensure that potential losses that could arise from these risks do not exceed the enterprise pain threshold (EPT), which is the financial or other indicator point established by the ENT$_{MGT}$.

- For discussion and defense of management practices and controls, it is essential to be able to define what the enterprise seeks to do; how it controls the processes that it uses; how it ensures the integrity of the records that are used by, and result from, its business processes, as well as how it manages or provides for losses that could significantly damage or destroy the enterprise. Although there is no overall security regulator seeking these explanations at the present time, many of the industry regulators such as financial services, food and drug, and health regulators now take a closer look at security governance. Consequently, ENT$_{MGT}$ will need to be able to explain what is and has been done to them in relevant concepts and terms. This would be especially important where it may be necessary to influence them regarding enterprise or industry views and practices, or if it is necessary to defend existing practices and controls.

- For the information security profession (albeit a new and developing one), practitioners need know where the scope and boundaries lie. These help us to form and develop the profession; they help us to recognize what is within and what is external to our profession; and they also help us to have an intelligent dialogue with other colleagues who may have an interest in our work (such as auditors and risk managers). These, in turn, help with our daily jobs as security managers — they help with recruitment, with development of business cases, and with knowing what we are responsible for!

Putting Theory into Practice

We would like to suggest how the information security governance concept could be applied at the enterprise level to establish and maintain an adequate control environment. To do this, we will use an example to:

■ Identify an enterprise-level information risk
■ Assign responsibility for managing that risk
■ Implement and manage controls

Identification of Enterprise-Level Risks (ENT$_{RISK}$)

ENT$_{MGT}$ are the only people who can identify which risks are enterprise-level risks. Because they are, by definition, enterprise-level risks, they will own them as the primary risk owner. These risks, and their associated controls, are also likely to be directly managed by a secondary risk owner(s) as assigned by ENT$_{MGT}$.

As a specific risk example:

$$ENT_{RISK} = \text{Adequacy of enterprise financial information controls}$$

The enterprise's financial information systems do not have adequate controls to manage the enterprise's financial assets in a manner that meets the management, public reporting, and regulatory requirements.

As with all enterprise-level risks, by definition, these will be risks that could exceed the enterprise's pain threshold. For information risks, they will involve confidentiality, integrity, and availability, and for convenience, they will be designated respectively as EPT$_C$, EPT$_I$, and EPT$_A$.

EPT$_C$ risks include those where sensitive information in the system *could* be:

■ Accessed by people or processes that are not authorized to do so
■ Disclosed by people or processes without authorization to do so
■ Or disclosed by people or processes prior to an authorized disclosure date

The direct impact to the enterprise (as measured by the EPT$_C$) of an information confidentiality failure *could* include:

■ Action against the enterprise by stockholders and regulatory authorities
■ Insider trading allegations
■ Damage to share price of the enterprise
■ Damage to the share price of companies doing business with the enterprise

EPT$_I$ risks include those where significant information in the system *could* be:

- Accessed by people or processes that are not authorized to do so
- Modified and deleted by people or processes without authorization to do so
- Or deleted by people or processes that are not authorized to do so

The direct impact to the enterprise (as measured by the EPT_I) of an information integrity failure *could* include:

- All of the confidentiality impacts
- Significant incorrect decisions being taken based on incorrect information
- Significant loss of money related to incorrect decisions being taken

EPT_A risks are those where the business process cannot function because the information or the information system is not available for use by authorized persons or processes when it is needed. The direct impact to the enterprise (as measured by the EPT_A) of an information or IT resources availability failure *could* include:

- Significant decisions related to cash management may be delayed or not taken
- Significant required corporate reporting may be delayed or missed
- Share price value may be reduced significantly
- Shareholder and regulatory actions may be initiated against the enterprise

Assignment of Risk Management Responsibilities

For our example, the management of this risk is delegated by ENT_{MGT} to the enterprise's controller (or in some organizations it may be the financial director) as the secondary risk owner because the financial information systems are part of the controller's business information process/operations. This assignment of responsibility includes making sure that the risk is managed within an appropriate control environment and keeping enterprise management advised that the risk is being managed adequately, or advising otherwise if it is not being managed adequately.

Implement Appropriate and Reasonable Controls to Manage the Risk

As noted above, the controller, as the financial information business process owner, would be expected to ensure that appropriate controls to manage the risk(s) are in place. In this example, the controls would be implemented within an information protection program that will secure the confidentiality, integrity, and availability of the information and IT assets.

To meet the delegated risk management responsibility, the controller would need to make sure that an adequate general controls environment is in place, and that specific appropriate and reasonable controls are defined and implemented, and are working effectively. For commercial enterprises, in contrast to national governments, expectations as to what may be "appropriate and reasonable" may vary significantly, and some security failures might be "acceptable" or tolerated if there are adequate liability mitigation measures in place.

Therefore, to meet information security governance requirements, the definition of "appropriate and reasonable controls" should be:

■ Specific to the enterprise's industry and operating environment
■ In compliance with what the enterprise had communicated as privacy expectations to those people whose personal information is to be used as part of its operations
■ In compliance with the enterprise management's interpretation of legal and regulatory requirements

Implementing and ensuring the ongoing effectiveness of both the general and specific controls could be addressed as part of a business process information risk management (BPIRM) approach. Coles and Moulton suggest a BPIRM approach in *C&S*, volume 22 number 6. Their BPIRM approach recommends that the business process owner understand the real risks that may arise as a result of the process and the information that it uses, that there be absolute clarity of responsibilities for who is managing the controls related to these risks throughout all aspects of the process. (This is different from actually managing the people, processes, and technology that comprise an information protection program.)

In short, it is our view that to support fully and meet the objectives of information security governance, the information protection program should provide a reasonable level of assurance that it:

■ Operates within the enterprise's expectations for a general operating controls environment
■ Meets, and continues to meet, the risk owner's specifically stated control expectations, including expected loss containment/mitigation and recovery positions in the event of a disruption or a security failure
■ Provides a defensible position for ENT_{MGT} if information or information systems are used in a manner which causes or results in a loss (or losses), or if the adequacy of the ENT's information controls is challenged by shareholders, or by a legal, civil, or regulatory authority. And, it should be able to do so in generally understandable concepts and terms.

Recap

- New legal requirements have significantly changed enterprise management's governance responsibilities.
- An information security governance approach can provide a better framework, meet new requirements to manage risks within the enterprise, communicate more effectively within the enterprise as well as with external parties, including regulators, and to further the security profession by clearly establishing governance and protection roles and responsibilities.
- Implementing an information security governance program starts with enterprise management identifying the full scope and context of the real risks that the enterprise is up against, and includes the process for managing those risks.
- Absolute clarity of primary and secondary risk ownership and management responsibilities is essential to understand and appropriately contain and minimize the impact(s) of a possible control failure.
- Both primary and secondary risk owners must demand that the enterprise's information protection program provides the opportunity and ability for them to be directly involved in the governance loop to make certain that appropriate and cost effective controls are implemented and continue to function as intended.

Note

The material in this chapter is based on "Moulton, R. and Coles, R. S. (2003). Applying information security governance, *Computers & Security,* Vol. 22 (7)."

Chapter 14

Building Management Commitment through Security Councils

Todd Fitzgerald

One of the most common concerns voiced at the various security conferences and security associations around the country is, "How do we get our management to understand the importance of information security?" Individuals who have been unable to secure the attention or financial commitment from the senior leadership of their respective organizations typically voice these concerns. The question is usually accompanied with frustration as a result of multiple attempts to obtain budget, only to be faced with flat budgets, cuts to the current expenditure levels, or the elimination of separate information security budgets. Although each organization has different values, principles, and strategies to move the business forward in a secure manner, this article explores some techniques for building management commitment through the implementation of a successful information security council. Experience indicates that security councils are excellent mechanisms for establishing buy-in across middle management, senior management, and the end users of the organization.

Establishing the Security Council

The information security council forms the backbone for sustaining organizational support for comprehensive information security programs. Additionally, the security council serves as the oversight or governance function for the information security program. The vision of the security council must be clearly defined and understood by all members of the council. Before the appropriate representation of the council can be decided, the purpose of the council must be decided upon. Although the primary purpose is to provide oversight for the security program and provide a mechanism to sustain the organizational security initiatives, the purpose that will be most meaningful to the specific organization will depend upon the current organizational culture and the maturity of information security practices, as discussed in other sections of this book.

A clear vision statement should be in alignment with and support the organizational vision. Typically, the statement would draw upon the security concepts of confidentiality, integrity, and availability to support the business objectives. The vision statement is not technical and should focus on the advantages to the business. People will be involved in the council from management and technical areas and have limited time to participate, so the vision statement must be something that is viewed as contributing to the business. The vision statement should be short, to the point, and achievable.

Mission statements are objectives that support the overall vision. These become the road map to achieving the vision and help the council clearly view the purpose for its involvement. Some individuals may choose nomenclature such as goals, objectives, and initiatives. A sample mission statement is shown in Figure 14.1. Effective mission statements do not need to be lengthy, as the primary objective is to communicate the goals so those technical and nontechnical individuals readily understand them. The primary mission of the security council will vary by organization, but should include statements that address:

- *Security program oversight:* By establishing this goal in the beginning, the members of the council begin to feel that they have some input and influence over the direction of the security program. This is key, as many security decisions will impact their areas of operation. This also is the beginning of management commitment at the committee level, as the deliverables produced through the information security program now become "recommended or approved" by the security council versus the Information Security Department.
- *Decide on project initiatives:* Each organization has limited resources, i.e., time, money, and people, to allocate across projects to advance the business. The primary objective of information security projects is to reduce the organizational business risk through the implementation of reasonable controls.

The Information Security Council provides management direction and a sounding board for the ACME Company's information security efforts to ensure that these efforts are:

Appropriately prioritized

Supported by each organizational unit

Appropriately funded

Realistic given ACME's information security needs

Balance security needs to be made between cost, response time, ease of use, flexibility, and time to market.

The Information Security Council takes an active role in enhancing our security profile and increasing the protection of our assets through:

Approval of organizational-wide information security initiatives

Coordination of various workgroups so that security goals can be achieved

Promoting awareness of initiatives within their organizations

Discussion of security ideas, policies, and procedures and their impact on the organization

Recommendation of policies to the ACME Company IT Steering Committee

Increased understanding of the threats, vulnerabilities, and safeguards facing our organization

Active participation in policy, procedure, and standard review

The ACME Company Information Technology Steering Committee supports the Information Security Council by:

Developing the strategic vision for the deployment of Information Technology

Establishing priorities, arranging resources in concert with the vision

Approval of the recommended policies, standards, and guidelines

Approving major capital expenditures

Figure 14.1   Sample security council mission statement.

The council should take an active role in understanding the initiatives and the resulting "business" impact.

■ *Prioritize information security efforts:* Once the security council understands the proposed project initiatives and the associated positive impact to the business, it can be involved with the prioritization of the projects. This may be in the form of a formal annual process or may be through the discussion and expressed support for individual initiatives.

■ *Review and recommend security policies:* Review of the security policies should occur through a line-by-line review of the policy, a cursory review of the procedures to support the policies, and review of the implementation and subsequent enforcement of the policies. Through this activity, three key concepts are implemented that are important to sustaining commitment:

1. Understanding of the policy is enhanced.
2. Practical ability of the organization to support the policy is discussed.
3. Buy-in is established for subsequent support of implementation activities.

- *Champion organizational security efforts:* Once the council understands and accepts the policies, it serves as the organization's champion behind the policies. Why? Because the council was involved in the *creation* of the policies. The council may have started reviewing a draft of the policy created by the Information Systems Security Department, but the resulting product was accomplished only through council review, input, and participation in the process. The security leader must involve the business areas in the creation of policies to create ownership of the deliverable, which generates a desire to see the security policy or project succeed within the company.
- *Recommend areas requiring investment:* Members of the council have the opportunity to provide input from the perspective of their individual business units. The council serves as a mechanism for establishing broad support for security investments from this perspective. Resources within any organization are limited and allocated to the business units with the greatest need and the greatest perceived return on investment. Establishing this support enhances the budgetary understanding of the other business managers, as well as the chief financial officer, which is essential when obtaining the appropriate funding.

A mission statement that incorporates the previous concepts will help focus the council and also provide the sustaining purpose for its involvement. The vision and mission statements should also be reviewed on an annual basis to ensure that the council is still functioning according to the values expressed in the mission statement, as well as to ensure that new and replacement members are in alignment with the objectives of the council.

Appropriate Security Council Representation

The security council should be made up of representatives from multiple organizational units that are necessary to support the policies in the long term. Possible participants include the following:

- The Human Resources Department is essential to provide knowledge of the existing code of conduct, employment and labor relations, termination, and disciplinary action policies and practices that are in place.
- The Legal Department is needed to ensure that the language of the policies is stating what is intended, and that applicable local, state, and federal laws are appropriately followed.
- The Information Technology Department provides technical input and information on current initiatives and the development of procedures and technical implementations to support the policies.

- The individual business unit representation is essential to understand how practical the policies may be in carrying out the mission of the business.
- Compliance Department representation provides insight on ethics, contractual obligations, and investigations that may require policy creation.
- And finally, the security officer, who typically chairs the council, should represent the Information Security Department and members of the security team for specialized technical expertise.

The security council should be comprised primarily of management-level employees, preferably middle management. It is difficult to obtain the time commitment required to review policies at a detailed level by senior management. Reviewing the policies at this level is a necessary step to achieve buy-in within management; however, it would not be a good use of the senior management level in the early stages of development. Line management is very focused on their individual areas and may not have the organizational perspective necessary (beyond their individual departments) to evaluate security policies and project initiatives. Middle managers appear to be in the best position to appropriately evaluate what is best for the organization, as well as possessing the ability to influence senior and line management to accept the policies. Where middle management does not exist, then it is appropriate to include line management, as they are typically filling both of these roles (middle and line functions) when operating in these positions.

The information security officer (ISO) or the chief information security officer (CISO) should chair the security council. The ISO is in a better position knowledge-wise to chair the council; however, politically it may be advantageous for the chief information officer (CIO) to chair the council, where they may be able to better communicate support through the information technology department. It is our experience that the stronger argument is for the council to be chaired by the ISO, as it provides for better separation of duties and avoids the "chicken in the hen house" perception if the CIO chairs the council. This is true even if the ISO does not report through the information technology organization. In addition to the ISO, the council should also have 1 to 2 members of the systems security department available to (1) provide technical security expertise and (2) understand the business concerns so that solutions can be appropriately designed.

Many issues may be addressed in a single security council meeting, which necessitates having someone record the minutes of the meeting. Because the chairperson's role in the meeting is to facilitate the discussion, ensure that all viewpoints are heard, and drive the discussions to decisions where necessary, another participant should record the proceedings. Recording the meeting is also helpful to capture key points that may have been missed in the notes, so that accurate minutes are produced.

"Ing'ing" the Council: Forming, Storming, Norming, and Performing

Every now and then, an organization will recognize that collaboration is not taking place between the functional departments and it is time to talk about enhancing the team development process. This is usually the result of poor or no communication between the departments. Why wait for the problems to occur? When committees are formed, they are not magically functional the moment they are formed, but rather must go through a series of necessary steps to become an operational team. Following are the classical four phases of team development:

1. Forming
2. Storming
3. Norming
4. Performing

Let's review each of the concepts briefly and see how they apply to the security council:

- *Forming:* This is the stage where the efforts are moving from an individual to a team effort. Individuals may be excited about belonging to something new that will make a positive change. The tasks at hand and role of the council are decided (as described earlier). Teams should be communicating openly and honestly about their likes and dislikes, deciding what information needs to be gathered to carry out their mission, and should be engaging in activities which build trust and communication with each other. It is critical to draw out the responses of those who may appear to be "silent" in the meetings, as they may be thinking some very valuable thoughts, but may be afraid at this stage that their ideas may be rejected. It is important to have patience at this stage and "let the team" form and not rush the discussion. The leader must serve as a facilitator for bringing the parties together, but not be overly authoritative, as that can jeopardize or slow down the buy-in process.
- *Storming:* Now that the objectives are understood and the team has had the chance to discuss some of the challenges that it is tasked to resolve, doubt may settle in. Some members may become resistant to the tasks and return to their old comfort zones. Communication between members starts to erode and different sections of the team form alliances to counter-positions. The team becomes divided and there is minimal collaboration between the individuals. At this stage, it may be necessary to reestablish or change the rules of behavior for the council, negotiate the roles and responsibilities between the council members, and possibly return to the forming stage to answer any open questions about the purpose and clarity of the council. And finally, listen to the concerns of the council members and let them vent any frustrations; they may have some very valid concerns that need to be addressed to

be successful. The leader must continue to re-emphasize the importance of the security council and the importance of gaining alignment with objectives that everyone can "live with." Specific frustrations of members should be explored, and brainstorming sessions with the entire council should be engaged in to resolve the frustrations. The leader must recognize that this dissension is a critical step for individuals to feel that their individual concerns will be heard and reacted to during the long-term operation of the council.

■ *Norming:* At this stage the members of the council begin to accept their roles, the rules of behavior, their role on the team, and respect the individual contributions that others on the team can provide. Now wouldn't it be nice if the "storming" stage could be skipped and the security council just moved to this stage? Think of a child learning to ice skate. The concept of ice skating is explained in vague terms such as, "Put these skates on your feet, then stand up, and skate around the rink." The child has an idea of how this works because he or she has seen others skating and it looks pretty easy. However, when the child stands up, he's in for a big surprise ... boom! The same applies for teams: as much as individuals have seen other teams' success, worked on other teams, until the issues are worked on, the team cannot feel how bad the fall will hurt until this particular team falls down. As the norming stage progresses, competitive relationships may become more cooperative, more sharing is present, the sense of "we are a team" evolves, and the team members feel more comfortable working together. This stage of development should focus on detailed planning, creation of criteria for completion of goals, and continuing to encourage the team to build upon the positive behaviors demonstrated within the team and change the unhealthy ones. The leader must seize the opportunity provided during the team "norming stage" to focus on meaningful work. The council will lose patience if there are still discussions in this stage about what the vision statement should be, as the council has limited time and needs now to see progress toward the objectives.

■ *Performing:* The team is now functioning as a unit focused on the objectives of the security council. The team has the best opportunity at this stage to meet deadlines, utilize each member's unique talents, and produce quality deliverables. The members of the team have gained insight into the unique contributions of everyone on the team and recognize that the team can accomplish much more than any one individual on the team. The leader must recognize in this stage that the council can slip back into earlier stages if individual concerns are ignored. Council members also may change over time and new council members need to be assimilated into the process.

The security council may be formed in a day, but does not become a team in a day. Understanding the path that every team traverses can be helpful in knowing where the team is currently functioning, as well as to permit the application of strategies to move the team to the next stage. Depending on the organizational culture and the individuals involved, the security council may become a functioning team within weeks or months. What is important is that the commitment to getting to the team stage has a level of persistence and perseverance equal to the passion to build a successful security program within the organization.

Integration with Other Committees

As indicated earlier, management has limited time to be involved in efforts that may not seem to be directly related to its department. Examine the performance objectives and performance reviews of the management of most organizations, and it becomes readily apparent that the majority of the performance rewards are based on the objectives of the individual department's goals. There is typically little incentive for participating to "enhance the corporate good" even though that may be communicated by the organization's vision, mission, goals, and objective statements. Therefore, committees where there is not a direct benefit or their involvement is not seen as critical will be met with a lukewarm reception.

So when the information security department decides to "add a few more committees," this is likely to be met with resistance. A practical approach is to leverage the committees that are already established, such as an information technology steering committee, electronic commerce committee, standards committee, a senior management leadership committee, or other committee that has a history of holding regularly scheduled (and attended!) meetings. Tapping into these committees and getting 30 minutes on the agenda reserved specifically for security will provide ample airtime for security issues and the appropriate linkage to the company decision makers. In committees such as the information technology steering committee many of the issues discussed have information security issues embedded within them and being present provides the mechanism to be at the table for these issues.

Because the time allocated for discussing information security issues tends to decrease as the management chain is traversed to higher levels of management, it is important to ensure that the security council is well established and performing in the norming or performing stages. Participation at the higher levels should be limited to review, discussion, communication of initiatives, and primarily decision making (approval of policies and projects). The senior management stamp of approval is necessary to win broad organizational support and is a key component for successful implementation. If the security council does not perceive that the recommendations are important to the senior leadership, it will lose interest. If the senior leadership does not approve the security policies, organizational management and staff support will also dissipate. Therefore, it is important to get on the agenda and stay on the agenda for every meeting. This also creates the (desired) perception that security is an ongoing business process necessary to implement the business objectives.

Once it is decided which committees would be the best candidates for integration, then the process for how the committees will function together needs to be decided. Is the IT steering committee the mechanism for policy and project approval? Is there a dollar threshold required for its approval? How are changes to the security policies made at this level? Do they go back to the security council for re-review, or are they changed and considered final at this point? Much of this will depend on each individual cultural norm of how teams and committees function.

Establish Early, Incremental Success

Organizations tend to get behind individuals and departments that have demonstrated success in their initiatives because they believe that the next initiative will also be successful. Organizations lose patience for 15-to-18-month initiatives (these tend to be labeled as long-term strategies these days). Projects should be divided into smaller discrete deliverables versus trying to implement the entire effort. This allows the organization to reap the benefits of the earlier implementation while waiting for the results of the longer-term initiative. The early initiative may also help shape or redefine the longer-term initiative through the early lessons learned.

The early initiatives should provide some benefit to the organization by making their processes easier, enabling new business functionality, providing faster turnaround, reducing paper handling, and making more efficient or effective processes. The primary objective should not be something that benefits the information security department, but rather provides benefit to the business (although it most likely will provide information security benefit even though this is not the "sell"). Management may be skeptical that the investment in information security will produce an equal amount of benefits. Nothing helps future funding opportunities more than establishing a track record of (1) developing projects that contribute to the business objectives, (2) establishing cost-effective aggressive implementation schedules, (3) delivering on time, (4) delivering within budget, and (5) delivering what was promised (at a minimum).

Let Go of Perfectionism

Imagine being a dancer of 15 years, dancing since you were 2½ years old, practicing a couple of nights a week, learning jazz and ballet. Imagine the hours of commitment to a discipline that makes movements that would be difficult for most of us appear to be purposeful, graceful, and flow with ease. Imagine that it is the big night for showcasing this enormous talent, the recital, and the dancer is rightfully filled with excitement in anticipation of performing in front of friends and family. As the curtain rises, and the dancers are set to begin the performance, a dancer's hairpiece falls off. Oh no, what to do? Does the dancer stop and pick up the hairpiece? Do the dancers look at the floor to avoid stepping on the hairpiece? Does the dancer break into tears, stop, and say, "I messed up"? No, none of the above. Although it is preferred that the dancers firmly attach their hairpieces, and that is what was planned for and practiced, in the scope of the dance, it is not a big deal. In fact, few people in the audience would actually notice it unless it was pointed out by the dancer. The dancer dances on, smiling with great pride, demonstrating the skill that she has possessed to the audience's delight.

We should all strive to perform to the best of our ability. The argument could be made that the security profession is made up of many individuals who are primarily detail-oriented, are control-oriented, analytical, and logical decision makers. These personality preferences suit the profession very well, as these attributes are many times necessary to master the information security skills. However, one of the traits also represented by the profession is that of perfectionism, the need to "get it right," "do the right thing." Security professionals often speak in terms of "musts" and "wills" versus "shoulds" and "mights." For example, imagine a written policy that would state, "As an employee, you may choose to create an eight-character password made up of a combination of letters, numbers, special characters, or you may choose something with less characters if you have a hard time remembering it. If KATE123 or your dog's name is easier to remember, then just use that." That would be absurd — we tell users not only the rules, but how to implement them, and that they must do that action.

Carrying the perfectionist standard forward into every project is a recipe for failure. First of all, resulting project costs will be higher trying to get everything right. Second, the time to implement will be longer and opportunities to create the business benefit when needed may be missed.

When other individuals across the business units are asked to participate in security initiatives, they may not have a complete understanding of what is expected of them, and some tolerance for this gap in understanding should be accounted for. It may be that they believe that they are supplying the right level of support or are completing the deliverables accurately, given their knowledge of what was communicated to them. The minimum expected deliverable for security initiatives should be that if 80 percent of the goal is completed, then the risk absorbed by the company is considered as reasonable. Achieving the remaining 20 percent should be viewed as the component which, if implemented, would return increased benefits and opportunities, but not necessary to achieve the minimum level of risk desired. Taking this posture permits the information security initiatives to drive toward perfection, but not require attainment of complete perfection to maintain a reasonable risk level. This approach keeps the costs of security implementations in balance with the reduction of risk objectives.

Sustaining the Security Council

Humpty Dumpty sat on the wall, Humpty Dumpty had a great … well, we know the rest of this story. Putting the pieces back together again is much more difficult than "planning for the fall." As mentioned previously in "Ing'ing the Council," the team will go through various stages. Frustration, boredom, impatience, and inertia may set in as the sizes of the efforts are realized or roles in the process become blurred. When we know that something is likely to occur, it is much easier to deal with. Understanding that these events will occur can be helpful to the leader of the security council to continue the mission and not give up hope. Members of the organization may view the security council as a vehicle to deposit their security issues for resolution. Alternatively, the council may be viewed as a committee that produces no tangible benefits and consumes the most valuable resource — time. The truth is that both views will exist simultaneously within the organization based on how the council personally affects each person's individual role. There will be periods where individuals will become disinterested, and it may be necessary to bring some new blood into the council, thereby expanding the knowledge of the council. It is also a good practice to periodically bring new individuals into the council to inject new ideas and skills to the team. As this is done, it is important to revisit the mission and vision steps as this person and the rest of the team (with respect to the new individual) is repeating the forming, storming, norming, and performing process.

End-User Awareness

The existence of the security council and the relationships with the other committees should be embedded in the security awareness training for every end user within the organization. By establishing the message that the security policies are business decisions (versus information technology decisions emanating from the Information Systems Security Department), there is likely to be greater acceptance for their implementation. If the message is constructed in such a way that it is clear that middle management and senior management have reviewed and agree with all of the policies line by line, this can be a very powerful message. Line managers and supervisors are less likely to ignore the policies, as they understand that the directives are coming from management and not another functional unit, which they consider to be their peer. This assumes that the organization is following the necessary practice of training all management with the security training as well as the end users.

If there are multiple organizational units participating in the policy development/review process in addition to the security council (i.e., IT steering committees, executive leadership team reviews, focused business and or technical workgroups), then the relationships between these committees and their associated functions should be explained in concise terms at a high level. For example, if the role of the security council is to review and recommend policies to the IT steering committee, which approves the policies, then state these basic functions so that the end users understand the role. If the role of the security council is to establish the security strategy for the organization, prioritize projects, and implement the mission through these initiatives, then state that as well. The advantage to having the end users understand the role of the security council is three-fold: (1) helping them to understand how these policies are created, (2) conveying that their management is involved in the direction of information security (versus security mandates), and (3) providing individual understanding to keep their own management in line with the security policies!

Is end-user awareness of the security council's existence really a critical success factor? To answer that question, we need to look no further than what the ultimate goal of a security program should be — to have every user of an organization's information protect it with the same diligence as if it was the purse around their shoulder or the wallet in their back pocket. The answer is, you bet! Although they may not need to understand the working dynamics of the security council, they do need to understand that the organizational structure exists, is operating, and is effective at balancing the needs of security and the need to operate the business.

Establishing the security council may be seen as threatening to some managers at first, as it means that now some decisions will not be made by the security manager/director/officer, but rather by the security council. Some security leaders may not want that sort of insight into or control of their activities. However, to be truly effective and truly maintain management commitment, the continued participation by business unit managers is essential. This can also be established informally without a security council, but the time commitment is much greater and the collaboration between the business unit managers is less likely to occur.

The security council is not the answer to resolving all of the management commitment issues, as there will always be other business drivers impacting the decisions. Mergers and acquisitions may put security efforts on hold. Debates over the constraints of the technology on the business operations may stall projects. Budget constraints due to a drop in sales volume or public sector funding may preclude security investments. Acceptance of risk by insurance or outsourcing initiatives may change the company's security posture. Other company high-priority projects may consume the needed internal resources for security projects. Each of these can serve to limit the information security focus and related investments. These are normal events in the course of business. However, consider the individual responsible for information security having to address these issues alone (lack of management commitment) versus acting on these issues with the collaboration of the security council (supportive management commitment), and the advantages of the security council can be readily appreciated.

Final Thoughts

The word *commitment*, according to the *Merriam-Webster Dictionary of Law*, is defined as "an agreement or promise to do something in the future." According to the *Merriam-Webster Medical Dictionary*, *commitment* is defined as "a consignment to a penal or mental institution." As security practitioners, hopefully we would agree that the former definition is much preferred over the latter! Alternatively, if we fail to get the lawyers' definition of commitment, we might end up with the medical definition of commitment!

Management commitment is not something that can be held, touched, or seen, but rather, it is a state of being. It is also a current state, subject to change at any moment. The level of commitment is arrived at by management's memory of historical events that led up to the present and paves the path for the future. If these experiences have not been good, then their commitment to spending large investments on future security initiatives will also not be good. Therefore, appropriate care must be taken to deliver on the promises made through the security council by the security team, information technology departments and the business unit representatives, or the next project will not be met with enthusiasm. Security councils are an essential element to building management commitment, and continued delivery provides the necessary oxygen to keep the council functioning.

Commitment is the two-way street — if commitment is expected from management, once it is obtained, the security program must also be committed to deliver on the expectations agreed upon. Doing less makes withdrawals from the goodwill that has been established, doing more creates increased satisfaction and confirmation that the investment choices supported by management were, in fact, the right choices. This also increases their trust in their own ability to make decisions supporting the security program.

Finally, each security officer should evaluate his or her own commitment to enhancing the security of the organization and the current cultural view towards security. Where does the organization stand? It will feel uncomfortable at first to establish the council, but it is well worth the effort. So assemble the security champions from legal, information technology, human resources, the individual business units, and begin. Today.

Recap

- The security council provides an excellent mechanism to serve as a sounding board for the information security program and test the vision, mission, strategies, goals, and objectives initiated by the security department.
- The security council is an excellent mechanism for establishing buy-in across middle management and subsequently senior management and the end users of the organization.

- Without a security council, the information security officer is working in isolation, trying to move initiatives forward obtaining business management support one person at a time.
- The security council is much more effective in establishing the necessary collaboration and ensuring that all points of view are provided a chance to be expressed.
- The security council must produce some early successes to sustain the commitment of the individuals, each of whom has limited time that could be expended elsewhere. When it comes to committee involvement, people have a choice. Yes, it may be possible to get the individuals to physically show up for a few meetings, but to win their hearts and active participation, there must be a purpose that the council is driving toward. There will be periods of time where this purpose may not be clear; however, the council must still be sustained by the leader's belief in the value of the council and the creation of activities where decisions are needed.

Chapter 15

Measuring Security

William Hugh Murray

Abstract: This chapter will discuss useful metrics that can be applied to security. The subtext is that security is inadequately measured, and that for our purposes it must be well measured. These metrics will include state, progress, activity, service level, attack traffic, losses, spending (planned and unplanned), compliance, effectiveness, and efficiency.

Introduction

Science tells us that unless one can measure something, one cannot recognize its presence or its absence. This often surprises those who treat security as binary, present or not, secure or insecure. We do not seem to have good metrics for IT in general and IT security in particular. Historically, only the most mature IT and security programs have been measured in the same way that we measure other business functions like design, assembly, and distribution. Such mature programs are few and far between.

However, measurement is essential to our effectiveness, success, and to our being recognized as successful. It is one way that we communicate our accomplishments to our peers and superiors.

Why Do We Not Measure?

Although we have usually measured security programs, e.g., number of services provided, we have not measured their effectiveness. We have not measured the security of the enterprise.

In part, we thought that security was not material, that the difference between secure and insecure was not significant or material, that it had little or no significance to the profitability of the enterprise, that it did not "hit the bottom line." When one suggested that security should pay, security people were among the first to howl. Instead we relied upon anecdotes to talk to management about what we did and how effective we were.

Many of us tend to think of security as binary, as a state or condition, achieved and maintained or not. We see it as a point rather than as a vector with length that we can measure. When there was one system, scaled to the enterprise, we saw it as secure or not rather than more or less secure than some other system. Both the single-system paradigm and by the language trapped us, i.e., "security," a condition that applied to an application in the system environment.

Historically, we did not measure security because it was an immature business function. Indeed, we can recognize the maturity of a business function by the fact that it is measured. In part we have not measured because we did not know how or what to measure. In large part, we have not measured because we never started; we did not start because we did not know how or where to start. Even when we were ready to start, we were often stymied by trying to measure the immeasurable. This chapter intends to address that.

What Can We Not Measure?

"Enterprise Security"

We cannot directly measure the "security" of the enterprise. It is an abstraction, sometimes defined by policy, sometimes not. There is no direct metric. Instead, one judges it indirectly from what one can measure.

Trust

Trust is similarly abstract. It is best recognized by its absence. However, there is no way to measure it directly. Generally, trust in a network, system, application, person, or enterprise is granted in the context of a relationship and a purpose. One may trust a network or system for one purpose, but not for another. One might trust one's personal computer to protect one's personal data, but not a database of personal data of others. Trust defies measurement.

Single Systems

Measuring the single system was the effort that first discouraged measurement. The measurement was seen as one or zero, most often zero. It was not sufficiently granular to be of any use.

Cost of Losses

Finally, we cannot measure losses, at least locally or in the short term. Locally and in the short term, losses are so sparse and irregular that they cannot be measured.

What Can We Measure?

There are a number of things that we can and should measure. These include system state, not of single systems, but across populations of systems. We can measure compliance with expectations and progress toward compliance. We can measure cost and spending. We can measure the cost of programs, losses, prevention, and remediation. We can measure attack traffic, successful versus prevented attacks, and the time to detect and remediate. We can measure service level and customer satisfaction. We can measure risk and risk acceptance.

Having said that we can measure such things raises questions.

State

One can measure the state of each network, system, and application. Although one cannot measure its "security," one can measure things that are related to its security and compare them to similar objects. First, one can identify all networks, network segments, systems attached to each of those network segments. One can identify the networks in which each system participates. One can identify the applications for each of those systems, e.g., whether it is a server or a personal computer. If it is a server, one can identify whether it is an application, database, file, print, or other kind of server.

One can ensure that each system is properly configured for its application, that there is a properly configured firewall and current anti-virus protection. We can measure:

- Network (e.g., LAN segments, address range(s))
- System (SN, type and model)
- Applications (e.g., personal, application, server, proxy, gateway, firewall, etc.)
- Operating systems (OS)
- Currency

- OS version
- Patches applied
- Anti-virus (date and version of last update)
- Firewalls (hardware, software)

Populations of Systems

Although one cannot only describe the state of single systems and compare that state to that of others in a similar environment and performing similar applications, one can say much more about populations.

Compliance

Like any other aspect of security, one cannot recognize compliance with law, regulation, contract and other agreements, policy, standards, essential practices, guidelines, and required procedures without measuring them. In practice, many enterprises measure these things late, that is, they are measured exclusively by the auditors. One problem with this is that the measured functions spend the time between audits correcting variances. Often, all variances are treated the same without any priority.

One can measure compliance with law, regulation, contract, policy, standards, essential practices, guidelines, and procedures. This is what auditors do. However, they do it at a point in time; staff should do so routinely. The auditor spends a great deal of time and energy identifying that with which the enterprise must comply. It is telling that auditors most often, not to say always, discover these expectations themselves; they have not been documented, much less measured, in advance by staff. If the security program has not done this in advance, compliance will be ad hoc, not to say sparse. In such cases the auditors find that compliance is limited and is more accidental than by design and intent. Management and staff then spend the time between audits responding to them.

If compliance is to be proactive rather than reactive, it is essential that management and staff measure it routinely, rather than simply respond to audits. Reacting to audits is inefficient and ineffective. It may result in auditors rather than management, setting agendas and priorities.

Compliance with law, regulation, contract, and policy is much easier to measure if the essential practices, standards, guidelines, and procedures have been demonstrably chosen to implement them.

Mature enterprise security programs measure compliance proactively and routinely. They do not wait for the auditors. When the auditors arrive, they are able to say to them:

- These are the requirements that we are trying to comply with.
- These are the places where we are in compliance.

- These are the variances.
- These are the variances that we intend to correct, and the schedule on which we plan to fix them.
- These are the variances that we do not plan to fix, here's the business justification, and so-and-so is the deciding executive.

Because the auditors now need only test what they are told, the audit is much more efficient. Compliance is also more efficient.

Note that the opposite of compliance is not noncompliance, but a (short) list of known and enumerated variances. Some of these variances will be fixed to improve security effectiveness. A shorter list will be accepted as a means of ensuring efficiency.

Measurement of compliance should include the number of variances, their life, and their significance. Over time, all of these should be going down.

Service

At least in the presence of rigorous service level agreements, one can measure service. Unfortunately, for far too long in far too many enterprises, the default service level has been "IT best efforts" and, consequently, has not been written. The CISO must ensure that any and all security service levels are responsive to the constituent's requirements, expressed in measurable terms, and then reconciled to those terms, and summary reports provided to the constituents.

Risk

Within boundary assumptions of uncertainty, we can measure risk.[1] We can measure both natural and man-made threats and hazards, our vulnerability to them, and the potential consequences to our resources and assets. Although risk assessment is not an exact science, it is a useful decision-making tool. It makes it possible for us to make efficient decisions as to which risks to mitigate, which to assign, and which to accept. Moreover, for purposes of security measurement, we can use it to determine whether the accepted residual risk is going up or down over time.

Risk Acceptance

One of the most powerful security controls is documented risk acceptance. Under this system, identified and accepted risk is documented by staff and accepted by business unit executives. The purpose of this control is to ensure that the decision to tolerate or mitigate a risk is made by the executive best able to understand the net impact on the business. Normally these acceptances expire on the earlier date of implementation of mitigating measures, a scheduled date specified in the acceptance, with the tenure of the accepting executive, or one year, whichever occurs first.

For purposes of measurement, it is useful to know the number of outstanding risk acceptances and whether this number is going up or down. We can also track the average life, the number retired, and the number renewed.

Attack Traffic

Attack traffic is an important measure of threat. Attack traffic may be defined as any traffic observed by a network, application, or system that is not intended or expected. Note that this is easier to measure if the policy for each of these is restrictive rather than permissive. The policy can be expressed and measured in terms of properties of the traffic including origin address (e.g., domain or IP address), protocol (normalized for tunneling), destination, content (e.g., attachment file types, known malicious code), protocols, rate, and delta rate.

A high rate of attack traffic may suggest an attempted denial of service (DoS) attack. A high delta, depending upon where measured, may suggest an increase or decrease in the general threat level. Temporary increases in either may suggest target identification probes.

Resistance to Attack

In addition to measuring attack traffic, we can measure our resistance to attack. This can be expressed in part as the ratio of successful attacks to total or detected attacks. We can measure it in terms of the cost of attack to the adversary. His cost of attack is some combination of work, access, indifference to detection, special knowledge, and time to detection and corrective action. A useful mnemonic for this is W.A.I.S.T.:

Work is measured in terms of the number of trials the attacker must use or avoid for a successful attack. The maximum work is the number of trials for a successful brute-force attack. For example, the amount of work for a brute force or exhaustive attack goes up with the number of possible passwords. One can never know what the minimum work might be because it is a function of what the attacker may already know.

Access can be expressed in terms of the capabilities and privileges that he must have or obtain to get access to the resources or control that constitute success. For example, an attacker might require hands-on access for some attacks; for many attacks, the ability to send a message to the system is sufficient.

Indifference to detection is the measure of the penalty the attacker fears for being caught in the act of the attack. For example, Megazoid was in Russia and his target was in New York. If he had been detected in the course of his attack, he might have to find a new target, but he would not likely pay any other penalty. The Wiley Hacker went through so many layers that tracing him to his origin took years.

Special knowledge is what the attacker must know or learn for a successful attack. For example, he must know or learn the identity of a suitable target. For example, if he knows the root password and has sufficient access to send a log-on message to the target system or control, his attack will be cheaper than if he must learn that password or bypass log on.

Time to detection and corrective action is the maximum time that the attack can take before it triggers an alarm or automatic remedy. For example, he might need enough time for a brute-force attack against a password or encryption key before it is changed.

Notice that a sufficiency of any one of these will reduce his requirement for any of the others. For example, the more special knowledge he has, the less work he must do, access he must obtain, risk of detection and penalty he has, or time that he needs. Notice also that both work and special knowledge can be encapsulated in a computer program (think scripts for kiddies or "exploits") so that those otherwise lacking in the motivation or skill for a successful attack can use them.

The managers of a network, application, or system can both measure and control this cost of attack, at least at the expense of some other value. For business systems or Internet-facing systems, this cost should be high enough that it cannot be paid by amateurs using readily available tools and sufficiently higher than other systems in the same environment that skilled hackers would choose those other systems first. Very sensitive systems should be "hardened" so that the cost of attack is higher than the expected value of success.

Because the only way to eliminate all possible attacks is to raise the cost of attack to infinite, we must expect and measure the cost of some attacks. Because the cost of detecting and remediating an attack may be cheaper than preventing it, we must also measure these.

Spending

Mature enterprises and programs will measure spending, i.e., cost of both security and losses, broken out by planned and unplanned. Over time one would expect the cost of security to rise slowly, the cost of losses to fall, and the sum of the two to fall. Boundary assumptions will be helpful in taking theses measurements.

The generally accepted mechanism for measuring cost is the budget, that is, actual cost compared to plan. Budget is well accepted because it is both powerful and flexible. However, in information protection, we are much better at planning for programs and initiatives than for the overall cost of security measures or losses. The primary thesis of this section is that if one does not measure it, one cannot control it. If we do not measure the cost of information security, we cannot expect to influence it, much less control it.

This is not to suggest that the measurement of the cost of security is either easy or routine. It is to say that, for any enterprise of sufficient scale to have a CISO, it is both possible and necessary.

Because it is so widely and sparsely dispersed, and material only at the business unit level, although most enterprises budget for the cost of the security function, few budget for the true and total cost of security. For example, although the cost of identification and authentication is material, most of the cost is paid in productivity of individual users where it is barely noticeable and difficult to measure. Similarly, the cost of errors is treated as a cost of something else. The cost of fraud or disasters is so irregular that it is treated as an exception and never properly classified as a loss. Similarly, the unplanned work of incident response is often absorbed as lost productivity and not properly identified or classified. Still if one does not properly recognize, identify, record, classify, and measure these costs, one cannot hope to control them.

The cost of security measures and losses are not the only costs in business that are like these. A similar cost is that of employee benefits or the cost of employee relocation. However, we have a number of accounting and budgeting techniques to ensure that these costs are properly recognized and allocated. For example, we use such mechanisms as burden, capitation, head count, relocation, and allocation. The accountants are skilled and adept at doing these things. It is time for us to ask for their help instead of assuming that it is possible or necessary.

Availability

For many applications and environments, availability trumps both confidentiality and integrity.[2] Most enterprises measure the percentage of scheduled time that a network, application, or system is available. However, to ensure that availability meets requirements, it is also necessary to measure and control mean time before failure (MTBF) and mean time to recovery (MTTR).

For MTTR to be meaningful, one must know what constitutes acceptable recovery. This might be something as easy and cheap as close of business at the end of the previous month to something as difficult and expensive as recovery of all transactions to the last transaction completed in real-time. Only very rarely and for very special applications will it be necessary to recover to the point of failure.

Responsiveness

For services, one should measure responsiveness. One should measure the total number of service requests by type. One should measure the average time to close requests. For open requests, one should measure its age as well as the time since the last activity.

Customer Satisfaction

Customer satisfaction can be measured as the inverse of the number of complaints. However, because some customers may be very dissatisfied and still not complain, one should still undertake proactive measurements like customer satisfaction surveys. These may be particularly useful for complex services like application design assistance, walk-throughs, or code reviews.

Progress

Finally, one can measure progress. Is enterprise security getting better? Is the sum of the cost of security measures and losses going down? Are successful attacks and their cost going down? Are the time to detection and the cost of remediation going down? Progress can be usefully measured period-to-period, period-to-same-period-prior-year, and year-over-year.

Progress may be the best single measure of the effectiveness of a security program or officer. However, one can recognize progress only in the context of other measurements.

Measuring the Security Program

It is safe to say that, although few security officers measure security, most measure the performance of the security function. This section will discuss the metrics that they use and suggest some that are useful or otherwise indicated.

Plan

In a study of "world class" security programs by Deloitte & Touche, security officers were asked how they measured the performance of their own departments. The one metric that all respondents mentioned was plan. They all compared what they did to what they said they were going to do. These plans were expressed in terms of activities, the things that the members of the security function spend their time doing, the products, mostly documents, that they produce, and initiatives, i.e., tools, controls, or programs that they implemented.

Budget

They reported that they measured themselves against their financial plan of budget. That is, did they spend the amount of money that they had agreed to with their management? The budget was expressed in terms of expense categories like salaries, travel, training expense, presentations, and other artwork, etc. It should be kept in mind that the security officer had more discretion over some of these items than others. For example, while he has discretion over travel expense, this is small when compared to salaries over which he has little discretion.

Few budgets associated expenditures with the program's products, services, and initiatives. Even those programs that had large administrative functions did not tie the expenses to those programs. If one is spending a large portion of one's resources changing passwords, it would be nice to know that when considering password alternatives.

Constituent Expectations

Most reported that they were concerned about constituent service, but few reported that they had formal mechanisms to define or measure those expectations. Although a few reported that they used constituent surveys, most of them admitted the instruments were primitive.

Peers

Although most reported that they measured themselves against their peers, this too was informal, or "seat of the pants."

Industry Practice

Most reported that they measured themselves against their industry peers. However, this too was informal, and for the purpose of being able to answer the management question, "What does my competition do?"

"Best" Practice

Some report that they measure their programs against "best" practice. However, for the most part, this means comparing one's practice to the "state" of the practice rather than to the best. It is used as much, or more, to justify what one intends to do in any case, rather than to justify improvement.

How and Where to Start

We have outlined a significant number of possible, useful, and recommended security metrics. However, we recognize that one cannot implement all these at once. Where then to start?

Identify Targets of Reports

We recommend that one start with an inventory of networks, systems, and applications along with the responsible manager and organizational unit for each. Start with servers; count personal computers, desktops, and laptops; and treat as two classes. Classify applications by sensitivity in no more than three or four classes.

Require Responsible Managers to Report

Ask the managers to report the state (see State above) of each system on no more than one piece of paper. Ask the auditors to reconcile a representative sample existing systems to satisfy themselves that reporting is complete. Similarly, ask them to reconcile the actual state of networks, applications, and systems to the state reported to satisfy themselves that the reports are accurate. This information should now be put into a database to facilitate analysis, feedback, reporting, and future measurement.

Report

Provide ranked feedback to the reporting managers so that they can see how they are doing, as recognition that management knows how they are doing, and as motivation to do better. Provide ranked reports to the responsible business unit executives. In subsequent periods you will measure the networks, systems, and applications identified in this step and against the baseline established by it.

Now repeat this process for compliance with standards, guidelines, and procedures. Ask managers to report their compliance. Solicit the assistance of the auditors to ensure the completeness and accuracy of the reports, give feedback to the reporting managers, and report to the responsible executives.

Go into this process with your eyes open. Reporting these things to you will not be high on anyone's list of priorities. You will have to do a lot of follow-up. You have to be willing to report incomplete results and identify some managers as nonresponding.

Automate

Automate the process. Use e-mail and Web pages, both to collect measurements and to give feedback. Put the results in a database. For example, information about unexpected attack traffic at the perimeter can be collected automatically, and subsequently measured to provide the necessary feedback.

Budget

A standard business metric is performance against plan. One of our most important plans is the spending plan of budget. Unfortunately, we do not budget for losses. We know that we will have them. Across a large enterprise and a long period they can be predicted with some precision. However, most enterprises do not plan for them or measure them; it seems like planning to fail. On the other hand, failing to plan is planning to fail. Those who budget for and measure losses report good results. They say that measuring losses results in their being reduced over time. Budgeting for them provides an offset for those security initiatives intended to reduce them. If one budgets for the costs of leaks of personal profiles ($135 just to notify the victim, more to make him whole for any losses), then one can draw from those budgets to pay for initiatives like awareness training and file system or database encryption.

Assess and Iterate

Keep in mind that information is in the change, the delta. A report or a measure that never changes period to period conveys no information. Therefore, periodically assess all your measures; when a measure no longer reflects progress, replace it.

Measuring for the CEO and the Board

The time of the CEO and the boards of directors is both scarce and finite. They must look to staff to organize information in a way that makes best use of their time. One way to do this is through policy. One way to think of policy is that it originates with general management. However, in practice, general management simply does not have the necessary special knowledge, the words, in which to express the policy. Therefore, policy is negotiated between general management and staff.

Modern security policy is negotiated between general management and the CISO. At a minimum, such a policy must express the level of risk that general management is comfortable with, who is held accountable, and how success and failure are to be measured. It is the responsibility of the CISO to ensure that the policy requires measurement in meaningful and useful terms.

To craft this language, the CISO must know what the CEO and the board of directors are interested in. As a general rule, the CEO and the board are more interested in the conclusions than in the supporting measurements. The following paragraphs speak to their concerns. Metrics must be in place to support conclusions on these concerns.

Damage to Brand

The CEO and the board are concerned about the integrity of the brand. Security policy must require that managers protect the brand and remediate any damage on a timely basis. Simply being in business constitutes a risk to the brand, but policy must speak to what level of risk to the brand general management will tolerate. For example, policy might say that any damage to the brand will be dealt with before it results in material financial loss or damage to the health and continuity of the business. Such a policy would require that all such incidents be tracked and that time to detection and corrective action be measured, recorded, and reported both to line management and the security staff.

Employee Awareness and Morale

Because it is essential to any security program that employees understand their roles and responsibilities, policy should make management responsible for developing and maintaining employees' awareness of their roles and responsibilities and require that programs and training intended to develop this awareness be measured.

Because the diligence of employees in carrying out their security responsibilities and their resistance to destructive acts are a function of their morale and satisfaction, then the CISO will want to monitor these measurements, e.g., employee satisfaction surveys, and report those to the CEO and board of directors.

Damage to Competitive Position

The CEO and board of directors are concerned about leaks of intellectual property that compromise products or otherwise damage the competitive position of the enterprise.

Material Impact on the Bottom Line

Should there be a security event or events that have a material effect on the bottom line, the CISO should report that to the CEO and board of directors. In the meantime, he should measure the total cost of losses as a percentage of net income.

Legal, Contractual, and Regulatory Compliance

As noted above, there should be a system in place to measure the compliance with law, regulation, and contract. Because the directors may be held liable for noncompliance, compliance measures should be routinely reported to the board.

Effectiveness and Efficiency of Security Programs and Measures

The most efficient security posture is where the sum of the cost of losses and the cost of security programs, mechanisms, and measures is at a minimum. Interestingly, at this point the costs are roughly equal. As noted above, these are difficult to measure and compare in the short term, but easier over time. They are useful to the CISO in regulating his programs and useful to the CEO and the board of directors in assessing the job the CISO is doing. If he is spending more money on his program than he is measuring in losses, he is either spending too much or, as likely, not identifying all the losses.

Changes to Threats, Attacks, and Vulnerabilities

Changes in threat sources or rates, the use of classes of attacks, or the vulnerabilities targeted may be of interest to the CEO and the board of directors. Such changes have been enormous over the last 50 years.

As noted above, threat should be routinely measured. Although threat is normally relatively stable, with natural threats dominating man-made, with rate being higher for outsiders than insiders, and consequences being higher for insiders, every now and then there is a new threat that seems to surprise management. Many enterprises seem to have been surprised by the increase in outsider attacks, particularly distributed DoS attacks that emerged with the Internet.

Management should identify novel attacks and measure the rate of all attacks. For example, although worm attacks relying on pervasive vulnerabilities in targets of opportunity may decrease, spoofing attacks against the customers of targets of choice may increase.

Changes in Posture since Last Report

The CEO and board of directors are interested in significant changes in the security state or posture of the enterprise from period to period. For example, few managements noted or reported to their boards when the target of crime shifted from property to information. Systematic measurement and analysis might have provided early warning.

Final Thoughts

Measurement is hard work and there are no silver bullets. No one ever said that measurement, security, or leadership were supposed to be easy. That is why it is called leadership, why only a special few can do it, and why they receive extra recognition and compensation.

Compliance with restrictive policies is usually easier to measure. It is easier to identify variances from a policy that says, "Do not permit anything that is not on this (short) white list." For example, there are an infinite number of permissible filename extensions, but the average enterprise uses only a few dozen.

Measurement is how we tell our superiors and our customers what we are doing. Are we effective? Are we efficient? Are we getting better? It is how we identify our most productive subordinates so that we recognize and reward fairly and equitably. Perhaps even more important, it is how we demonstrate that we know what we are doing. Are we methodical, systematic, reproducible, rigorous, and disciplined, or are we simply winging it? Measurement is a major difference between professional managers and pretenders. No one can aspire to leadership who has not mastered it.

It goes without saying that the "early bird gets the worm." He who measures early, who sets the example for his peers and colleagues sets himself apart and identifies himself as a leader.

Recap

- Measurement is essential to our effectiveness, success, and to our being recognized as successful.
- There are a number of things we can and should measure:
  - System state (across populations of systems)
  - Compliance with expectations and progress towards compliance
  - Cost and spending
  - The cost of programs, losses, prevention, and remediation
  - Attack traffic, successful versus prevented attacks, and the time to detect and remediate
  - Service level and customer satisfaction
  - Risk and risk acceptance
- If compliance is to be proactive rather than reactive, it is essential that management and staff measure it routinely rather than simply respond to audits.
- One of the most powerful security controls is documented risk acceptance. Under this system, identified and accepted risk is documented by staff and accepted by business unit executives; this ensures that the decision to tolerate or mitigate a risk is made by the executive best able to understand the net impact on the business.

Notes

1. Donn Parker has argued that there is insufficient information to do a valid information security risk assessment, and there are better ways to justify and prioritize security. The authors believe that, although we may do it by the seat of our pants, we do it in any case. We believe that, at least in enterprises large enough to have a CISO, it should be methodical, rigorous, and disciplined.
2. Although we may measure confidentiality, integrity, and availability separately, they are really separate manifestations of a single property. Each is essential to the other. One cannot achieve availability without integrity and confidentiality.

Chapter 16

Privacy, Ethics, and Business

Rebecca Herold

Editor's Note: Ethics and privacy of consumer information do not fit as neatly under the topic of leadership skills as some other competencies and skills such as communication, confidence, and understanding organizational culture. However, acting in an ethical manner is a nontechnical behavior worthy of note in this anthology, especially when it's the security officer doing the acting. Bottom line — we decided to include this well-written chapter in the book because it does have merit.

Businesses Need to Have a Conscience[1]

One of my favorite movies of all time is *It's a Wonderful Life.* A scene that still resonates with business today is when Mr. Potter offers George Bailey a high-paying job. George is amazed and flattered with the offer, considering how much more money and prestige it will bring him, until he shakes Potter's hand; he can feel it isn't right, rubs his fingers together as though he's feeling the oily residue that has rubbed off of Potter's unethical soul onto his hand, and you can see on his face that he realizes he is being manipulated by Potter, the "scurvy little spider."

In January 2006 I got an unsolicited package in the mail from a security software vendor, whose name I will not promote here. I opened it up, and there was a copy of Enron's 2000 "Code of Ethics" booklet, which also contained the corporation's information security policies. This surprised me. Hmm; what was this all about?

Reading the letter I found that this vendor was promoting their product by encouraging potential customers to view a site they set up with a copy of all the Enron e-mail messages, "over 85,000 records," that were on the Enron system at the time of the Enron collapse and sending the Enron policies to demonstrate the noncompliance. The vendor tried to rationalize this by indicating that because the information "is already posted on the Web by the Federal Energy Regulatory Commission," the vendor "believes that it is not harming anyone." However, right before this the vendor indicated that it "believes that most Enron employees are (and were) hard-working, honest people who are (and were) trying to do a good job. We respect them and apologize for any embarrassment that this content may cause them." They have documented that they realize they are probably embarrassing or harming someone by their actions, but they are following through with those actions anyway.

Embarrass a Person to Win a Prize![2]

The vendor then goes on to offer three separate contests, each with a prize of iPod shuffles, to the people who, after searching through the Enron e-mails, can find the best e-mails that:

- Would be grounds for firing
- Contained the funniest jokes
- Were the most embarrassing to the sender

So, they are now encouraging others to embarrass the people named in the e-mails further.

The vendor indicated it had scrubbed the e-mails of "really personal information." However, all the people's first and last names are clearly seen in the text that the people in the contest have submitted onto the vendor's site that were copied from the Enron e-mail database. Gee, full names are rather personal, don't you think? Also, how was "really personal information" actually removed from the 85,000 messages? If they had really removed such information, would there have been any information left to support their contests?

Does this feel right or ethical to you? As I read the letter, I felt as though I had just shaken hands with Mr. Potter. It is one thing for the government to post evidence under public access laws, but it is quite another thing for a vendor to actually make a copy of the information and post it, stating that they realize their actions will cause embarrassment to the people named therein; people who have lost their jobs and life savings, probably many people mentioned who weren't even employees at Enron, solely for the purpose of promoting the vendor's security product. And then to go on to have three separate contests encouraging the public at large to continue to embarrass them is really the icing on the cake!

There were around 28,000 Enron employees who lost their jobs, in addition to another 85,000 Arthur Andersen employees who also subsequently lost their jobs. And now the vendor is taking opportunistic advantage of the situation, and government regulations regarding evidence, blatantly to promote their security product and even go a step further and explicitly embarrass anyone named in the now "public" documents in the name of their marketing gimmick ... just because they can ... and it will help their sales.

It is as if this vendor set up a circus around a train wreck and created carnival sideshows around the scattered victims. Does this seem right to you? Does this seem ethical? If the vendor has CISSP, CISM, CISA, CIPP, or other certified professionals on staff who went along with this, are they in violation of their codes-of-ethics promises?

The Enron trial started January 31, 2006. I'm sure the Internet searches for information related to it were high. I'm sure this vendor had a very high hit rate on its site. No, I did not search the e-mail database at its site; its justification for doing the macabre marketing stunts were disgusting. The longer you think about this the more your gut, heart, and conscience should tell you this is wrong.

It is ironic that an organization in court for being so unethical now has other organizations doing actions that are also ethically questionable. It is similar to the mob mentality, isn't it? If someone else is doing bad things, then others will often join in just because they think they won't get singled out and will in fact get some benefit from it.

Aren't Teddies Fair Game?[3]

Why should organizations worry about revealing personal data if doing so does not explicitly break any regulations? If it would take human and dollar resources to make the changes necessary to protect the nonregulated personal data, then why do anything? Consider the potential negative business impact along with the embarrassment factor of the individuals involved.

Recall the incident that occurred with Victoria's Secret in 2002. An error within its website application code allowed visitors to the site to be able to view all the other customers' orders, including their full names and the specific types of intimate apparel they had purchased. Very embarrassing indeed for many of the customers! This information could also have been copied onto other sites, prolonging the embarrassment factor long after the application was fixed. The customer information could also have been obtained by other organizations and used for their marketing campaigns.

It was widely reported that the problem was not fixed right away after a customer notified the company; there were no laws or regulations explicitly requiring the data available for viewing to be secured. True, it is doubtful there is any law explicitly requiring information about teddies and thongs to be protected. However, the programming flaw was fixed after publicity regarding the incident occurred. The incident was viewed as an incident of gross privacy invasion, and also a violation of the company's posted privacy policy. Under the settlement, Victoria's Secret had to compensate New Yorkers whose personal information was accessible via the Internet, pay a $50,000 fine, and implement a series of improvements for its website security.

Even if It Isn't Illegal, Actions Perceived as Unethical Hurt Business[4]

Embarrassment resulting from privacy invasions of personal information that may not be covered by any specific laws certainly can have an impact on organizations. Embarrassment is a component of privacy that often gets overlooked by organizations that are focusing only on the "letter of the law" for what is legally allowed when handling personal information and when trying to get an edge on the competition. Not only can the resulting legal actions impact a business, but the damaged reputation and lost customers resulting from the bad publicity and perceived callousness could have a much longer-lasting impact. Using personal information in ethical ways, in addition to ways that comply with the law, are ultimately good for business.

After a presentation I did on privacy at a conference some time ago, one of the attendees chatted with me for a while afterwards about the use of "found" personal information. During the presentation I had talked about the importance, particularly for international data protection law compliance, of getting consent from individuals to use their personal information. The attendee indicated his marketing area had figured out a way to harvest the names and contact information from unprotected retail Web servers and include them within their marketing databases. There was no law against this, was there? After all, the individuals had probably consented to having their information collected by those Web servers for marketing purposes. Hmm ... interesting logic. Be very, very careful. If I give my consent to Company X for them to use my personal information, it does not mean I have consented to having every other Company Y and Z deluge me with its marketing arsenal.

Greed Is Good?[5]

Today, the ease of collecting and disseminating personal information is unprecedented. Yes, legally, in the United States at least, individuals have a right to view databases of public records, which the Enron e-mails have become as an effect of being evidence for the trial. Technologically it is easy to post them on the Internet. But just because it can easily be done does not mean it should be done.

Unguarded moments, careless words of youth or naïveté, or even messages spoofed by others, can now be viewed by an audience of millions, following those victims for years to come. Recall the 15-year-old known as the Star Wars Kid. He became famous because a video of him was posted on the Internet as a joke, reportedly causing the young man considerable embarrassment and raising many privacy discussions. The video remains widely circulated and will be something that will follow him the rest of his life. The people being made the butt of jokes in the Enron e-mails will quite possibly be impacted for the rest of their lives. But, the vendor is getting good publicity at their expense, and it is not breaking any law, so that makes it okay, right? Well, they are certainly getting publicity, and many organizations may decide they do not want to do business with such an organization.

This reminds me of the quote from the 1987 movie *Wallstreet* with Michael Douglas and Charlie Sheen: "Greed is good!" It is sad that this motto is paid homage to by organizations through the use of public access laws and exploiting the misfortunes of others, ironically to promote an information security and privacy product.

Even if you can use "found" personal information with potential financial gain without breaking any laws, should you? Well, Mr. Potter kept his found money from the trash can in his bank, knowing and delighting in the harsh impact his actions would have upon George Bailey and many others in Bedford Falls and how it would benefit him financially. Do you want your organization to follow Mr. Potter's example?

Does your organization have an ethics code? If so, does it address privacy issues? This may be a good time for you to review your existing code, or create one if it does not exist. When creating it, it will be helpful first to know a little about the history of computer ethics and the associated privacy impacts.

Computer Ethics Origins[6]

The consideration of computer ethics fundamentally emerged with the birth of computers. There was concern right away that computers would be used inappropriately to the detriment of society, or that they would replace humans in many jobs, resulting in widespread job loss. To fully grasp the issues involved with computer ethics, it is important to consider the history. The following[7] provides a brief overview of some significant events.

1940s and 1950s

Consideration of computer ethics is recognized to have begun with the work of MIT professor Norbert Wiener during World War II when he helped to develop an anti-aircraft cannon capable of shooting down warplanes. This work resulted in Wiener and his colleagues creating a new field of research called "cybernetics," the science of information feedback systems. The concepts of cybernetics, combined with the developing computer technologies, led Wiener to make some ethical conclusions about the technology called information and communication technology (ICT), in which Wiener predicted social and ethical consequences. Wiener published the book, *The Human Use of Human Beings* in 1950, which described a comprehensive foundation that is still the basis for computer ethics research and analysis.

1960s

In the mid-1960s, Donn B. Parker, at the time with SRI International in Menlo Park, California, began examining unethical and illegal uses of computers and documenting examples of computer crime and other unethical computerized activities. He published "Rules of ethics in information processing" in *Communications of the ACM* in 1968, and headed the development of the first Code of Professional Conduct for the Association for Computing Machinery, which was adopted by the ACM in 1973.

During the late 1960s, Joseph Weizenbaum, a computer scientist at MIT in Boston, created a computer program that he called ELIZA that he scripted to provide a crude imitation of "a Rogerian psychotherapist engaged in an initial interview with a patient." People had strong reactions to his program, some psychiatrists fearing it showed that computers would perform automated psychotherapy.

1970s

Weizenbaum wrote *Computer Power and Human Reason* in 1976 in which he expressed his concerns about the growing tendency to see humans as mere machines. His book, MIT courses, and many speeches inspired many computer ethics thoughts and projects.

Walter Maner is credited with coining the phrase "computer ethics" in the mid-1970s when discussing the ethical problems and issues created by computer technology, and taught a course on the subject at Old Dominion University. From the late 1970s into the mid-1980s, Maner's work created much interest in university-level computer ethics courses. In 1978 Maner published the *Starter Kit in Computer Ethics*, which contained curriculum materials and advice for developing computer ethics courses. Many university courses were put in place because of Maner's work.

1980s

In the 1980s, social and ethical consequences of information technology, such as computer-enabled crime, computer failure disasters, privacy invasion using computer databases, and software ownership lawsuits, were being widely discussed in America and Europe. James Moor of Dartmouth College published "What is computer ethics?" in *Computers and Ethics* and Deborah Johnson of Rensselaer Polytechnic Institute published *Computer Ethics*, the first textbook in the field, in the mid-1980s. Other significant books about computer ethics were published within the psychology and sociology field, such as Sherry Turkle's *The Second Self*, about the impact of computing on the human psyche, and Judith Perrolle's *Computers and Social Change: Information, Property, and Power*, about a sociological approach to computing and human values.

1990s

Maner Terrell Bynum held the first international multidisciplinary conference on computer ethics in 1991. For the first time it assembled philosophers, computer professionals, sociologists, psychologists, lawyers, business leaders, news reporters, and government officials to discuss computer ethics. During the 1990s, new university courses, research centers, conferences, journals, articles, and textbooks appeared, and organizations like Computer Professionals for Social Responsibility, the Electronic Frontier Foundation, and ACM-SIGCAS launched projects addressing computing and professional responsibility. Developments in Europe and Australia included new computer ethics research centers in England, Holland, Italy, and Poland. In the UK, Simon Rogerson of De Montfort University led the ETHICOMP series of conferences and established the Centre for Computing and Social Responsibility.

Regulatory Requirements for Ethics Programs[8]

When creating an ethics strategy, it is important to look at the regulatory requirements for ethics programs. These provide the basis for a minimal ethical standard upon which an organization can expand to fit its own unique organizational environment and requirements. An increasing number of regulatory requirements related to ethics programs and training now exist, including the following:

- The 1991 U.S. Federal Sentencing Guidelines for Organizations (FSGO) outline minimal ethical requirements and provide for substantially reduced penalties in criminal cases when federal laws are violated if ethics programs are in place. Reduced penalties provide strong motivation to establish an ethics program. Effective November 1, 2004, the FSGO was updated with additional requirements.

■ In general, board members and senior executives must assume more specific responsibilities for a program to be found effective:
  − Organizational leaders must be knowledgeable about the content and operation of the compliance and ethics program, perform their assigned duties exercising due diligence, and promote an organizational culture that encourages ethical conduct and a commitment to compliance with the law.
■ The Commission's definition of an effective compliance and ethics program now has three subsections:
  − Subsection (a) the purpose of a compliance and ethics program
  − Subsection (b) seven minimum requirements of such a program
  − Subsection (c) the requirement to assess periodically the risk of criminal conduct and design, implement, or modify the seven program elements, as needed, to reduce the risk of criminal conduct

The purpose of an effective compliance and ethics program is "to exercise due diligence to prevent and detect criminal conduct and otherwise promote an organizational culture that encourages ethical conduct and a commitment to compliance with the law." The new requirement significantly expands the scope of an effective ethics program and requires the organization to report an offense to the appropriate governmental authorities without unreasonable delay.

The Sarbanes–Oxley Act of 2002 introduced accounting reform and requires attestation to the accuracy of financial reporting documents:

1. Section 103: Auditing, Quality Control, and Independence Standards and Rules requires the Board to:
   a. Register public accounting firms.
   b. Establish, or adopt, by rule, "auditing, quality control, ethics, independence, and other standards relating to the preparation of audit reports for issuers."
      i. New Item 406(a) of Regulation S-K requires companies to disclose:
         − Whether they have a written code of ethics that applies to their senior officers
         − Any waivers of the code of ethics for these individuals
         − Any changes to the code of ethics
      ii. If companies do not have a code of ethics, they must explain why they have not adopted one.

The U.S. Securities and Exchange Commission approved a new governance structure for the New York Stock Exchange (NYSE) in December 2003. It includes a requirement for companies to adopt and disclose a code of business conduct and ethics for directors, officers, and employees, and promptly disclose any waivers of the code for directors or executive officers. The NYSE regulations require all listed companies to possess and communicate, both internally and externally, a code of conduct or face delisting.

In addition to these, organizations must monitor new and revised regulations from U.S. regulatory agencies, such as the FDA, FTC, BATF, IRS, ERISA, and many others throughout the world. Ethics plans and programs need to be established within the organization to ensure that the organization is in compliance with all such regulatory requirements.

Computing Ethics

Within the everyday application of business work responsibilities, there are many times when ethical issues will arise. Many of these situations are related to information processing. For example:

- *Personal information privacy:* Who should have access to personally identifiable information (PII)? Who needs access?
- *Industrial espionage:* Is it right to use the information a new employee brings from another competitor organization? What if that new employee still has access to their former employer's systems; what should you do?
- *Criminal hacking:* Is it right to try to break into a system or application just to see how it works, but with no intent of doing damage?
- *Illegal copying of software and music:* Are you using unlicensed software within your organization? Do you know if the MP3 music and video files your personnel download are legal?

Throughout your career as an information assurance leader, you will encounter many times when you will need to consider and discuss the ethical considerations of security and privacy policies, laws, regulations, and so on. It will be helpful for you to have a bit of theoretical background to help you with these situations.

When applying ethical considerations to business decisions, you typically will need to decide between multiple possible actions. You will often need to be able to determine that even though something is legal or in compliance, it may still be unethical in the context of your business situation. You will need to consider the consequences of your decisions and actions:

- Upon others
- Upon yourself
- Upon your employer
- Upon society

Ethical issues related to computers and the associated uses and data are sometimes difficult because of the technologies involved, the speed with which activities can happen on a computer, the seemingly anonymous behaviors involved with using a computer, and the apparent impersonality of interactions with computers. People's behaviors in using computers will often be drastically different from their behaviors offline. Think about people you may know who do not think twice about making illegal copies of software or illegally sharing MP3 music files with their friends, but would never, ever consider stealing something from a store or never drive over the speed limit. However, it is important to remember the ethical issues are fundamentally the same as with interactions with living breathing humans.

Computers can store information about millions of people, and they can transmit data, also to millions of people, in the blink of an eye with the press of one key. Technology has actually increased exponentially the negative impact of an unethical decision far more than in the past when someone may have done something like modifying a business letter the manager wrote to a customer, or even posting customer information on a physical bulletin board.

From a privacy standpoint, the search and compare capabilities for going through PII, and doing a wide range of data mining activities, are very large concerns. Huge ethical struggles visit personnel in all companies when deciding how to use PII. However, because many, if not most, people do not actually imagine other people being associated with the PII, they depersonalize their activities and do not think about personal impacts, only that their actions and decisions are capable through using computers, and therefore must be okay to do. It is likely many people do not even realize that what they're doing through their computers has ethical dimensions. Effective business leaders must help their personnel to understand how to make ethical decisions during the course of their work.

Ethical Decision Making

At a very high level, information assurance professionals must make use of the following ethical decision-making steps:

■ Know the law.
■ Follow policies and guidelines.
■ Examine the ethical principles.

Know the Law

You must know the laws your organization must follow, and you must establish an ongoing relationship with your legal counsel and discuss related business issues with him or her. It is important to understand that legal issues and ethical issues overlap, but are certainly far from being identical. In fact different business actions can fall into four general categories:

1. *Ethical and legal:* For example, establishing safeguards to ensure only those with a business need can access PII.
2. *Ethical and illegal:* For example, providing medical information to the domestic partner of a critically ill, comatose patient.
3. *Unethical and legal:* As the earlier example with the vendor posting the Enron e-mails for their contest shows, just because an action is legal does not make it ethical.
4. *Unethical and illegal:* For example, making copies of a single purchased software package and installing it to use on all employee computers.

Follow Policies and Guidelines

Organizations must ensure formally documented guidelines and policies exist to help personnel make the right ethical decisions. Ethical guidance should be included in documents such as corporate policies, regulatory compliance documents, corporate code of ethics, and professional codes of conduct.

Personnel should also be encouraged and taught to look inward when faced with ethical dilemmas at work if guidelines do not exist for their particular situations. They should consider:

- *Using the "Golden Rule."* Consider the situation with reversed roles. What would be the right thing to do if the shoe was on the other foot?
- *What Mom would say.* What would happen if they discussed the situation with a parental figure? Would their decision make Mom proud?
- *What the news media would report.* Would it be okay if everyone outside the organization read a news story about the ethical decision?
- *Their own instinct.* Does this feel like the right thing to do? Does your gut tell you that it is or is not right? Intuitive feelings of people who are at the ethical core are often correct.

Examine the Ethical Principles

In addition to knowing the laws and following documented guidelines, personnel can also make use of some long-standing ethical principles to help them make their decisions.

Deontology

Deontology is the study of rights pertaining to groups and individuals and duties toward others. What are the rights we expect others to allow us? What are the duties we have for giving others those rights? Both of these become important questions in deciding whether we are considering a reasonable course of action, or if we are considering something that would violate our normal standards. Within a work context, these considerations follow your professional duties, such as respecting your professional relationships, exercising professional efficacy, protecting confidentiality, and exercising impartiality.

Sometimes within our profession we have special obligations. For example, when using proprietary software the seller may have provided for specific kinds of use by you, the buyer. You have a duty to comply with the agreements in the terms of use. The seller offered you the right to use the intellectual property in specific ways, and you try to respect the terms of that contract. That's an example of rights and duties being exchanged on both sides.

As a general rule, if you exercise rights, then there will usually be a corresponding duty. And similarly, if you have a duty, then there is likely to be a corresponding right.

Consequentialism

Consequentialism is generally the observation and consideration of what happens to other people. It involves three types of results:

1. *Egoism:* Maximizing benefit or minimizing harm to yourself
2. *Utilitarianism:* Maximizing benefit or minimizing harm to your group
3. *Altruism:* Maximizing benefit or minimizing harm to others at your expense

This involves looking at the consequences of actions. One approach, based upon immature perspectives, is a completely egotistic approach to decision making where everything revolves around you. In the long run, it doesn't work very well for business decisions, even though it is often the model used. It's a primarily antisocial approach that does not take into account the consequences to the wider society of the actions that would benefit you. An example would be stealing something from someone else, perhaps a competitor or even a co-worker, because it would be useful and benefit you within your profession. However, there are consequences to that act. There is degradation of trust and increase in suspicion. There may also be the actual loss of utility of the stolen material or object from the original owner or user, plus many other potential consequences.

Utilitarianism goes one step beyond egoism. It looks at group benefits. And even though this is better, if it is done using a narrow definition of the group, the value realized by the group could still cause damage to a wider group such as the entire company, all customers, society, or even the planet.

Altruism is maximizing the benefit to the group even if there is an expense or a cost to you. Although this can be useful in the long run, it can also be destructive. You have to examine this carefully. A totally altruistic life, to the point of becoming a martyr, could quickly end your profession, and then be of little benefit to anyone else. On the other hand, a complete lack of altruism could make for a life devoid of kindness or generosity.

Categorical Imperative

Immanuel Kant[9] proposed the ethical notion of categorical imperative. Basically, it is considering the harm that would result if everyone did what he or she proposed. For example, in 2007 Google Earth replaced the most up-to-date satellite images of New Orleans with images taken before Hurricane Katrina in 2005.[10] Residents impacted by Katrina were upset that the images showed the city as being completely back to normal, and members of Congress charged "that the company and civic leaders were conspiring to portray the area's recovery progressing better than it really is." If Google had followed the categorical imperative of ethical consideration the company would have considered how their decision to replace the newest satellite images showing the still-remaining destruction from the hurricane with the pre-hurricane images would have impacted the residents of the city and general public perception, and perhaps they would have made a different decision as a result.

Stakeholders

Another ethical principle involves looking at everyone involved and being sensitive to all stakeholder interests. Stakeholders include everyone impacted by a decision. Business owners, shareholders, employees, customers, families of affected people, and anyone dependent upon the organization are considered as stakeholders. This is typically a pretty broad group of people. When you are making a business decision, it is important from an ethical standpoint to look at the stakeholders and consider the consequences of the decision upon them. Note the groups who will bear negative consequences because of the decision as opposed to who will benefit from the decision. If your organization is benefiting at the expense of others, and if your organization is not planning to compensate those expenses, then the chances are high that this is an unethical decision; for example, the vendor promoting the contest based upon the Enron e-mails at the expense of the reputation, feelings, and possible related monetary losses of those whose e-mails it posted.

High-Level Steps for Integrating Ethics into Business

When addressing ethics and privacy issues within information assurance activities, use the principles and guidelines previously described. Provide ongoing ethics and privacy training to your personnel. Go through case studies dealing with realistic issues your organization faces during the course of business. And of most importance, model ideal ethical behavior when addressing information security and privacy dilemmas.

- *Be a good example.* This is your most important job. Personnel emulate their leaders' behaviors, so be cognizant of the ethical implications involved with the business decisions you make and your day-to-day behavior.
- *Make developing your personnel's ethical practices a priority.* Provide ongoing awareness and training.
- *Develop an ear and an eye for how well your personnel adopt the ethical concepts.* Control the flow of ideas and images you provide that will influence your personnel's ethical behavior.
- *Use the language of ethics.* Clearly indicate when there are situations that are ethically right and wrong.
- *Consistently apply sanctions for unethical behavior.* Personnel must know there are consequences for not working in an ethical manner.
- *Learn to listen to your personnel.* Take their concerns seriously and set aside time to listen.
- *Get involved with your personnel.* Helping personnel handle difficult situations will develop and strengthen their ethical decision-making capabilities.

Example Topics in Computing Ethics[11]

When establishing a computer ethics program and accompanying training and awareness programs, it is important to consider the topics that have been addressed and researched. The following topics, identified by Terrell Bynum,[12] are good to use as a basis.

Computers in the Workplace

Computers can pose a threat to jobs as people feel they may be replaced by them. However, the computer industry has already generated a wide variety of new jobs. When computers do not eliminate a job, it can still be radically altered. Computers in the workplace also create many concerns about the privacy of employee information and activities on the network. In addition to job security concerns, another workplace concern is health and safety. It is a computer ethics issue to consider how computers impact health and job satisfaction when information technology is introduced into a workplace.

Computer Crime

With the proliferation of computer viruses, spyware, phishing and fraud schemes, and hacking activity from every location in the world, computer crime and security are certainly topics of concern when discussing computer ethics. Besides outsiders, or hackers, many computer crimes, such as embezzlement or planting logic bombs or keyloggers, are committed by trusted personnel who have authorization to use company computer systems.

Privacy and Anonymity

One of the earliest computer ethics topics to arouse public interest was privacy. The ease and efficiency with which computers and networks can be used to gather, store, search, compare, retrieve, and share personal information make computer technology especially threatening to anyone who wishes to keep personal information out of the public domain or out of the hands of those who are perceived as potential threats. The variety of privacy-related issues generated by computer technology has led to re-examination of the concept of privacy itself.

Intellectual Property

One of the more controversial areas of computer ethics concerns the intellectual property rights connected with software and electronic files ownership. Some people, like Richard Stallman who started the Free Software Foundation, believe that software ownership should not be allowed at all. He claims that all information should be free, and all programs should be available for copying, studying, and modifying by anyone who wishes to do so.[13] Others such as Deborah Johnson argue that software companies or programmers would not invest weeks and months of work and significant funds in the development of software if they could not get the investment back in the form of license fees or sales.[14]

Professional Responsibility

Computer professionals have specialized knowledge, usually with positions of authority and respect. Computer professionals have a wide range of professional relationships. Such relationships can sometimes conflict with each other. Computer professionals need to be aware of possible conflicts of interest and try to avoid them. The codes of conduct for various computer professional organizations require members to have a professional responsibility for their actions and decisions.

Globalization

Global networks such as the Internet and conglomerates of business-to-business network connections are connecting people and information worldwide. The following globalization issues include ethics considerations:

- Global laws
- Global business
- Global education
- Global information flows
- Information-rich and information-poor nations
- Information interpretation

The gap between rich and poor nations, and between rich and poor citizens in industrialized countries, is very wide. As educational opportunities, business and employment opportunities, medical services, and many other necessities of life move more and more into cyberspace, gaps between the rich and the poor may become even worse, leading to new ethical considerations.

Recap

- Ethical issues related to computers and the associated uses and data are sometimes difficult because of the technologies involved, the speed with which activities can happen on a computer, the seemingly anonymous behaviors involved with using a computer, and the apparent impersonality of interactions with computers.
- Using personal information in ethical ways, in addition to ways that comply with the law, are ultimately good for business.
- When creating an ethics strategy, it is important to look at the regulatory requirements for ethics programs. These provide the basis for a minimal ethical standard upon which an organization can expand to fit its own unique organizational environment and requirements.
- You must know the laws your organization must follow, and you must establish an ongoing relationship with your legal counsel and discuss related business issues with him or her. It is important to understand that legal issues and ethical issues overlap, but are certainly far from being identical.
- Organizations must ensure formally documented guidelines and policies exist to help personnel make the right ethical decisions. Ethical guidance should

be included in documents such as corporate policies, regulatory compliance documents, corporate code of ethics, and professional codes of conduct.

Notes

1. Herold, R. Privacy Ethics Embarrassment. *CSI Alert Newsletter,* March 2006.
2. Ibid.
3. Ibid.
4. Ibid.
5. Ibid.
6. Herold, R. Ethics section, in *Official (ISC)² Guide to the CISSP CBK*, H. Tipton and K. Henry (Eds.), pp. 71–86, Auerbach, Boca Raton, FL, 2006.
7. Stanford Encyclopedia of Philosophy, Terrell Bynum, 2001. http://plato.stanford. edu/entries/ethics-computer/.
8. Herold, R. Ethics section, in *Official (ISC)² Guide to the CISSP CBK,* H. Tipton and K. Henry (Eds.), pp. 71–86, Auerbach, Boca Raton, FL, 2006.
9. Stanford Encyclopedia of Philosophy. http://plato.stanford.edu/entries/kant-moral/. Obtained March 31, 2007.
10. CNN News. http://www.cnn.com/2007/TECH/03/31/katrina.google.maps.ap/ index.html. Obtained March 31, 2007.
11. Herold, R. Ethics section, in *Official (ISC)² Guide to the CISSP CBK,* H. Tipton and K. Henry (Eds.), pp. 71–86, Auerbach, Boca Raton, FL, 2006.
12. Stanford Encyclopedia of Philosophy, Terrell Bynum, August 2001. http://plato.stanford.edu/entries/ethics-computer/.
13. Stallman, Richard. Why software should be free, in *Software Ownership and Intellectual Property Rights,* Terrell Ward Bynum, Walter Maner, and John L. Fodor (Eds.), 35–52, Research Center on Computing & Society, 1992.
14. Johnson, Deborah G. Proprietary rights in computer software: Individual and policy issues, in *Software Ownership and Intellectual Property Rights,* Terrell Ward Bynum, Walter Maner, and John L. Fodor (Eds.), Research Center on Computing & Society, 1992.

Chapter 17

Leading through a Crisis: How Not to Conduct a Security Investigation

Mark D. Rasch

> *Editors Note:* While chapter 16 (Privacy, Ethics, and Business) was deemed to have merit for the security officer, the security officer must possess the leadership skills necessary to exercise good judgment and make good decisions when handling crisis situations under fire. Failing to be prepared to execute under these circumstances could significantly reduce the CISO's credibility and ability to receive continued management support for the strategies and projects previously supported and articulated within other chapters.

The Phone Call

It is the moment that every CISO dreads. The phone rings and one of the system administrators says, "We have a problem..." This could mean a network outage, a power loss, a disruption of service, but in this case it means that someone has broken into your network and obtained unauthorized access to files, programs, and data. How you handle this situation may very well impact not only your job and future with the company, but in some situations, the future of the company itself. There are many ways to handle an incident — *all of them wrong in some way.* Effectively, your job as the CISO is to pick the least wrong one of them and learn from what has happened to prevent future similar attacks. We learn more from what we do wrong than from what we do right.

How Not to Conduct an Internal Investigation

There are many steps to an effective incident response capability, the first of which are policy, planning, and training. Believe it or not, every entity has an incident response plan — it is just that some of them are being written at 2 o'clock in the morning, as the incident is unfolding. A better approach is for the plan to have been developed in advance, vetted, tested, and disseminated. The truth is, in a real crisis situation, one of the first steps is to abandon all prior plans, but the incident response plan will, at a minimum, provide a framework for what to do, whom to contact, and to whom to report. It can also provide a checklist for things like data recovery, data forensics, and regulatory compliance. Moreover, many state "data breach disclosure" statutes permit companies to delay public disclosure of breaches of databases containing personally identifiable information (PII) if such a delay is pursuant to a written incident response policy. A variety of laws, including the Gramm–Leach–Bliley Act,[1] and its implementing regulations,[2] the Payment Card (credit and debit card) Industry Data Security Standard,[3] HIPAA regulations,[4] as well as various state laws,[5] mandate that regulated entities not only protect data, but also that they have workable and effective incident response plans to investigate and respond to potential data breaches.[6] But what makes an incident response plan "effective?"

What Mistakes Do Companies Make in Responding to Incidents?

The First Step: Know You Have a Problem

The first step in incident response is incident identification and notification. Someone has to notice something unusual, and tell someone. This can be something simple like noticing a misconfiguration or a bad log-in attempt, to something more serious. Unless you have a procedure to identify anomalous activity (including intrusion detection and prevention, scanning, etc.) you aren't going to have an incident — or at least aren't going to know about it until it is too late. We also speak about training the "first responders" — the IT security staff or others — about computer forensics and incident response. However, it is incredibly unlikely that these will be the true "first responders." By the time the IT security staff becomes involved, there may have been as many as a dozen people trying to figure out what is going on, altering files or evidence, and changing the forensic character of the evidence. Not that there is anything unusual about this, but it is something to keep in mind when you are forced to testify about the forensic nature of the investigation. Remember also that the situation described may bear little relation to the actual situation that you find. What you *think* you are investigating may be completely different from what you are *actually* investigating.

The Next Steps

Determine Goals and Objectives

Among the first questions to ask during an incident investigation are, "What do I want to have happen here? What would be a *successful* outcome? Do I want to find out who is in my network, or do I just want to get them out? In other words, what am I doing, and why am I doing it?" Another set of questions that should be addressed is, "What am I going to do with the results of the investigation? Are there liability or law enforcement issues I need to address? Should this investigation be covered by attorney–client privilege? What do I want to know, and why?" There is an old saying that if you don't know where you are going, any road will take you there. The same is true with forensic investigations. You need to have a clear idea where you are going to know how to proceed.

What Triggered the Internal Investigation?

Some "event" caused you to start your investigation. It could be a help desk issue, a network intrusion, a call from Human Resources about misbehavior by an employee, or an inquiry by Legal about theft or misuse of trade secrets. Internal investigations may also be launched as a result of external factors like SEC inquiries, grand jury subpoenas, formal or informal investigations, external litigation, shareholder actions, audit reports or investigations, or other needs to "find out what happened." The CISO needs to know what triggered the investigation, to know what they are looking for and why. If there are likely to be criminal or regulatory concerns, the CISO needs to proceed differently than in cases where there are merely internal operational concerns.

The Nature of the Evidence

Some evidence may be literally "too hot to handle." Internal investigations may relate to abuse of the system for distributing prohibited materials, including obscene materials, child pornography, or other materials, the mere possession of which may lead to criminal or other liability. Other evidence may create particular Sarbanes–Oxley (SOX) compliance issues, audit issues, or regulatory noncompliance issues. *What do you do if you uncover criminal activity being committed by the company?* Part of any incident response plan must be to determine what evidence will be collected, where it is likely to be located, how it is to be collected, and by whom.

Another problem with data collection is knowing how to collect the data. How the data is collected is directly related to what you intend to do with it. It is important to remember, however, that at the outset of an investigation, you may not truly know what you will eventually do with the data. Is it possible that the data will be needed for litigation later on? If you discover that an attack, damage, or even a malfunction was caused by the actions of an employee, might a competitor or a vendor sue you to collect damages? Are your damages covered by some form of insurance policy, which might reimburse the company for the expenses related not only to damages, but also to the cost of investigation? All too often CISOs forget that insurance policies may pay not only for the damages resulting from an investigation, but also for assessments or proactive measures which might have prevented the incident in the first place. Thus, CISOs should be prepared to coordinate their activities not only with the HR and legal staff, but also with compliance, risk management, and insurance professionals.

Special Problems with Smut

Many incidents that CISOs may have to deal with may involve the misuse of company networks or computers for the improper transfer or storage of "inappropriate" materials. These range from tasteless jokes to obscene materials. While HR policies and general practice may dictate disciplinary actions against employees who misbehave, these materials present a potential land mine for evidence collectors and handlers — and the CISO to whom they report. Laws in the United States and other countries make it a criminal offense to "knowingly possess," copy, or transfer certain kinds of materials, including "obscene" materials and child pornography. Thus, the mere act of imaging a hard drive or network share may itself constitute a felony. Providing a copy of that drive to HR or the General Counsel for review may constitute an additional felony. These types of records present special issues with respect to authenticity, chain of custody, and whether and how to coordinate with law enforcement agencies. More importantly, the CISO may have to decide whether the evidence collected demonstrates a genuine threat to the health, safety, or welfare of others, and, if so, determine the best way to mitigate that threat. Concerns about the reputation of the company and its employees must also be weighed. In other words, the CISO must endeavor to "do the right thing" without a great deal of guidance about what the "right thing" is in any individual case. Every case is unique, and solutions which may have worked in the past may not work today.

Legal counsel may be necessary to make the distinction between "ordinary pornography," which may be the appropriate subject of internal disciplinary actions — and child pornography or obscenity, which may require law enforcement intervention.

Retain Yourself

In any data collection, the objective is to find out what happened in a precisely defined and well-controlled manner. However, the essence of electronic evidence is its ephemeral nature. Some data, such as e-mails, documents, or other electronic records, may persist for days, weeks, months, or years (of course, the data may not be useable as the hardware or software requirements may have changed), but some electronic records may persist for minutes, hours, or days. Thus, IP history files, records of dynamic Internet protocol addresses, electronic communications through intermediaries or other similar records may have a very short shelf life. Relevant records are likely to be found not only on your computers and systems, but also on those of your vendors, suppliers, partners, ISPs, and unrelated third parties. An incident response plan must include examination of document retention and destruction policies, not only of your company, but also of third parties. Counsel may also have to be engaged to request (and possibly insist) that third parties (like ISPs) retain or produce relevant records. These records may not be only electronic documents. They may include phone records, physical access logs, voicemail records, surveillance cameras, and other records. Finally, you need to consider whether you want to retain records, which may later be used to demonstrate liability. If you are going to ask third parties to retain their records, how long do you want them to retain the records, who will pay for the retention, and what is your legal authority to ask them to keep them? In some cases, it may be better to make friends with your ISP (or its counsel) and make a polite request for retention and production, rather than a sternly worded demand.

Dramatis Persona

Another issue for the CISO in incident response is whom to bring into each incident, and who takes the lead. Parties who may be involved include both internal and external counsel, forensic document experts and consultants, HR staff, security staff, legal and regulatory compliance experts, insurance experts (on possibility of filing claims for damages), as well as the possibility of contacting law enforcement agencies.

Legal

The legal staff of the company is frequently one of the last entities involved in an incident. However, contacting legal staff early can allow the entire investigation potentially to be covered by either the attorney–client privilege or what is called the attorney work-product doctrine. Counsel — either internal or external — can assist in developing procedures for data collection that comport with relevant evidence laws, including those on originality, chain of custody, and authenticity. In addition, in investigations, there are invariably questions about employee privacy, third-party privacy, wiretapping and surveillance, and interview procedures. Well-trained and knowledgeable legal counsel can be invaluable to formalizing the procedure. Counsel can also review contractual obligations of the company or third parties to learn whether the company has a right of access to records, and what liabilities it may have in terms of notification of possible breaches involving different kinds of information. Finally, any coordination with law enforcement agencies should be done (absent a life-threatening emergency) only with the input from counsel.

Whether the CISO decides to use internal or outside counsel will largely be a function of the availability of each, the expertise of each, and the nature of the incident. Inside counsel will be more likely to know the parties involved, the general practices of the entity, and the regulatory environment in which the entity finds itself. Outside counsel, or a legal or forensic consultant, is much more likely to have developed a specialty in evidence collection. Outside experts may also have developed relationships with third parties (ISPs, law enforcement), which may prove useful in your incident response.

In addition, the CISO will likely wish to retain the services of a forensic data collection expert. These individuals will likely have the expertise and tools necessary to collect evidence in a way that it is preserved if it is later needed for legal process. This preserves your flexibility to proceed with litigation (or prosecution) if you want, or not to if you don't want. If evidence is collected forensically, it can be used; if it is not, there may be problems with admission later on.

In addition to forensic data collection, the CISO may also want to work with forensic document analysts as well. These analysts may use special tools or databases to determine patterns (e.g., e-mail trails, correspondence, cross-referencing different databases). They may also be experts in things like evaluating losses and damages for insurance or litigation purposes, and can testify as an expert if you need them to.

IT Department

Naturally, the IT Department will be involved in any incident response. They know the infrastructure, the personnel, and the procedures used. They also know where the evidence is likely to be located, and the nature of controls on the IT infrastructure. But when it comes to conducting investigations, the IT staff should participate, but not always lead the investigation. In data breach or other electronic investigations, it is important that those conducting the interviews and investigation be knowledgeable about the IT infrastructure, but also that they be unbiased, and not perceived as being invested in any particular solution or solution set. Moreover, in many cases the unauthorized activity may have involved either the participation or the negligence of someone within the IT staff, which highlights another point about the CISO's role in incident response: question everything. Do not assume that because you require anti-virus software, the system you are looking at actually had such software. Don't assume that controls that have been implemented, audited, and tested are actually in effect. Remember that the hacker needs to find only one way in, but you must prevent every possible means of access.

HR Department

Perhaps the most important thing to review in preparation for incident response is the company's policies — not just those on incident response, but overall privacy and security policies. For example, it may be easy to say that employees have no expectations of privacy in their corporate e-mail, but it is another thing to demonstrate that this is, in fact, the case. Have you considered employees' privacy interests in personal items left on their desks — an iPod, a personal computer, a cell phone or PDA, CD/DVD, a briefcase, or purse? May you examine each of these things? May you reveal the contents of what you find? May you listen in on employees' conversations online? Voice-over-IP calls? Regular telephone calls? Cell phone calls? Does it matter whose equipment they are using? Who is paying for it? Who is reimbursing for it? If an employee accesses the company network via a Virtual Private Network, may you examine the contents of their home PC? If they access Webmail from work (or from a work-provided asset), may you read that personal e-mail, intercept their user ID and password? May you use their log-in to read their mail when they aren't there? May you attach a keystroke logger on their computer to capture everything they are doing? May you turn on their Webcam or microphone and monitor or listen in on their conversations?

All of this points out that the question of expectations of privacy of employees, contractors, vendors, or third parties (including customers) are not so straightforward. They are established by law, policy, custom, and contract. As a general rule, you should assume that employees do have privacy interests in what they are doing, and that your rights or ability to monitor their activities are the exception rather than the rule. Too many companies begin with the alternative assumption — that there are no privacy interests. Thus, rights to monitor are generally creatures of contract. The policy is a form of contract between the user and the provider of services. It must be clear, concise, well-documented, and well-distributed to be effective. Monitoring in violation or in excess of policy may give rise to personal criminal liability.

The HR Department is also the repository of the past experiences of the company. What has the company done in similar situations in the past? How has the company handled similar types of misconduct in the "physical" or real world? If an employee goes to a pornographic Website, is this grounds for immediate termination, or is the policy more flexible than that? Are the policies being enforced in an even-handed and rational manner that does not discriminate against persons for prohibited reasons? Are there other protected forms of expression (e.g., union-organizing activities) that the company is infringing on? A well-trained and informed HR staff can be essential for an effective incident response.

Outside Investigators

Outside investigators, whether forensic investigators or private investigators, can be invaluable in providing you with access to tools, techniques, databases, or experiences that you would not otherwise have access to in an internal investigation. But beware. Investigators are like power tools — very effective if you retain a strong control over them. Otherwise, they can create a swath of devastation. The classic example is the internal investigation of the board of directors of Hewlett Packard. Company executives, concerned that members of the board might be leaking damaging internal information, retained outside counsel, who in turn retained private investigators to look into the actions of the board of directors. Thus, the investigation was being conducted by individuals three steps removed from those who were seeking the investigation.

In a cyber investigation, it is the responsibility of the CISO or his or her delegate to know not only what is going on, but to be familiar with the tools and techniques by which evidence is being gathered. In the HP case, the private investigators conducted illegal wiretaps and "pretext" calls to obtain information. The PI would call some institution — a bank, a telephone company, etc.— and pretend to be the data subject seeking access to his or her account information. In other contexts, the PIs would access the data subject's account by establishing an online access account using the subject's personal information. Because the data subject did not have an online account, the PI would create one, using his or her own user ID and password.

So the lesson for the CISO is that if a PI or consultant offers to get information, but tells you that you don't want to know where it came from, you probably do want to know, and you probably want to think about getting another investigator. Moreover, there are many other ways to get into legal trouble during an investigation. Fraud, deception, and trespass into other systems, hacking back, causing damage to other systems, or even leaving Trojan horse programs for others to download may also cause legal problems.

So the top mistakes a CISO can make during an investigation include the following:

- Not having a detailed plan, or not being willing to abandon one.
- Not taking the consequences of the investigation too seriously, or taking them too seriously.

- Not having a theory of how the event occurred, or not being willing to depart from that theory when the facts fail to support it.
- Not having enough management input, or having too much management input.
- Not having enough people on the overall team, or having too many people on the team.
- Losing control over the investigation, or retaining too much control over the investigation.
- Bringing in outside experts, or failing to do so.
- Not paying attention to the public relations aspects of incident response, or paying too much attention to PR.
- Doing things the way they have always been done, or doing things differently from how they have always been done.
- Not learning from your mistakes.

Again, there is no right way to conduct an investigation. As CISO, your job is to find the least wrong way.

Recap

- The security leader has a variety of options to choose from to respond to a crisis, all of them slightly wrong in some manner.
- The best approach is for plans to be vetted, tested, and disseminated in advance. Even then, these serve as a framework when faced with an actual crisis.
- The security officer needs to define what a "successful" result looks like at the start of the investigation by defining the objective.
- Departments such as legal, human resources, and risk management and the business units must be involved in the process.
- Policies must be clear and concise with respect to privacy issues, or the security officer could be leaving the company open to liability during an investigation.
- Asking the tough questions in advance of an actual crisis versus assuming that the organization knows how to respond will better equip the security officer to manage through a crisis.

Notes

1. Pub. L. 106-102 (Nov. 12, 1999).
2. 16 C.F.R. Part 314.4(b)(3).

3. See Payment Card Industry, Data Security Standards (PCI-DSS), Requirement 12.9, available at https://www.pcisecuritystandards.org/pdfs/pci_dss_v1-1.pdf.
4. 45 C.F.R. 164.308(a)(6)(i).
5. See, e.g., Cal. Civ. Code 1798.81.5.
6. (Arizona) A.R.S. § 44-7501 (2006); (Arkansas) A.C.A. § 4-110-105 (2006); (California) Cal. Civ. Code § 1798.29 (2007); Cal. Civ. Code § 1798.82 (2007); (Connecticut) Conn. Gen. Stat. § 36a-701b (2006); (Delaware) 6 Del. C. § 12B-102 (2007); (Florida) Fla. Stat. § 817.5681 (2007); (Georgia) O.C.G.A. § 10-1-910 (2007); (Hawaii) HRS § 487N-1 (2006); HRS § 487N-2 (2006); (Idaho) Idaho Code § 28-51-105 (2007); (Illinois) 815 ILCS 530/10 (2007); 815 ILCS 530/12 (2007); 815 ILCS 530/25 (2007); (Indiana) Burns Ind. Code Ann. § 24-4.9-3-2 (2006); Burns Ind. Code Ann. § 4-1-11-5 (2006); (Louisiana) La. R.S. 51:3072 (2006); (Maine) 10 M.R.S. § 1347 (2006)10 M.R.S. § 1348 (2006); (Michigan) MCLS § 445.72 (2006); MCLS prec § 445.61 (2006); (Minnesota) Minn. Stat. § 325E.61 (2006); (Montana) Mont. Code Ann. § 30-14-1704 (2005); (Nebraska) R.R.S. Neb. § 87-803 (2007); (Nevada) Nev. Rev. Stat. Ann. § 603A.220 (2007); (New Hampshire) RSA 359-C:20 (2007); (New Jersey) N.J. Stat. § 56:8-163 (2007); (New York) NY CLS Gen. Bus. § 899-aa (2007); NY CLS State Technology Law § 208 (2007); (North Carolina) N.C. Gen. Stat. § 75-65 (2006); (North Dakota) N.D. Cent. Code, § 51-30-02 (2007); (Ohio) ORC Ann. 1347.12 (2006); (Oklahoma) 74 Okl. St. § 3113.1 (2006); (Pennsylvania) 73 P.S. § 2302 (2006); (Rhode Island); R.I. Gen. Laws § 11-49.2-3 (2007); (Tennessee) Tenn. Code Ann. § 47-18-2107 (2007); (Texas) Tex. Bus. & Com. Code § 48.103 (2006); (Utah) Utah Code Ann. § 13-44-202 (2006); (Vermont) 9 V.S.A. § 2435 (2007); (Virgin Islands) 14 V.I.C. § 2208 (2006); (Washington) Rev. Code Wash. (ARCW) § 19.255.010 (2007); Rev. Code Wash. (ARCW) § 42.56.590 (2007); (Wisconsin) Wis. Stat. § 895.507 (2006).

Chapter 18

Security Pitfalls

Todd Fitzgerald

There are many books on leadership that one can read to gain some ideas of how to approach management situations. There are many books on technical security skills that one can read to understand the technical approaches to resolve specific technical situations. There are many books that one can read about the business vertical in which one is employed to understand the challenges within the business environment. But where do these challenges for the security leader come together? Presented here are some challenges that have been communicated through the 2006 Security Leader Survey, as well as an expansion of some potential lessons learned and approaches to mitigate the situations, or preferably avoid them in the first place. These stem from actual experiences of security leaders, and although their business environments, organizational culture, management structure, relevant importance of security, and skill level may vary from organization to organization, some of these events have the potential of occurring within any organization. The mitigation strategies may or may not be different; however, it is useful to think about these situations and anticipate the question, "What would I do if this happened in my company?" Just as incident response plans are developed well before the actual event, the security leader needs a "security management incident response plan" to deal with the various situations that may arise.

Executive Meeting, Failure to Prepare Adequately

Executives have very limited time and must deal with a multitude of business issues, some seemingly unimportant and time consuming for their role, such as a potential employee termination for misuse of company assets, and others with a more strategic focus, such as discussing business opportunity strategies, opening of new offices, and increasing revenue share. Their day is filled with a mix of initiatives, and depending upon the executive's view of the importance of information security to the business sustenance of the organization, they may be willing to devote much time or a little. Therefore, when the security leader has the opportunity to interface with the executives, through board meetings, IT steering committee meetings, security councils, management meetings, etc., it is critically important that the message is focused and the time required is minimized. Much energy can be put into the presentation; however, if it does not meet the focus, executive perspective of the situation, expectations, and ability to understand the issues, the presentation will be unsuccessful. Executives like to know (1) what is the problem, in clear, concise business (non-techie) terms; (2) what are the potential alternatives to resolve the problem; (3) how much will each alternative cost? (4) the recommendation and expected benefit; and (5) how long will this take and cost and what other business risks must be considered? These also need to be presented quickly, without 50 PowerPoint slides to get the point across. In fact, each of these areas should be addressed in 1 to 2 slides at the most. Some executives may prefer more detail, and this should be available, as a separate document, for those who would like to understand the information at a deeper level. Some may want this information just as a validation check that the security leader and the team have done due diligence and homework in coming up with the alternatives presented. Therefore, it is essential to know the audience that is being presented to and what its style of review will be.

The security leader must also think like a sales person, and anticipate the questions which will be asked so that the presentation will yield the results expected. Is the objective of the presentation to just "share" information? Is it to reach a decision? Is it to ascertain the support that may be provided for a proposed initiative? Knowing the expected outcome will appropriately position the presentation and provide the focus necessary. If the objective is to just "share" information, the objective should be revisited. As indicated earlier, executives are busy people and want to spend their time dealing with real problems that need to be addressed. If the security leaders are always bringing information to the executives to simply share how well the security program is performing, without some suggested courses of action to improve, the program risks obsolescence and lack of attention from the executives. On the other hand, appropriate metrics are very important: if results of a phased strategy are made available and the relationship of how business operations, compliance, or reduction of risk can be continuously demonstrated, the security leader has a greater chance of obtaining an ongoing revenue stream to address the future security challenges.

Completely Relying on Security Vendors

Security consultants and security vendors provide a very useful complement to any organization. Without the proper level of automation, many of the tasks simply could not be performed. Without leveraging the expertise from those consultants, who work with a multitude of clients and have gained experience from various success and failures, organizations may spend more time and resources investigating different products, approaches, and implementation possibilities on their own than they would by leveraging the resources of a consultant.

Even though the security consultant may bring to the table an enormous amount of expertise, he or she may not have a firm grasp on the particular organization or how it operates. The security leader needs to recognize that, no matter how much planning has gone into the project, there needs to be committed involvement from someone within the organization to ensure the success of the effort. The individual within the organization has established the relationships necessary and speaks the same language as the organization. The technology implemented is useful only if it is applied, taking the specific norms and constraints of the organization where the solution is being implemented. Thus, many organizations will have a project manager allocated from the security consulting firm or vendor, as well as a project manager internally within the organization that is applying the solution. Without this structure, the risk increases, as there becomes an implicit assumption that the security firm will have the same priorities and business drivers as the implementing company, which is typically not the case. Naturally, the external firm wants to see the project succeed; however, they may not be fully aware of the internal challenges and politics required to achieve the goal.

Even Security Departments Are Not above Company Policy

It is probably obvious that security departments are not "above the law" in the execution of daily tasks. However, what if the intentions are good, but the results end up representing a violation of policy? For example, disabling or bypassing some of the security features to perform an internal penetration test/vulnerability assessment may produce the unintended consequences of opening up the environment to viruses or internal/external exploits. Or, suppose an effort to review the strength of passwords across the organization involved using a password-cracking tool, which revealed the results of the passwords? In this case, a control that was not to be shared, and was to be "kept secret" by the company users, was now revealed to the security team. Suppose those secrets revealed the passwords of executives, and they were concerned that the security team or other information technology individuals now had access to their personal data, such as salary information in the Human Resources system, or their e-mail messages. This could be very detrimental to the security leader's job situation. Further imagine that the passwords revealed information the executive did not want known, say, for example, that his password was the name of a girlfriend or boyfriend, which was now disclosed? The password vulnerability scan may also reveal that the executive had not lived up to his or her vocal support of the security program, and had not followed the rules by making an easy-to-guess password, such as "password," their spouse's name, or the name of their favorite sports team.

To avoid this situation from happening, the security leader could discuss the proposed test in advance with the appropriate and responsible executives and obtain their approval before proceeding. This protects the security leader by having obtained the support up front, and would avoid embarrassment. It could be argued that the executives are also responsible for complying with the rules, just like everyone else. Although this is true, this is where judgment must be exercised by asking the question, "What do I expect to gain from this approach?" If the objective is to embarrass some key executives who are necessary to support the security program, then get approval from a higher executive first, and also proceed while simultaneously preparing the resumé! If, on the other hand, the objective is to strengthen the password controls within the entire organization, then soliciting the permission up front is a wiser move.

Acquiring Tools to Solve the Problem

Security tools, as noted earlier, are many times necessary to achieve the efficiency and quality of security operations. Log files are many times too voluminous for most large organizations to manage without intrusion detection systems, event correlation solutions, and investigative tools. Although the tools serve to support the manually intensive process, they cannot replace the functionality with adequate care themselves. A mistake that organizations make is the assumption that the tool is going to solve the problem, and manual effort (manpower) can be significantly reduced, without considering that the work is not eliminated. Someone must still update the tool, install new releases, understand the new functionality of the tool, and, most time consuming, follow up on the reported anomalies from the tool. Failing to recognize the ongoing support required can cause an organization to bring in too many tools at once, with having the manpower required or the expertise to manage the tool. Each of these tools has a learning curve associated with the tool itself, plus the application of how best to utilize the tool also requires time.

A mitigating control for the tool is to ensure, during the Request For Proposal (RFP) stage of tool selection, that the ongoing internal and external (tool vendor, additional security consulting) costs are identified and appropriately recorded. Funding requests must include the total solution for tool acquisition and ongoing support. Reviewing customer references from other companies that have implemented the tool is a good place to start. In the end, the rationale for acquiring the tool may not result in cost savings, but instead may be positioned as a product and process that will improve the quality and effectiveness of the security operations.

Developing Security Policies without Management Buy-In

Prior to the role of the security leader obtaining prominence within many organizations, and still the case today for many others, security policies were developed in the "basement of IT" by a security manager. When these policies were written, they were then distributed to the rest of the organization as "the policy." This may have been done this way for speed, as it is much faster to write the policies and issue them, than to take the time to ensure everyone is in agreement with the policy.

The difficulty with the write-it-then-issue-it approach is that it is seldom fully supported by management. Many times this may not even surface as a problem until there is a violation of the policy, and then it becomes a question of under whose authority the policies were issued. The biggest problem is that management may be unaware of the policy until there is a problem. Or, the security policy is an IT policy, which is just another business unit, which has no more authority than its own operational department. After all, information technology exists to support the business, right?

To avoid the difficulty of not getting the appropriate management support when it is most needed, it is critical that management get involved in the development of the policies. This requires strong communication and influencing skills of the security leader. To gain consensus, the security leader must be willing to listen to alternative points of view to obtain the management commitment necessary. More on obtaining management commitment can be reviewed in Chapter 14, Building Management Commitment through Security Councils. If end users within the organization understands that the security policy was developed with management involved, especially senior management, they are much more likely to support the security policy in their daily activities. Therefore, a structure which has the policies come from the senior management and the security officer is much more effective than one whose policies have been issued solely from the security department. This process may take longer initially to obtain all the buy-in; however, the time will be saved on the back end, reducing the likelihood that every security violation will be challenged as to whether or not it should be a large concern.

Involving stakeholders to obtain buy-in individually before presenting to a larger group is also a very good technique for obtaining the support of others. This is especially true if it is known that certain individuals will be particularly resistant to the new or changed security policy. This is also true if the organization is decentralized, and the decentralized groups are accustomed to making their own decisions.

Presenting the information on a one-on-one basis can prevent embarrassment or conflict for the security officer.

Solving It All, Today

Audit issues can cause immediate attention to the concerns, as the desire is to "make the audit issue go away." This is similar to playing the popular arcade game, "whack-a-mole," where each audit issue is chased individually. This approach may be useful, especially if there is added pressure by senior management to get the control environment under control. However, this approach may lead to disparate solutions that are not part of a cohesive solution set. This typically occurs in organizations where a security vision and associated plan have not been well thought out. With this approach, as the audit issues arise, a determination can be made to implement that piece of the architecture that is in the plan, or to live with the audit issue in the short term. This may be acceptable if the risk is perceived as low, or if a major systems upgrade is planned to mitigate the problem in the near future.

Implementing manual point solutions all at once are also a drain on the information technology team. The team may not have the expertise to implement each of these solutions, making them less than effective.

The best business strategy for the security officer is to take an honest assessment of the entire security infrastructure, viewing the management, operational, and technical controls, and critically examining where the gaps are. Then, a road map can be developed as to what controls need to be implemented across each of these areas and a subsequent plan of action put in place. Funding time available and management interest/attention will most likely not be available for completion of all of these initiatives, so they must be prioritized by risk. Then, when the audit issues do occur, there is less of a propensity to acquire a point solution that will solve that immediate problem. Solutions can be re-evaluated as to how they integrate with other solutions which have been thought out in advance and specified in the road map.

Implementing Technology before It Is Ready for Prime Time

Technology is a great thing — when it works and when it addresses a business problem (versus looking for one). As the Gartner "hype cycle" so eloquently addresses the phenomenon, there is typically a lot of excitement at the suggestion of a new product to solve an existing business problem. Many early adopters jump at the opportunity to become involved, hoping that it will provide their organization with a competitive advantage. These organizations typically understand that not all of the oil wells will result in oil, but after taking risks on multiple initiatives over time, some of them will yield substantial advantages in efficiency and effectiveness of the service the organization is providing. Therefore, they are willing to take the risk. As these products move down the hype cycle, the reality sets in, and some of the realities of the technology are more defined and more understood. As the product finally matures, the initial design flaws are worked out and the expectations become more realistic. The product becomes more of a commodity at this point and is adopted by more companies as a solid solution to their business problems.

So, if the organization is an early adopter, the risks typically surface and contingency plans are put in place. However, if the organization is not accustomed to the potential failure of these new products, or does not understand that they are early in the hype cycle, and attempts are made to implement them as mature products, there can be frustration with technical components not working, implementation delays, and higher risks of schedule and budget overruns. Therefore, it is important for the security leader to recognize that understanding the maturity of the product, actual production implementations, and the specific problem the solution was intended to solve can mitigate the risk of choosing the wrong product. Public key infrastructure (PKI) implementations typically failed due to the fact that the theory of implementation sounded like a great idea, but the costs, scalability, and technical feasibility of the solution made it unworkable for most organizations.

The security leader must stay involved within the industry, collaborating with others who have implemented the technology. Technology products need to be evaluated with a critical view, understanding the risks involved with implementing or not implementing the product, and developing the appropriate contingency plans.

Making Your Own Manager Security-Aware

As security leaders, it is taken for granted that it is part of your role to educate the organization on the importance of complying with security policies. It is especially important not to take for granted one person in particular — the boss. Depending on the reporting structure, this may occur in many different parts of the organization, but these days it is most likely to be the individual responsible for the information technology organization.

It is important to make the boss the security leader's "best customer" so that he or she can sell and support the initiatives.

Fight Hard for External Security Program Reviews

Sometimes external consultants are listened to more than the internal staff. To put the security program on the right path, it is sometimes advantageous to push for an independent security risk assessment and review of the security program. This can provide the extra credibility needed to change some of the current practices. An external consultant can also relate the activities to what other companies are doing within the particular industry and provide management with another viewpoint. In highly regulated environments, this process naturally occurs through the high use of external and internal audits, many times with overlapping reviews of the same information, but with a slightly different focus/intent.

Prioritize According to Business Priorities versus Best Practice Orientation

Not perform security according to best practices? Blasphemy! Lower the standards? Ridiculous! Well, not really. Many times there is a tendency of security professionals, most of which are very detail-oriented, to want to dot every "i" and cross every "t" on every security control. After all, who doesn't want to implement a best practice in their profession? The reality is that security controls need to incorporate the concept of risk, just as the business makes decisions about new product launches, services to be provided, markets to go into, based upon business risk. There are typically more potential business opportunities than a business can typically be engaged in at one time without losing focus and spreading itself too thin. The same is true with security initiatives; these must be prioritized to support the business priorities versus being prioritized to meet the implementation of a best practices model, assuming one did exist. Understanding the business context of the security control is essential to being able to appropriately prioritize the initiative.

One could proceed down the ISO17799 path, or the COBIT path, or any other framework, but at some point, if these initiatives did not involve the business areas in their development, then this most likely will be met with resistance. This is especially true if the organization is not required to meet the regulation (i.e., as part of an ISO certification).

Executives Accepting Risk

At the end of the day, the business executives own the decision as to how much risk should be accepted by the organization. The security leader has a responsibility to educate the senior executive on what "accepting the risk" means. This requires the security leader to translate the risk into nontechnical, business terms, which communicate that the security area is not acting as a department with the paranoid switch being in the "always on" position, but truly understanding what the impact and probability of the threat will mean to the business.

If the security leader has also taken the time to explain the risk, and the business executive is willing to accept it, it may still be beneficial to reach this consensus across the business leaders. For example, the HR business owner of an employee benefits application may be willing to accept the risk of lower authentication standards, but the CFO may have a different viewpoint of the exposure. However the risks are articulated, the security leader should have the business leader sign off on the results of the risk assessment related to the situation and formally provide the business justification and authorization to accept the risk. Amazingly, this process tends to make individuals more accountable and less willing to accept the risk. Typically, the only risks that end up being accepted are those risks that would cause major business disruptions or would be too costly to mitigate.

The security leader should not view this scenario as the ability to abdicate the decision to the business leader. The reality is that the security leader must act as if he or she owns the decision and therefore would perform due diligence to ensure that the decision has considered all the relevant variables. In the end, the security officer must then own the decision as well, and as new information changes the risk profile of the decision, be diligent in ensuring that the executive is informed to make a possible change in direction. Taking this approach promotes a business partnership between the security officer and the executive and has the impact that the next time there is a significant issue, the security officer is more likely to be seen as credible in communicating the risks and discerning which ones are most critical.

Security Awareness Programs Should Not Be Boring

Security leaders need to ensure that the security awareness programs are not viewed as being dry and boring. Security leadership is about engaging the organization to understand security as it pertains to its role and ensure that they are performing those functions. This cannot be accomplished if the message is not heard by the end users in the first place. Security awareness programs that are designed to deliver all the security information by slides in one hour are not effective in achieving long-term support for the security initiatives. Influencing end users to care about security requires that the security leader is viewed as caring about their functions, and is viewed as working toward making their job easier. This can be accomplished by creating programs where the end user feels free to engage with the security department after the training has been completed. After all, they are the hands and feet of security. They are the source of many security violations. They need the education and, for the most part, are willing to "do the right thing." Oral communication skills, not demonstrations of technical excellence, are what is necessary here. The ability to get a simple, concise message across as to how their failure to comply with the security policies puts their jobs, the organization, and the information entrusted to their care at risk, must be the mandate of the security leader.

Trust, but Verify

The security leader needs to take a "show me" position when receiving assurances from other areas that certain processes have been implemented. For example, a network services manager may provide assurances that the systems have been patched to the appropriate level in a timely manner. However, a virus outbreak may expose the fact that not all servers and desktops had the appropriate patches or updated virus control software. The security leader must be persistent enough to ensure that the proper evidence is being collected to attest to the effective implementation of the control. In this situation where the patches were not appropriately applied, the business executives would not be asking the question, "Who was responsible for applying the patches?" but most likely would be looking to the security leader and asking, "Don't we pay you to ensure that the company is appropriately adhering to the practices to reduce our risk?" or "Why did we lose one day of productivity due to this virus?" or "Wasn't the patch management initiative that we approved 12 months ago supposed to protect us from this situation?" It is hard to argue with the business executive that it is the responsibility of the security leader to ensure these events are happening. Therefore, in situations where the impact would be high it would be pragmatic for the security leader to sample on a periodic basis the control environment to ensure that the controls are working.

Information technology departments have not been known historically for maintaining current and accurate documented processes, let alone their execution. Unless there have been internal reviews or audit issues, the lack of documentation has typically not been a problem as long as the systems were available for the business operations. Over the past few years regulations have changed this view, along with control frameworks that promote documented controls are the best way to achieve quality and repeatable process execution. In fact, in today's environment, if a process is not documented, from an audit perspective, it does not exist.

Treating a Business Project Like a Technology One

Implementing a project like identity management involves the use of technology implementations to manage the roles assignments, role profile development, movement of users across the organization, user provisioning, role maintenance, authentication, and reporting. However, implementing identity management has many more cultural components to it and changes the flow of how people work. Treating this as a technology project without the involvement of the business users to define the roles, decide on how roles will be assigned and changed, and leverage the functionality of the implementation is apt to result in a technical implementation which falls far short of the expectations. Security leaders who embark on projects of this sort without understanding the business benefits and focus on "deploying the tool" will miss the full benefit of the implementation, and may find the project cancelled if the business fails to see the benefits in its terms. Rarely is a security problem solely a technology one, but rather a combination of process, people, and technology that requires management support and attention.

External Client Relationships

Imagine this scenario: on a company Website, it appears that an employee of a client company was trying to exploit a vulnerability. The immediate security incident response may be to contact the client company and inform it of the infraction. However, what if this client happens to be one of the top 10 customers? The business may be very reluctant to even approach the other organization, especially if all the relevant facts are not known. As they say, it takes five times as much effort to obtain a new customer than to retain an old one, and with the largest customers, these may be nearly impossible to replace. Security leaders must be cognizant of the business relationships that are held with external clients and should not attempt to make contact without the appropriate support or involvement of the business department. It may be advisable/imperative to involve the legal area as well to ensure that the proper expectations, protocol, and contractual obligations are adequately represented. In situations where there are external customers, it would behoove the security leader to have these discussions with the business executive before such events occur.

Just Say "No"

Eventually, just saying "no" will cause departments to find ways around the security department to accomplish their business objectives. It is important to build a reputation as a can-do person who works toward finding secure solutions to the security problems. Using phrases such as "Yes, and" or "Yes, if we consider" are apt to build better business relationships. Keeping abreast of the newer technologies and thinking outside the box will better position the security leader as a true leader who views company success as the foremost objective.

Combining Security Operations with Security Oversight and Strategy

Day-to-day activities have a way of taking over the whole show. When the operational, security administration, and monitoring functions are managed by the same individual, these tend to become the "highest priority of the day" to resolve. Due to the nature of the work, the solutions tend to be implemented in a hurried, quick-fix, short-term solution. The long-term strategy is not causing as much immediate pain, so the effect is that little time, if any, gets allocated to developing it. There are also potential issues with the segregation of duties, as the same area is providing the security oversight as the area implementing the controls. Separating the operational and security administration functions from the security leader to enable the proper focus to be provided toward crafting the overall security program can provide the mitigation.

Reacting to Security Incidents in a Timely Manner

These sound like motherhood and apple pie, or may elicit a big "duh" from security leaders. However, the reality is that in many organizations, the security incident response procedures are outdated, individuals have changed positions, the reporting requirements are unknown, incidents are not clearly defined, or there has not been a "major" incident in a while which ensures that the process is being followed and improved on a regular basis. Therefore, sometimes the security leader may be out of the loop in responding to the incident, as the technical staff handles it.

With the lack of documentation and training for incident response, it may be unclear who is actually in charge and responsible for ensuring that the incident is appropriately followed up. It is important the security leader and his department be viewed as being "front and center" with respect to the security issue. Sometimes the scope or the potential damage possible by an incident is not immediately known. For example, the loss of a hard drive, memory stick, or laptop may be inconsequential to an organization if it does not contain financial or protected health information (PHI), but it may contain these items, or the Social Security numbers of someone useful to identity thieves, or a business strategy that would be useful to a competitor. The security leader needs to be able to exercise good judgment early in the process to ascertain the potential impact to the business. There will be many times when they will have to rely on the facts provided by the information technology staff, the security department, and the business users to determine the actions required.

The security leader needs to have excellent facilitation, oral communication, and active listening skills to work through an incident. The ability to remain calm, permit the technical analysis to occur without requesting updates so frequently that the technical staff cannot do the investigation, and the ability to know who within the organization is needed to resolve the problem are key determinants of how quickly and accurately the problem will be resolved.

Summary

The security leader faces various situations, any one of which has the potential to cause large financial losses to the organization. Obtaining the appropriate management support with the business area and working toward a mutual solution that balances the risk of the security vulnerability with the business risk associated with it can mitigate many of the situations presented as lessons learned. The security leader should be open to new ideas and approaches and, especially, leverage the experience from their peers in the industry to avoid similar failures. For example, if marketing is proposing a new Web-based service involving online credit card payments, it may be useful to talk with some individuals who have gone through the implementation to understand the business relationships, ongoing communication, technical knowledge, and political hurdles that needed to be addressed to ensure the success of the project. Learning from others and applying the lessons to the particular project at hand can reduce the risk of making major mistakes.

Chapter 19

Security Leader Horizon Issues: What the Future Holds

Steven Skolochenko

The challenges, or opportunities, depending on your point of view, facing the IT security leader are daunting. The accelerating advance of technology coupled with the need for qualified staff make keeping up with the security needs to support the conduct of business in a secure and timely fashion will present a true challenge for the IT security leader. The situation is made even more complex in that most of the issues faced are not isolated. They can be successfully addressed only through a multifaceted approach that includes organizational, managerial, and operational aspects of the IT security issues associated with doing business.

By definition the IT security manager is going to be concerned with the management issues faced by his or her company. The question of how to deal with these issues is not addressed here, as it would vary from firm to firm. However, the issues themselves need to be recognized and understood so IT security managers can plan how to address them.

Several of the issues are being faced now. They will continue and grow in importance in the future. One of the most pressing is that of hiring qualified and competent staff. Generally speaking, colleges and universities pay short shrift to information security in information and computer science classes at the undergraduate level. Their graduate degree programs produce the master of science in information security. This forces the IT security manager to bring in staff who have several years of IT security experience if they are to hit the ground running, but where will they get them and at what price? Will IT security managers have the luxury of a developmental program where they can hire new computer science graduates and train them? And what about career progression of the staff? If managers wish to keep their trained and competent staff, they must be able show them a career path and commensurate remuneration.

The management issues are shown in Table 19.1, operations issues in Table 19.2, and technology issues in Table 19.3.

Table 19.1　Future Management Issues

Continuing or Future Issue	Impact on ITSec Manager	Area
Hiring technically competent staff and keeping them	Description: Technology is changing rapidly. Keeping staff up to date, retaining and hiring competent staff will be a challenge. CISO issues: The IT security manager must be able to identify and hire personnel with the needed competencies. There will be continued competition for qualified personnel. Can they be grown in-house? Will CISOs be able to not only attract qualified staff, but will they be able to retain them?	MGNT
Convergence of ITSec into Corporate Security and out of OCIO	Description: Changing organizational structures and relationships. CISO issues: Organizational structure may change. Where will IT security best be managed? Private industry is leaning this way. Government has statutes that place IT security under the CIO. Should, can, will this change?	MGNT
Protection of intellectual and proprietary property	Description: The continued vulnerability of systems, and ability of hackers and insiders to purloin vast amounts of information presents challenges to the IT security officer to ensure controls are adequate. Heightened competition will spur demand to get the jump on competitors and save money by stealing others' research and development	MGNT

Table 19.1   Future Management Issues (continued)

Continuing or Future Issue	Impact on ITSec Manager	Area
	knowledge. In the 21st century, intellectual property may become much more significant to the business for some organizations than the physical property and plant assets. CISO issues: The entire organization must be aware of the value of its information. How to best accomplish sensitizing the staff to this? Managing identification, authentication, and authorization in a teaming and partnering environment will be a major challenge.	
International laws/privacy/ piracy	Description: Compliance with requirements of various nations will require a holistic view of the IT security process and supporting functions. Care and storage of virtual documents must be addressed with a long-term view. CISO issues: Keeping up with changes in statutory requirements from all nations in which the organization does business will require significant attention. There may also be political issues involved as well as conflicts between the laws of different nation-states.	MGNT
Software development process	Description: These processes are changing. They are becoming more dynamic, e.g., the team software and personal software processes will require close attention to security requirements early in the development process. CISO issues: How will the CISO support demands for participation in these processes? Will staff with the necessary expertise be available?	MGNT
Use of standards	Description: As complexity increases, the use of standards becomes a very desirable mechanism to improve uniformity of processes and functions. CISO issues: Standards may have to be acceptable and used in more than one country. How are standards identified? How are they implemented?	MGNT

Table 19.1   Future Management Issues (continued)

Continuing or Future Issue	Impact on ITSec Manager	Area
Increased importance of IT security governance	Description: As the security of intellectual and proprietary information becomes more visible, boards of directors, etc., will change information security governance to support business and regulatory requirements and reduce risk to stakeholders. CISO issues: Compliance and metrics are important; they must be identified and feedback mechanisms can be put in place to gather the data, which must be interpreted.	MGNT
Contract management	Description: The outsourcing of various aspects of IT services, to include security, is gaining in acceptance. CISO issues: Some of these services may be provided by foreign countries with laws different from those of the country in which the services are provided. Might this be a problem with regard to audit, record-keeping, etc.?	MGNT

Table 19.2   Future Operations Issues

Continuing or Future Issue	Impact on ITSec Manager	Area
Disaster recovery planning and COOP	Description: The need for due care with regard to recovery from disasters such as tsunamis, hurricanes, etc. increases the emphasis on complete, tested, and up-to-date disaster recovery plans. May not be the bailiwick of the IT security manager, but IT security vulnerabilities at stressful times must be managed. CISO issues: Although it is more difficult than in normal operations, it is essential to maintain security across a disaster, recovery, and return-to-normal operation.	OPNS

Table 19.2 Future Operations Issues (continued)

Continuing or Future Issue	Impact on ITSec Manager	Area
Keeping staff up to date	Description: Technological change will alter the way business is conducted in that business will take advantage of technological advances faster than full understanding of control and security issues. IT security personnel must be kept up to date to identify and understand the impact on the organization and how it does business. CISO issues: How are competent people hired and retained? How will training and education budgets keep up with technological changes?	OPNS
Surveillance of work	Description: Corporations may find themselves forced into using tools such as keystroke monitoring to ensure compliance with policy and reduce insider threat. This includes inappropriate use of IT assets. Such processes must be carefully implemented and managed. CISO issues: Who will do the monitoring? Who sets thresholds for reporting, what will be reported, and how will it be reported? CISO will have to answer or be part of the answer to these types of questions.	OPNS
More information and resource sharing	Description: As costs of doing business increase, there will be more pressure to share the burden, thus creating coalitions between governments, agencies, and businesses. IT security governance in this environment will be challenging. CISO issues: How to provide needed access to corporate information to partners without giving away the farm will be a challenge.	OPNS

Table 19.3 Future Technology Issues

Continuing or Future Issue	Impact on ITSec Manager	Area
Introduction of Vista Operating System by Microsoft and its successor	Description: Deciding on security settings and how these impact current and planned applications. CISO issues: Security settings must be reviewed for impact of the new OS. Understanding new security features must be understood to take full advantage of their capabilities. Staff will have to be brought up to date on the new OS and its impact on systems under development and to be developed.	TECH
Vulnerability management	Description: Software with tens of millions of lines of code with bells and whistles will have vulnerabilities. These must be discovered, patches developed, tested, and implemented. Example is Vista. CISO issues: This is not new, but will need added emphasis with the advent of a new operating system and the deluge of fixes/ patches that will succeed its introduction. Additionally, the updated third-party software will create vulnerabilities that must be managed also. Hiding the information assets that are more vulnerable until they can be corrected may also be a temporary option.	TECH
Increased connectivity and speed of communications	Description: Increased speed of communication means that attacks will be able to proliferate faster. Plans to deal with this must be part of the incidence response planning. CISO issues: The speed of propagation of malware requires extraordinary incident response capability to protect the enterprise. Various types of protection must be decided upon, acquired, and implemented.	TECH
Blurring of traditional electronic perimeter	Description: With the exponential increase in connectivity and improved facilities to foster seamless connectivity between devices and systems,	TECH

Table 19.3   Future Technology Issues (continued)

Continuing or Future Issue	Impact on ITSec Manager	Area
	vulnerabilities will increase as will the difficulty in managing them. While we must continue to strengthen the perimeter and push it outward, we must also strengthen other layers, identifying the "crown jewels," sucking them in, and pushing them down into the ground. We must provide alternatives to exclusive reliance on the perimeter. These will include user-to-application-layer encryption using SSL and IPSec. CISO issues: Keeping track of IT assets, their location, both logical and physical, connectivity will be a major undertaking.	
Increased system connectivity and complexity	Description: Increases in complexity invariably lead to increases in vulnerabilities. CISO issues: The more connectivity between systems means that exposure to malware and other threats is greater. Speed and connectivity will accelerate the spread of malware, etc. Total system and network situational awareness will become more necessary than ever to respond in a timely and effective manner to an attack.	TECH
Increased dependence and requirements for robust access control and authentication	Description: Statutory and business requirements will lead to greater attention to this area of the IT security program. May see merger/convergence of logical and physical access control both for devices and facilities. CISO issues: The move toward two-factor authentication is gaining momentum. What two factors will provide the robustness needed at a cost-effective rate? These decisions must be made on an enterprisewide basis with attention paid to laws and culture that differ from country to country.	TECH

Table 19.3 Future Technology Issues (continued)

Continuing or Future Issue	Impact on ITSec Manager	Area
Radio frequency identification (RFID) tags	Description: RFID is an automatic identification method, relying on storing and remotely retrieving data using devices called RFID tags or transponders. An RFID tag is an object that can be attached to or incorporated into a product, animal, or person for the purpose of identification using radio waves. Chip-based RFID tags contain silicon chips and antennae. Passive tags require no internal power source, whereas active tags require a power source. CISO issues: Can information in tags be secured from rogue antennae? Can tags be altered after encoding? Can tags be copied?	TECH
Voice over IP (VoIP)	Description: Use of the IP to transmit voice traffic. CISO issues: In addition to knowing IP-related vulnerabilities, exposure to exploitation may be increased by installation and use of VoIP facilities and applications.	TECH
Computer forensics	Description: "The use of specialized techniques for recovery, authentication, and analysis of electronic data when a case involves issues relating to reconstruction of computer usage, examination of residual data, authentication of data by technical analysis, or explanation of technical features of data and computer usage. Computer forensics requires specialized expertise that goes beyond normal data collection and preservation techniques available to end users or system support personnel." (Kroll-OnTrack). This process often involves investigating computer systems to determine whether they are or have been used for illegal or unauthorized activities. Mostly, computer forensics experts investigate	TECH

Table 19.3 Future Technology Issues (continued)

Continuing or Future Issue	Impact on ITSec Manager	Area
	data storage devices, either fixed like hard disks or removable like compact disks and solid state devices. CISO issues: The IT security program manager must work out where this capability should reside within the firm. How extensive will it be? What training and tools are needed to provide the level of capability needed? At what point does a forensics effort start and when does law enforcement get involved? The IT security manager must address these and other questions.	
Open source software	Description: Open source describes practices in production and development that promote access to the end product's source materials — typically its source code — allowing users to create user-generated software content. Some consider it a philosophy, and others consider it a pragmatic methodology. CISO issues: Installation of open-source software on corporate systems may create exposures that are unknown to the CISO.	TECH
Web services	Description: The W3C defines a Web service as a "software system designed to support interoperable machine-to-machine interaction over a network. Web services are frequently just application programming interfaces (APIs) that can be accessed over a network, such as the Internet, and executed on a remote system hosting the requested services." However, the ability of systems that do not know about each other to interoperate has the potential to increase the value of both. This value is likely to rise exponentially as the number of systems rises linearly. CISO issues: Maximizing the value of interoperation while minimizing the unintended consequences.	TECH

Table 19.3 Future Technology Issues (continued)

Continuing or Future Issue	Impact on ITSec Manager	Area
Grid computing	Description: "Grid computing" refers to the ability to provision and compose massive computing, communication, data, and storage resources late and as needed. It is intended for applications (e.g., weather or market simulations) that require a great deal of power for a short time. It is an emerging set of standards and protocols and computers that use them. These standards and protocols enable some participants to offer capacity and services and for others to discover and use them. Resource allocation and use in a grid is done in accordance with SLAs (service level agreements). The result appears to a user or application as a virtual computer represented by a directory. CISO issues: The grid architecture includes a number of security features. As with any shared resource computing, grids have the potential to leak information between users. CISOs in enterprises that participate in a grid must ensure that there are policies and practices in place to resist and minimize any such risks. Some enterprises will offer services to produce revenue. Their CISOs will wish to ensure that metering and billing mechanisms are resistant to tampering and work as intended. CISOs in enterprises that are users of grid services will wish to ensure that they pay only for those services that they contract for and use.	TECH
Service-oriented architecture (SOA)	Description: SOA is a paradigm which describes an application as a collection of services (and servers) connected to a network and using standard protocols to offer, discover and exploit, and compose the services. CISO issues: Increasingly, such services and protocols are used to offer applications, files, databases, communications, and even security	TECH

Table 19.3   Future Technology Issues (continued)

Continuing or Future Issue	Impact on ITSec Manager	Area
	services (e.g., identification and authentication (Kerberos, RADIUS)). Such services must be protected so as to resist contamination, interference, or unintended use.	
Instant messaging (IM)	Description: IM, or "chat," is a form of near real-time, connectionless, best-efforts, cross-domain (enterprise or other institution), informal communication between two or more people using software agent processes on their desktops and network services to establish addressability. AOL's AIM is the most common example. Although most IM is text-based, modern IM agents can exchange files, spoken words (an application of VoIP), images, and moving images. CISO issues: Issues that may concern the CISO include leakage of confidential information from a sending system, contamination of a receiving system, the default absence of any audit trail, and regulatory compliance. To comply with many regulations, CISOs will have to provide and ensure enterprise-level software that records and logs all traffic. They may have to monitor traffic to ensure compliance.	TECH
Authentication	Description: Authentication is the process of collecting and reconciling evidence that the person asserting an identity is that person. It is one of the earliest acting and most effective controls used. The evidence will be some combination of a secret that the person knows; something that only he can do, like speak or sign his name; some unique physical characteristic, such as his appearance or fingerprint; or something that he possesses, like a key, card, or other token The more evidence one collects, the lower the chance of	

Table 19.3 Future Technology Issues (continued)

Continuing or Future Issue	Impact on ITSec Manager	Area
	accepting an imposter, but the greater the potential of rejecting an authentic person. "Strong authentication" involves two or more of these kinds of evidence, at least one of which is resistant to replay. Most systems now support strong authentication. Examples are mag-stripe cards and PINS that qualify as "strong" only when used at trusted ATMs that resist replay. CISO issues: The CISO will wish to ensure that the appropriate strength of authentication is used for the intended application and environment. For example, four character passwords may work very well for single-user stand-alone devices like PDAs, and strong authentication will be indicated for sensitive applications done across the public networks, or applications where one wants to preserve strong accountability.	
Large-capacity portable storage (thumb drives)	Description: Storage is doubling in efficiency every 12 months. It is now possible to conceal in one's pocket and read or write in minutes quantities of data that 50 years ago would have required boxcars to carry and years to read or write. The size of storage devices continues to fall while the capacity increases. (At the time of this writing, one can buy a device (MiniSD card) for $60 that is the size of one's thumbnail (20 (22 mm) and will hold 4 gigabytes. CISO issues: Storage will continue to get cheaper, faster, and denser. Although the CISO may be tempted to focus on the media to resist data leakage, it will usually be more efficient to control access to the sensitive data. This will resist leakage by any means, not just on portable storage.	TECH

Table 19.3 Future Technology Issues (continued)

Continuing or Future Issue	*Impact on ITSec Manager*	*Area*
Encryption/cryptography	Description: Encryption is the process of hiding sensitive information from unauthorized parties by translating it from a public code into a secret one. This is usually done using a standard algorithm tailored to a specific use using a secret key. Encryption is used to hide data both in transit and at rest. The artful use of encryption is effective in hiding the information from the unintended while minimizing any burden on the authorized. Encryption can be used to preserve and demonstrate the integrity and origin of data and to involve multiple parties in sensitive duties. Encryption is usually far stronger than we need it to be and is rarely the weak link in our security. It is rarely broken, but sometimes bypassed. CISO issue: Like other good security, modern crypto is built in, rather than bolted on. The CISO must ensure that it is used as intended and provides the intended protection.	
Cross-domain identification and authentication	Description: A number of schemes have been proposed in which one service provider, the relying partner, will rely upon one or more other partners to vouch for the identity of users. MS Passport is one such scheme and OpenID is another. OpenID is differentiated from Passport in that it supports and encourages multiple vouching parties. A user can be registered with one or more of a number of vouching parties that participate in the OpenID scheme. The advantage to the user is that he need not register with those Websites that are prepared to trust participating sites with which he is already registered. He increases the number sites with which he can do business while reducing the number that must store and protect information about him.	TECH

Table 19.3   Future Technology Issues (continued)

Continuing or Future Issue	*Impact on ITSec Manager*	*Area*
	CISO issue: The CISO must advise management on the participation in any such scheme considering the increase in business that may result balanced against the risk of relying upon partners for information about customers.	

Index

T - #0105 - 101024 - C0 - 234/156/17 [19] - CB - 9780849379437 - Gloss Lamination